My dear Marg

Love, Gladys
Aug. 1999

PARENTING IN STEPFAMILIES

For Y.T. and Michael

Parenting in Stepfamilies

Social attitudes, parental perceptions and parenting behaviours in Hong Kong

GLADYS LAN TAK LAM-CHAN

Ashgate

Aldershot • Brookfield USA • Singapore • Sydney

Published by
Ashgate Publishing Ltd
Gower House
Croft Road
Aldershot
Hants GU11 3HR
England

Ashgate Publishing Company
Old Post Road
Brookfield
Vermont 05036
USA

British Library Cataloguing in Publication Data
Lam-Chan, Gladys Lan Tak
    Parenting in stepfamilies: social attitudes, parental
    perceptions and parental behaviours in Hong Kong. - (Social
    & political studies from Hong Kong)
    1. Stepfamilies - China - Hong Kong 2. Parenting - China -
    Hong Kong
    I. Title
    306.8'74

Library of Congress Catalog Card Number: 98-74644

ISBN 1 84014 969 8

Printed in Great Britain

Contents

Figures and tables

Acknowledgements

I wish to take this opportunity to express my deepest gratitude to the following persons who have given me invaluable support and advice from planning to completion of this study, on which my PhD thesis and this book are based.

First of all, I wish to thank the supervisor of my PhD study, Professor Olive Stevenson, for her very helpful advice, critical comments and unfailing guidance. Professor Stevenson has facilitated me to appreciate knowledge with breadth and depth. I feel rich and am blessed by Professor Stevenson's wisdom and support in helping me to face the challenges in this study. I must also thank my second supervisor, Professor Diana Mak most sincerely for her generous support and insightful advice. I am also grateful to the Hong Kong Polytechnic University for its staff development programme, which has given me generous support for my PhD study. Special thanks must be extended to Professor Phyllida Parsloe, the external examiner, and Mr. Bill Silburn, the internal examiner of my PhD thesis for their constructive comments.

This study could not have been completed without the useful suggestions and kind support of my friends in the field and colleagues at work. They have also shared my joy and frustrations, their kindness will always be remembered. I am especially indebted to the organizations who have given me help in the referral of informants or provision of figures and data; they are: the Family Service Department of the Caritas-Hong Kong, Against Child Abuse, and the Family and Child Care Division of the Hong Kong

Council of Social Service. Special thanks are due to the stepmothers, social workers and teachers who took part in this study. I am greatly touched by their life stories and their trust in me. Their openness in sharing with me their feelings and information have made the data collection process a most unforgettable experience.

This acknowledgement is not complete without mentioning some important persons in my life. I want to thank my colleague, the late Miss W.S. O for her encouragement to take up this study and her kind friendship. I am also grateful to Professor Margot Breton for her emotional support and understanding of the difficulties as a working mother embarking on such a demanding task on a part-time basis. I must also extend my deepest thanks to Dr. Julia Tao and Dr. Elsie Ho, who have always been caring friends and a source of strengths for me. I am also thankful to my parents for their frequent words of encouragement, my elder sister Julia, and my elder brothers Colin and Albert for sharing my worries and shouldering additional responsibilities in taking care of our frail parents when I was deeply involved in this study. Last but not the least, I owe a great debt to my husband, Y.T., and my son, Michael, for their understanding and unfailing support. I wish to dedicate this book to them as a token of my appreciation.

1 Introduction

That dear octopus we call the family, from whose tentacles we can never quite escape.

— **Dodie Smith, *DEAR OCTOPUS***

A family is a place where we are born and brought up. It brings us joy and gives us pain. We love it, we hate it. But once we are part of it, we will always be so. Some people aspire to harmonious family life and happy marriage, but their experiences are not quite what they anticipate. This book is a record of my investigation into the untold life experiences of some people in Hong Kong who expected better family life and happier marriages the second time. I shall begin by explaining why I was interested in exploring stepfamilies in the society in which I have been living since birth.

Background and Rationale for Pursuing This Study

In recent years, research into family life conducted by researchers and clinicians from developed countries has caused concern with the figures related to divorces and stepfamilies. From the United Nations Demographic Yearbook 1993, the crude divorce rate[1] of the United States was 4.76 in 1992; whilst that for the United Kingdom's was 2.96 in 1991. More refined measures of divorce rate[2] are causing the professionals involved greater

1

concern. Goode (1993) pointed out that the divorce rate for the married women in the United States in 1988 was 21 per 1,000. Marriage and Divorce Statistics of England and Wales (1993) show that the divorce rate for persons divorcing per 1,000 married population in England & Wales was 13.9 (HMSO, 1995). According to 'Social Trends 1995', divorces in United Kingdom increased sharply to 173,000 in 1992, that is, more than double the number in 1971 (Governmental Central Statistical Office, 1995).

In the United States, as predicted by its National Center for Health Statistics in 1990, one in two marriages will end in divorce, and 40% of children born in this decade will experience the breakup of their parents' marriage (Petersen & Steinman, 1994). Fine & Schwebel estimated 8.8 million of all children under the age of 18 in the United States (19.1%) live in stepfamilies and 5.8 million (12.7%) are stepchildren (Fine & Schwebel, 1991). McGoldrick & Carter predicted that by 1990 one in six children would live in a remarried family (Walsh, 1992).

In the United Kingdom, statistics in 'Social Trends 1995' show that 'remarriages grew rapidly in the 1960s and 1970s, from 14% of all marriages in 1961 to 34% in 1981 (Government Central Statistical Office, 1995, p.36). Overall, more than a third of all marriages in 1993 were remarriages and there were about half a million stepfamilies in Great Britain in 1991 (Government Central Statistical Office, 1996). The Stepfamily Information Sheet shows that it is likely that more than 1 million children are living in stepfamilies and that a further 1.5 million are currently living with a separated or divorced parent who may remarry. One in four children is likely to grow up in a stepfamily (Robinson, 1993). These growing figures have alerted the helping professionals to the fact that problems generated by stepfamilies and stepparenting should not be underestimated.

The city of Hong Kong, where I live and work, is also facing a rise in the divorce rate and a change of social attitude towards marriage, divorce, and remarriage. In 1972, the overall divorce rate was 0.09 per 1,000 population but it has increased to 0.97 per 1,000 in 1992 (Hong Kong Council of Social Service, 1993). Although the number of divorce decrees absolute granted in 1997 was only 10,492 (Hong Kong Judiciary, 1997) in a 6.6 million population (see Table 1.1 on p.3), it should be noted that the number of marriages ending in divorce dramatically increased almost four and a half fold between 1977 and 1987, and ten fold between 1977 and 1997. This increase does not take into account those who chose to dissolve their marital relationship through private arrangement.

Table 1.1
Divorce Statistics (Hong Kong)*

Year	Number of Divorce Decrees Absolute
1977	955
1978	1,420
1979	1,520
1980	2,087
1981	2,060
1982	2,673
1983	2,750
1984	4,086
1985	4,313
1986	4,257
1987	5,055
1988	5,098
1989	5,507
1990	5,551
1991	6,295
1992	5,650
1993	7,454
1994	7,735
1995	9,272
1996	9,473
1997	10,492

* Figures supplied by Judiciary Hong Kong

The Government White Paper 'Social Welfare into the 1990s and Beyond' (1991) has examined the impact of divorce on family members and confirmed a need to strengthen the relevant support services for couples and children. Unfortunately, the Census and Statistics Department of the Hong Kong Government has not collected data on the number of re-married persons or families. It is only since 1991 that the Hong Kong Council of Social Service -- a co-ordinating organization which has almost all of the non-governmental social welfare agencies as its members -- has collected minimal data on stepfamilies. The data is collected by asking one question: 'Is the family a stepfamily? -- yes or no' in an one-page face sheet to be completed by the social worker taking in a client. Due to constraints on manpower, the Council has not yet made full use of the information collected for facilitating the improvement of policies and services.

The limited information which I can gather at this time as regards the number of stepfamilies and their main problems reveals that stepfamilies only comprised about 3% of all the active cases handled by almost all the non-governmental family service agencies in 1996 in Hong Kong (see Table 1.2 below).

Table 1.2
Number of Stepfamily Counselling Cases Handled by Member Family Service Agencies of the Hong Kong Council of Social Service

Year	Number of Stepfamilies	Total Number of Active Counselling Case
1991	185	5,503
1992	245	6,978
1993	318	10,797
1994	351	11,482
1995	382	12,683
1996	439	13,603

Examining the raw data more closely, it is found that the stepfamilies in Hong Kong receiving family services had the following problems: marital relationships (30.1%), child care (13.2%), and parent-children relationships (10.7%) as recorded by the non-governmental organizations in 1996 (Hong Kong Council of Social Service Clientele Information Statistics) (Appendix 1). A special group of clients, i.e. stepparents who are known to be child abusers, comprised only 8.6% of the total active child abuse cases handled by the social workers of the social service units of the Social Welfare Department and the non-governmental organizations in 1996 and 1997 (Hong Kong Government Social Welfare Department Child Protection Registry 1996 and 1997 Statistical Reports) (Appendix 2). The only non-governmental child protection agency in Hong Kong, Against Child Abuse, has no record of stepparent-abusers receiving casework services in the year 1995-96 (Appendix 3). In 1996-97, only one stepfather was identified as potential abuser (Against Child Abuse Annual Report, 1997). Although the percentages outlined above seem insignificant, they are the only officially recorded figures. There are couples who have not gone through legal procedures in order to dissolve their marriage. Others are divorcees and widows/widowers who choose to cohabit and form new families without formally uniting through registry marriage procedure, and there are also child abuse incidents in stepfamilies which have not been detected. It would appear from observations of social workers in the field that these families 'in the dark' are not small in number and have not been included in these figures. They are the concern of helping professionals.

Owing to the fact that there is little statistical information and no findings of research studies available on this growing phenomenon, I wished to undertake a study on parenting in stepfamilies in Hong Kong for three reasons. Firstly, evidence shows that there has been a sharp increase in divorce within the past 20 years, albeit from a low base. Aspirations and relationships in marriages have changed and parenting practices are inevitably being affected. Secondly, there is plenty of evidence that trends in Western society influence social attitudes and behaviours in Hong Kong. It will therefore be interesting to examine how traditional values in marriage and parenting are challenged. Thirdly, I have a strong impression that there is a 'hidden dimension' to this phenomenon which is not revealed in the official statistics. The structural change and family dynamics in stepfamilies uncovered will be useful for understanding and helping these families in Hong Kong.

There are three major areas I wish to examine specifically in this study. My main interest is the parenting behaviours in stepfamilies, that is, the ways that stepchildren and biological children are parented by their stepparents and biological parents in stepfamilies. The emphasis is on stepparenting practised by stepmothers and parenting practised by their husbands as reported by the former. However, obtaining information on these is not sufficient in itself for an understanding of the dynamics of the stepfamilies: it is also necessary to uncover the factors affecting their practices. These influential factors are the parent's perceptions as shaped by values transmitted by their family of origin and by people who are significant to them in their life. As we are not isolated beings and are living in social environments, social attitudes which are

5

culturally specific and carry moral judgments inevitably affect parental perceptions. These perceptions have later formed beliefs in parenting, even though such beliefs may be myths. Perceptions, beliefs and myths affect parenting behaviours. Consequently the objectives of this study are to investigate the three interwoven areas of concern in stepfamilies: social attitudes, parental perceptions and parenting behaviours. The general and specific objectives will be outlined in the next section. The information for this study was collected from three batches of informants; the primary target being the stepmothers and the professionals who have frequent contact with stepfamily members, that is, teachers and social workers. The reasons why they were chosen as informants will be explained in Chapter 4 (pp. 85-86).

Objectives of this study

This exploratory study has five objectives. They were set with due consideration of cultural differences, gender sensitivity and the nature of the study. These objectives are:

1. to explore social attitudes towards stepfamilies and stepparenting from local informants who have personal experience or who have worked with stepfamily members;
2. to examine parental perceptions and beliefs about stepparenting in local stepfamilies whose members are willing to be interviewed;
3. to identify the difficulties of parenting in these stepfamilies;
4. to identify issues arising from parenting in these stepfamilies and to reflect upon their implications for social work practice; and
5. to make recommendations for social work policy and practice as to how Hong Kong stepparents and their families may be helped.

Organization of this Book

Chapter 1   **Introduction.** This chapter contains the layout of the book, the rationale for the choice of this topic, the extent and severity of the phenomenon, and the objectives of this study.

Chapter 2   **Social Attitudes, Parental Perceptions in Stepparenting and Parenting Behaviours of Stepfamilies: A Review of Western Literature.** This chapter contains a literature review and critique of predominantly Western references. Relevant concepts of the three specific areas under study are critically examined and discussed.

Chapter 3   **Traditional Chinese Beliefs and Current Views in Hong Kong Influencing Family Life and Family Relationships.** This chapter is concerned with culture-specific concepts relevant to the society in which this study was conducted. The presentation and discussion focus upon understanding the interplay of Western and Chinese thoughts and social changes in the context of Hong Kong Chinese society and upon the impact of these thoughts and social changes on stepfamilies in Hong Kong.

Chapter 4   **Research Methodology.** This chapter discusses the choice of the research method and why the qualitative method was chosen. Major perspectives guiding this study, the research design, and reflections on the process are also presented.

Chapter 5   **Social Attitudes and Parental Perceptions of Stepparenting in Stepfamilies in Hong Kong: Findings and Discussion.** This chapter contains the presentation and discussion of the findings of the first two major areas of the study. Reports of the stepmothers and information provided by the teachers and social workers are highlighted in order to show the attitudes of people outside the stepfamilies which have affected the perceptions of parents in the stepfamilies.

Chapter 6   **Parenting Behaviours in Stepfamilies in Hong Kong: Findings and Discussion.** This chapter focuses upon the findings and analysis of the profile and life course of the parents in stepfamilies as reported by the stepmothers as well as a thematic analysis and discussion on the dynamics in stepfamilies.

Chapter 7   **Reflections on the Themes and the Issues.** This chapter presents the central themes which stand out distinctively from the findings. Reflections upon those themes lead to the discussion of important issues in this study which help social workers to develop greater understanding of the difficulties experienced by stepfamilies in Hong Kong.

Chapter 8   **Implications for Social Work Practice.** The important points which have implications for social work practice are highlighted at the beginning of this chapter. Thereafter contextual reflections and discussions on the current debates are made from the ideology, policy and service perspectives. Suggestions for policy-makers and social workers are outlined at the end of the chapter preceding the epilogue.

Notes

1   Crude divorce rate means number of divorces per 1,000 population.

2   Refined divorced rate means number of divorces per 1,000 married women or married persons in a country/city.

2 Social Attitudes, Parental Perceptions in Stepparenting and Parenting Behaviours of Stepfamilies: A Review of Western Literature

Introduction

The understanding of parenting in stepfamilies requires an examination of theoretical concepts and a review of research findings so that they can serve as a guide to the researcher in goal-setting, data collection and analysis. Stepfamilies have been the topic of much professional literature in the last two decades, but the recognition of notice of stepfamilies as a social phenomenon had begun as early as the 1950s and attracted the attention of scholars and researchers. Literature and reports of studies over the years have reflected changes in society and values and their impact on stepfamilies. For example, the stepfamilies identified in the earlier years were those formed after the death of one spouse; there were more men remarried resulting in more stepmother families than stepfather families, and at that time there were not as many types of stepfamilies identified as in the 1990s. Nowadays there are more stepfamilies formed after divorces and the number of women remarrying has increased quickly. More liberal and accepting social attitudes have developed from these studies, and more 'hidden' stepfamilies which at one time covered themselves for fearing social labelling have now come to surface.

In selecting materials for this review from a large pool of literature, I have used works in the English language from the United Kingdom and the United States. One important criteria has guided the choice -- that there should be a balance between research conducted by social scientists and the observations of experienced clinicians. In drawing on materials from both the United Kingdom and the United States, I notice that there are culture-specific differences concerning social values and behaviour which is reflected in the work of the authors from these two countries. It is also important to note that these references should not be used for analysis of local observations without careful consideration of cultural and contextual differences. I have selected certain authors as of particular value, namely, Visher & Visher, the American authors who were among the first to focus their work on stepfamilies two decades ago. Their concepts such as myths and tasks of stepfamilies have been widely referred to and are used here in order to explore parental perceptions and parenting behaviours of stepfamilies. In addition, I have also chosen Robinson, a family therapist in the United Kingdom; her 30 years of clinical experience and her experience as a parent in a stepfamily have enriched her writings on stepfamilies as a system in transformation. Her work is thorough and complete in the context of the demographic data, the process of divorce-remarriage-stepfamily, and in providing discussion of the consequences and issues arising from the breaking up of a family and forming a stepfamily. Due to the comprehensiveness of Robinson's work, I have used it as a reference in all of the three areas I intend to study.

An examination of the literature over a period of time shows a change in the basic assumptions concerning stepfamilies. In the earlier studies the main contributors were clinicians who recorded their observations and experiences; later, social scientists had joined them and examined stepfamilies by conducting empirical studies using a 'deficit-comparison paradigm'. Stepfamily members were seen as somehow deficient when compared with family members in first-marriage families. More recent writings have been inspired by the 'normative-adaptive perspective' introduced by Visher & Visher (1979). Researchers do not place heavy emphasis on problems in stepfamilies or compare them negatively with other family forms. They have tried to explore the strengths in stepfamilies instead of focusing on deficits. This new direction stresses that biased perceptions and attitudes towards stepfamilies are not only held by the general public, some scholars and researchers have fallen into the trap as well. Therefore a review of the findings of studies conducted by social scientists is necessary and useful for understanding the social attitudes which have affected parental perceptions and parenting behaviours in stepfamilies. From amongst the researchers who have written on this topic for 20 years, Ganong & Coleman have been two of the most visible American writers in the past decade. Their specialisms are human development and family studies, and the findings of their works have influenced many authors who are interested in stepfamilies. Their discussions on cultural stereotyping, remarital and stepfamily relationships have facilitated the construction of the themes for this study. The analysis of social attitudes and parenting behaviours in this study has been particularly inspired by what they have written in these areas.

Since the literature is Western, cultural differences and social development over time have to be considered. For example, in the 1950s when divorces and stepfamilies in the West were few, social attitudes were rather negative towards remarriages and stepfamilies which resulted from divorces. Children whose parents had divorced were seen as 'pitiful and neglected'. However, 40 years later, remarriages and stepfamilies are very common in Western developed countries and such children are comparatively better off because social acceptance is greater which has resulted in greater social and familial support. Children are no longer considered as 'pitiful' and 'neglected' as decades ago. In Hong Kong, however, many Chinese families still uphold traditional values, and social attitudes are still rather conservative about divorces and stepfamilies despite the fact that divorces, remarriages and stepfamilies are growing in number and people seem to be more liberal in thinking. It was pointed out by Lee (1991) that divorce was viewed as a social problem and about half (47.1%) of the respondents in his study could not accept divorce (Lau et al, 1991, p.54). Moreover, the findings of a recent local survey exploring attitudes towards marriage also revealed that 42% of the respondents agreed that 'men generally will not consider marrying a divorced woman' (Yeung & Kwong, 1995, p.51). This is an example which illustrates the difference in pace of social change in different societies: although problems may no longer be negatively labelled in one society, another society may not yet have reached the stage of acceptance of stepfamilies. Therefore it is useful to review earlier Western literature in order to understand the dynamics of the stage through which Hong Kong stepfamilies are now going. In the next chapter there will be a review of literature from a culture-specific perspective which discusses the challenges of Western thought to Chinese values in Hong Kong.

Social Attitudes towards Stepfamilies and Stepparenting

Stepfamilies: What Are They?

Social attitudes reflect people's values at a particular time and in context. When families are called 'stepfamilies', people do not view them as merely 'families', they are families with special history, nature and structure. To understand why 'stepfamilies' are so-called, the social attitudes underlying the labelling language will be identified.

Stepfamilies are described with the prefix 'step', which means there were primary, original families before their formation. In Old English, 'step' is equivalent to 'steop' meaning 'bereaved' (Robinson & Smith, 1993, p.5). A stepfamily is formed following the loss or departure of one parent as a result of death or divorce and the remarriage of the other parent. The 'traditional' stepfamily is the family which is formed after a parent has died. It is noted by researchers that 'prior to the past 20 years or so, the death of a spouse was the most common precursor of remarriage' (Ganong & Coleman, 1994, p.xi). In stepfamilies which result from the death of a parent, clinicians advise adults and children alike to come to terms with their feelings of loss, mourning and loyalty conflicts which may occur when their former spouse or deceased biological parent are replaced (Visher & Visher, 1988; Papernow, 1993).

However, more recent research findings have noted that 'the stepfamily which is prevalent in the 1990s follows parental separation and divorce' (Robinson & Smith, 1993, p.xvi). Separation and divorce following the breakdown of marital relationship create life stress or life crisis for the couple. For children born from the primary family, it will be difficult and painful for them to experience the suffering and turmoil resulting from separation of their parents. After a divorce, many people attempt to enter into another intimate relationship through cohabitation or remarriage. The children in their care will then be brought into the newly formed family and will be confronted by difficulties caused by the transformation of the family structure and the development of complicated sets of family relationships.

How is stepfamily defined? Basically speaking, a stepfamily is 'a household in which there is an adult couple at least one of whom has a child from a previous relationship' (Visher & Visher, 1988, p.9). Different criteria have been used to construct a typology of stepfamilies in order to define and examine stepfamilies and also to understand the composition of their structure and the dynamics of the family relationships. Understanding the family structure and family process are the two main concerns of researchers and clinicians exploring families: these are also the areas social workers usually intervene. Definitions of stepfamilies based upon these two perspectives will, therefore, be presented below. In view of the family structure, a number of researchers have identified variations of stepfamily structure. For example, Clingempeel, Brand & Segal (1987) divide stepfamilies into nine types based on the presence or absence of children from the formal relationships, and upon the custody of the children; Pasley & Ihinger-Tallman (1982) postulated another nine types of stepfamilies based on the presence or absence of children from the former or the present relationships, the age of the children, and the custody of children from former relationships. Wald (1981) identified 15 types of remarried family configurations based on the residence of children from the former relationships of both adults. In view of the family process, stepfamilies can be classified according to the goals they set for their family life (Burgoyne & Clark, 1984) or according to the existence or lack of co-parenting relationship (Ahrons & Rodgers, 1988) or according to the levels of complexity in the stepfamily (Ihinger-Tallman & Pasley, 1987; Pasley, 1987).

The above writers have classified stepfamilies by considering their complexity in structure, relationship and process. Some typologies seem overly complicated. For a simple but clear classification, Robinson (1980) provides one that is based on the legalistic basis of marital relationship between the biological parent and stepparent: '(1) "legitimating", where the biological parent had not previously been married and the children were illegitimate; (2) "revitalized", where the biological parent had remarried following the death of the other natural parent; (3) "reassembled", where one or both partners have previously been divorced, and the biological parent brings into the family a stepparent who had not previously had children; and (4) a "combination" (first described by Shulman, 1972, 1981), where both parents have previously been married and have children from their first marriages, who may or may not live with the stepfamily full-time' (Robinson, 1993, p.122).

Social Attitudes Towards Stepfamilies and Stepparenting: Cultural Stereotyping and Feelings of Ambivalence

One of the major factors affecting adjustment and relationship-building in

13

stepfamilies is social attitudes influenced by cultural stereotyping. The language used by people reflects how people view stepfamilies; the change in the language used over a period of time reflects changing attitudes towards stepfamilies.

Stepfamilies have been variously termed over the past two decades. The changes made in reference to them reflect the fact that people have become less negative about them and, although there is still ambivalence, more neutral names are used to represent stepfamilies. For example, they are called 'reconstituted' (Duberman, 1975; Robinson, 1980; Shulman, 1981), 'blended' (Wald, 1981), 'remarried' (Wald, 1981; Sager et al 1983; Ihinger-Tallman & Pasley 1987), 'REM', 'extended', 'second', 'merged', 'combined', and 'reorganized' (Coleman & Ganong, 1987a). Stepfamilies are perceived as an 'incomplete institution' (Cherlin, 1978). These terms give the impression of regarding stepfamilies as not original or pure; they come together as 'second best' and their relationships are complex.

As pointed out in the last section, the word 'step' carries a negative connotation. Wald (1981) pointed out that the term encapsulates four basic aspects of human experience of the steprelationship: bereavement, replacement, negative connotations, and lack of institutionalization of this family form in the constellation of families (Coleman & Ganong, 1987a, p.20).

Stepparents are accepted with reservation and feelings of ambivalence. Bohannan (1970) noted that 'stepparent' originally meant a person who replaced a dead parent, not a person who was an additional parent. Stepfamily roles and stepfamilies in general are perceived more negatively than nuclear family roles and nuclear families (Ganong, Coleman, & Mapes, 1990). Visher & Visher (1979) have referred to stepfamilies as 'culturally disadvantaged families' because the term 'step' evokes the negative imagery found in fairy tales. For example, it is not unusual for stepmothers to be portrayed as 'wicked.' Wicked stepmother is a prominent character in many Western folk and fairy tales such as Cinderella, Hansel and Gretel, Snow White, etc. Stepfathers generally have escaped such portrayal in fairy tales, but the prefix 'step' is often considered a pejorative one for stepfathers as well as stepmothers (Leslie, 1982; Wald, 1981). Stepfathers are thought of as 'abusive' (Coleman & Ganong, 1987a; Fine, 1986; Bryan, Coleman, Ganong & Bryan, 1986; Visher & Visher, 1979; Wald, 1981). The negative stereotype of the abusive stepfather is regularly expressed in mass media through newspapers, television shows, and movies. The tragedies of Maria

Colwell (1974) and Wayne Brewer (1976) are classic examples associating child abuse in stepfather-headed families which have reinforced the ill-treating image of stepfathers and these cases are quoted repeatedly each time a child abuse case hits the news headlines. Stepchildren are associated with the thought of 'those poor children who fail to receive proper care and attention'. Society assumes that stepchildren may be rejected, neglected or cruelly treated (Maddox, 1975, 1976). Smith (1953) noted that there is a definite stereotype of the stepchild in popular thinking: he is a pitiful creature who suffers cruelty and neglect. 'The term "stepchild" has been consistently used to represent a negative experience or situation' (Coleman & Ganong, 1987a, p.20) and Wald (1981) notes that the use of the term 'stepchild' as a metaphor for neglect or abuse helps perpetuate a negative bias against stepfamilies. It should be noted that as stepfamilies have greatly increased in number in the developed countries over the past four decades and the number of stepchildren has also grown sizeably, there has been greater social acceptance of stepchildren. They have received more support from their families and communities and they are no longer considered to be neglected.

When social attitudes and perceptions of stepfamilies and stepparenting in Chinese culture was examined, it was rather disappointing to find that there was no known Western literature on this specific subject except for some sketchy description of negative views about divorced women. After failing to find any works using this source, much effort was made to look for Chinese folk tales and Chinese stories about stepfamilies. Only one record in a English book written about Chinese kinship was eventually found. It recorded a story in A.D.1403-25; a man aged 79 married a 17 year old girl, which was resented by the old man's elder son. The man insisted his young wife be called 'little mother' or 'madam', but the son refused to address his stepmother as 'mother'. He said: 'We cannot tolerate such a state of affairs and must not be too polite to her lest she should think too highly of herself' (Chao, 1983, pp.75-76). This was the only story found about negative social attitude towards stepmother after months of search. For stories depicting wicked stepmothers, two were found from the '24 Stories on Filial Piety' in traditional Chinese literature. One was about a stepmother who provided her own child with nice and warm clothes but gave her stepson flimsy clothes in cold winter. The stepson bore the sufferings because he did not want to hurt the feelings of his father. The other story told about a stepmother who disliked her stepson, she talked behind his back and made the stepson's father dislike him too. The stepson still practised filial piety when relating to his stepmother. He knew that she liked eating fish, he lay on an icy river, melted the ice and caught a fish for his stepmother. These stories glorify the practice of filial piety rather than unveiling the social attitudes towards the stepfamily. My search into the written work on Chinese stepfamilies reflects the fact that the subject matter is morally tabooed and that they are not encouraged to be openly depicted and discussed. I shall further explore the social attitudes of some people in Hong Kong in the next chapter.

Consequences of Cultural Stereotyping of Stepfamilies and Stepparenting in Western and Chinese Socieites: Negative Image-building and Problems in Adjustment

According to Hamilton (1979), stereotypes are 'standardized beliefs about an identifiable group' (Fagot, Leinbach, & O'Boyle, 1992, p.225). Most stereotypes are negative (Schneider, Hastorf, & Ellsworth, 1979) and tend to increase social distance (Allport, 1954). When a stereotype is negative, the individuals who are stereotyped may become the object of prejudice (Ehrlich, 1973; Schneider, Hastorf, & Ellsworth, 1979). 'The labels employed by public are rather negative and it may lead people to evaluate the stereotyped persons less favourably no matter what behaviour is observed' (Coleman & Ganong, 1987a, p.33).

Cultural stereotyping of the stepfamily tends to cast a negative image on the members of the family and create adjustment problems for them (Coleman & Ganong (1987a), Ehrlich (1973), Schneider, Hastorf, & Ellsworth (1979)), and other researchers have also noted that stepparents are perceived more negatively than those in similar positions in intact families. Jones (1978) added that 'interpersonal problems in a stepfamily are complicated by the mere categorization by society and itself as deviant' (p.220).

Social views developed through the years and perpetuated by the findings of researchers and mass media have a significant impact on adjustment and relationships in stepfamilies. It is common to perceive stepfamilies as deviant and complex family types with relationships in stepfamilies perceived as stressful and difficult: wicked stepmothers; abusive stepfathers; and neglected and abused stepchildren. The stereotyping of stepfamilies has a negative impact on the development of stepfamily members' self-image: they may live up to the negative images, play their roles negatively, and have difficulties in developing positive relationships with other members of the stepfamily.

There are two kinds of responses to lessen the negative effects. Firstly, there are responses from people in the society. Different terms are used to describe stepfamilies; they are 'euphemisms' for them and are used by both professionals and the general public (Coleman & Ganong, 1987a). Alternative labels are used to reduce biased reactions (Espinoza & Newman, 1979; Bernard, 1956; Coleman & Ganong, 1987a) such as those described in the earlier section (p.14). This change of labels has not been successful in improving the public image of stepfamilies and stepparents. As pointed out by Maddox (1975), 'if the connotation is unpleasant, the reason should be faced, not glossed over with change of label'. Secondly, there are responses from the stepfamilies. It is a common desire of stepfamily members to be regarded by others as a 'normal' family (Coleman & Ganong, 1985a; Duberman, 1975). Jacobson (1980), Johnson (1980) and Visher & Visher (1979) have pointed out that 'parents who play the roles of stepparents may tend to avoid the step label by denying, ignoring or refusal to recognizing their status' (Coleman & Ganong, 1987a, p.21).

Coleman & Ganong noted that 'clinical writers such as Visher & Visher (1979), Wald (1981) have argued that negative societal attitudes toward stepfamilies create stress for stepfamily members' (Coleman & Ganong, 1987a, p.22). Stepparents are most affected. As pointed out by Rallings (1976), stepparenting is considered to be difficult partly because of negative stereotypes and role ambiguity surrounding stepparenthood. As difficulties confronting stepparents would affect parenting beliefs and practice, Coleman & Ganong (1987a) noted that 'stereotypes of stepparent and stepchild may affect expectations of one another. It may also affect how they interpret each others' behaviour and subsequent interactions with each other, especially during the early phases of stepfamily development' (p.34). Moreover, as pointed out by Visher (1994), 'a mirror of negativity held up to stepfamilies can lead to a self-fulfilling prophecy -- they (stepparents) don't belong and are bound to fail' (p.338). As stepfamily roles and stepfamilies are perceived negatively, the perceptions are further reinforced; the societal beliefs about wicked stepmothers, cruel stepfathers, and unloved and neglected stepchildren. Stigma attached to steprelationships can result in less social support (Strong & DeVault, 1993). This is a vicious circle which has placed stepparents in a 'no-win situation': because they are seen as negative, they behave accordingly and fail to obtain sufficient support around them which, in turn, reinforces their negative self-image and parenting behaviours.

From a wider perspective, negative social perception of stepfamilies and stepparents has affected the kinds of help they need from the systems outside their families. As pointed out by Cherlin (1978), society has not responded to the needs and problems of these families, which are lacking in institutionalized support. For example, the school system, being the major socialization agent for children other than their own families and where social attitudes are developed, fails to respond sensitively, and regards stepfamilies as no different from intact, nuclear families (Walsh, 1992). Visher & Visher (1979) echo that 'the school reinforces the conflicts and hurt feelings in stepfamilies' (Skeen, Covi & Robinson, 1985, p.123). Hutchison & Hutchison (1979), Kompara (1980), and Visher & Visher (1979) speculate that the tendency for stepfamily members to seek clinical or counselling services is related to social pressure and the lack of acceptance of this family form. Jones (1978) added that 'interpersonal problems in a family are complicated by the mere categorization by society and itself as deviant' (Coleman & Ganong, 1987a, p.22). As the views of teachers and professional helpers have significant influence on parental perceptions and behaviours, I will examine how teachers and social workers perceive stepparenting and stepfamilies and explore the kind of help offered by them in Chapter 5 (pp.126-141).

Parental Perceptions and Beliefs in Stepparenting

Struggle of Stepparents against Generalized Social Expectations and Self-wishes

'Negative stereotyping has the cognitive confirmation effect which would result in behavioral confirmation effect' (Coleman & Ganong, 1987a, p.33). Since the 1970s many social scientists have used the 'deficit-comparison paradigm' to study stepfamilies, which has further reinforced the negative, problematic image of stepfamilies. 'Families do not exist in a social vacuum, and the structure of any given family is partly determined by the particular culture in which it exists' (Dallos, 1992, p.4). Social attitudes, together with values transmitted through the family of origin, will affect how parents in stepfamilies perceive and value themselves in parenting. 'What is of paramount significance, though, is how families translate these societal definitions for themselves and the continuous processes of mutual adjustments and redefinitions that are required in order to manage family life' (Dallos, 1992, p.5). Dallos further pointed out that 'families serve to maintain or reinforce the kinds of beliefs held by the individual members...a central element in a family is a sense of belonging, which is largely a learned cognitive and emotional state' (Dallos, 1992, p.4). In addition, Sigel, McGillicuddy-DeLisi & Goodnow (1992) pointed out the connection between parent cognitions and parent behaviours. They argue that the role of parent cognition is a central issue in the parenting process: 'parent cognitions are linked to parent behaviours, which in turn influence the child' (pp.xiii, xiv). Parents in stepfamilies, as Burgoyne & Clark state, 'typically visualize and act out their role obligations in terms of their actual experiences of parenthood and against a backcloth of generalized public expectations. The private experience of parenting is thus extremely vulnerable to images, constraints and ideologies which are generated in more public arenas' (Burgoyne & Clark, 1981, p.141).

Social attitudes, parental perceptions, beliefs and parenting practice are all inter-related. Social attitudes influence parental perceptions and in turn affecting parenting practice. Firstly, 'blood- parenting' is often seen as an important investment for ensuring a family's continuity and stability (Burgoyne & Clark, 1981). Such parenting is perceived as having many built-in positive aspects. Parent-child relationships which are not blood-related are thought to be lacking the same qualities of those with blood ties, and parenting functioning is questioned. Ganong & Coleman (1983) found that people believe stepmothers and stepfathers are less loving and less kind than mothers and fathers. Bryan, Coleman, Ganong & Bryan (1986) also pointed out that 'stepparents are regarded more negatively than are parents in nuclear families on the basis of social desirability, potency, activity, satisfaction, security, personal character and stability' (Coleman & Ganong, 1987a, pp.24-27). In societies where first-marriage families are predominant and stepparenting is negatively compared, stepparents will have greater difficulties in parenting (Lam, 1998). Secondly, parents' personal values and beliefs in parenting would affect their perceptions of their child as an 'easy or difficult child' to parent. Simons, Whitbeck, Conger & Melby (1990) argue for the importance of beliefs and values as determinants of parenting. They found that 'a mother's beliefs and values tend to affect the parenting of her husband, and they cautioned that destructive parenting by mothers was associated with perceptions of the child as difficult' (pp.386-388). Awareness should be enhanced about the effect of perceived difficulties in stepparenting. Stepparents may be led by their perceptions and see their stepchildren as

19

difficult to parent. It should be noted that parental values would affect his/her spouse and the perception of parents would influence parenting practice.

From the literature about stepparenting, 'myth' is a theme which frequently appears and affects parental cognition and expectation of stepparenting, and it is important to appreciate its place in forming parental perceptions and beliefs in stepfamilies. Let us first look at the definition of 'myth', and then examine its contents and discuss its relevance to this study. Birenbaum (1988) defines a 'myth' as 'a recurring theme or character type that incorporates information about cultural standards. Myths represent a way of viewing the world that embodies a culture's beliefs, regardless of whether those beliefs are accurate' (Dainton, 1993, p.93). There are two components which characterize myths: an externalization which is a 'corpus of images and identities', a cultural explanation of the way the world works; and an internalization whereby the cultural members internalize personal identities based upon the externalized corpus of ideas propagated by the myth (Bruner, 1960). Myths are individuals' personal aspirations reflected in their self-images and identities. The formation, and development of, and changes in those aspirations, however, are very much affected by the cultural beliefs, social attitudes and climate of the society in which individuals are living. Stepfamily members have not lived through an 'ideal' family life in their last family. The 'ideal' family is a picture powerfully painted by the media and generally people wish to have a certain type of family, for example, a happy family, a harmonious family, an intact family, a nuclear family, etc. These are common aspirations and reflect the attributes of the kinds of family few people can realize in real life. For stepfamilies, myths are not only the family's dreams, but also serve a purpose in helping them emerge from a rather undesirable past family life and sustain a hope for better prospects. They are buffers to combat the difficulties left from the past and the tension confronting them at present. By using myths as buffers to combat the troubles brought on by the turbulent past, they at least have dreams for betterment; by using myths as buffers to deal with the present difficulties, these myths lead them to believe, however false they may be, that if they commit or omit some actions in their stepfamilies the social stigma may be lessened. What are the myths held by stepfamilies?

It was noted by experienced clinicians that 'all families come complete with belief systems concerning how their family "should be". However, the belief systems of other types of families tend to be more congruent with reality than the beliefs held by stepfamilies' (Visher & Visher, 1988, p.122). Stepfamilies are found to hold the following myths: '(1) stepfamilies are the same as biological families; (2) stepfamily adjustment will be attained quickly; (3) love and caring will develop instantaneously; (4) working hard prevents the development of a "wicked stepmother"; (5) withdrawing a child from a biological parent enhances the relationship with the stepparent of the same sex; and (6) anything negative that happens is a result of being in a stepfamily' (Visher & Visher, 1988, pp.121-2).

Examining these myths more closely, some of them are for the family as a whole, whilst others are related to stepparent-stepchild relationships. The first, second and sixth myths reflect that stepfamily members wish their families to be the same as biological families, what they wish to happen may be what they have failed to experience in their last family. The first myth shows the influence of the common belief that biological families are 'good' and 'better' than other types of family which, in some cases, is not true. Stepfamily members wishing their family to be equal to the biological ones may feel outcast and do not want to be treated differently from the 'ordinary' families in the society. The second myth points out that stepfamily members wish to adjust quickly in their newly formed families. This reflects their wish to have 'one new happy family' emerging from the troubles they have been through, and again, this is hard to come by without taking considerable time for adjustment in a family where new ties are not strong. The sixth myth follows the second myth; if quick adjustment does not happen, stepfamily members find excuses to blame. It is easier to put the blame on a structure than on people as they feel stepfamilies are already socially stigmatized.

The remaining three myths relate to stepparent-stepchild relationships. The third myth is instant love and care when stepfamilies are formed. This myth is a false belief that people living under the same roof will automatically love and care for each other, whereas relationships need time to develop. Stepfamily members, who may very likely carry with them scars from the painful experiences in the past, may not be able to form trusting relationships and show affection to other members who are new to them. The fourth myth is a belief that stepmothers' hard work will be rewarded by the enhancement of their self-image. Again, this is something far from reality because, despite the increasing number of stepfamilies, some researchers have found that 'the myth of "wicked stepmother" shows no signs of losing strength' (Dainton, 1993, p.94). The fifth myth is that the exclusion of a same-sex biological parent of the stepchild will enhance the stepparent-stepchild relationship.

This seems to be too simply concluded because firstly, the establishment of the stepparent-stepchild relationship does not count on the inclusion or exclusion of the nonresident biological parent of the child alone. Secondly, inclusion of the biological parent may not be definitely a 'good' idea and the exclusion of the biological parent may not be absolutely a 'bad' idea. It depends upon whether the former family was a child-focused one with both parents having considerable emotional investment in their children's upbringing, and the intensity of the emotional upheaval felt by the children before, during and after the parental separation and divorce. Moreover, the willingness of the non-custodial biological parent to be involved in shared parenting also has to be considered.

Impacts of Parental Preception and Belief on Stepparenting: Examining Research Findings

Role expectations and duty-sharing in stepfamilies: Work overload or feeling overload? There are many studies on stepfamilies focusing on the stepparent role and/or stepparenting behaviours. Findings on the role of the stepparent which used data from the larger population, suggest that people perceive greater variability in the role of the stepparent than in that of the biological parent (Schwebel, Fine & Renner, 1991). In addition, the stepparent role is criticized pejoratively (Fluitt & Paradise, 1991; Ganong, Coleman & Jones, 1990; Sauer & Fine, 1988).

The most cited hypothesis used in stepfamily studies is Cherlin's (1978) notion of an 'incomplete institution,' which suggests that the lack of institutionalized support for remarriage after divorce from language, law, and custom is apparent. Stepfamilies are stressful because they lack social support and normative prescriptions for role performance. A lack of institutionalized guidelines leads to more frequent marital conflict in stepfamilies. This suggestion has often been used to relate social impact to role ambiguity in stepfamilies. Recent studies have examined the same suggestion from the angle of the impact of remarriage and stepchildren upon marital conflict in stepfamilies. Studies such as the one conducted by MacDonald & DeMaris (1995), found that remarriage and stepchildren are not necessarily associated with more frequent marital conflict. Stepfamilies have looser family rules which may make for an easier beginning. Moreover, their experiences in the past may help them to develop more realistic expectations. Contrary to the disadvantages suggested by the 'incomplete

22

institution' hypothesis and the myth about 'anything negative that happens is a result of being in a stepfamily', these recent research findings show the brighter side of living in a stepfamily and challenge the 'incomplete institution' hypothesis which has been frequently quoted since its first introduction in 1978.

However, there are other studies which have examined role expectations and enactment, and have focused upon the difficulties faced by parents in stepfamilies. Ihinger-Tallman & Ishii-Kuntz (1988); White & Booth (1985); and White, Brinkerhoff & Booth (1985) suggested that role ambiguity in stepfamilies can lead to stress and conflicts in family relationships. Compared with other parents, stepmothers are more loaded with responsibilities and are more stressed. Fine & Schwebel (1991) found that 'stepmothers are likely to have more parenting stress than stepfathers because of the greater expectations they and others have of them as stepparents, because of the greater role ambiguity they face, and because of the greater difficulties they have in developing attachments with stepchildren' (p.9). When literature on stepparents' roles and stress is reviewed, it is important to note whether one is considering the findings with a deficit assumption. If so, one is led to focus on the facts of family breakdown, and may overlook why some families still stay together in misery and stress. It is necessary to compare intact and stepfamilies objectively and also to measure their family functioning, children's well-being, etc. in order to obtain a balanced picture of the real situation.

There are many tasks to be taken up by parents in a stepfamily in daily parenting practice. The members of a stepfamily progress at different pace during the adaptation period when they first join the family. Visher & Visher have observed tasks to be taken up by a stepfamily when it is newly formed in order to go through adjustment and the building of integration and solidity. The tasks are to: '(1) deal with losses and changes; (2) negotiate developmental needs of different family members; (3) establish new traditions; (4) develop solid couple bond; (5) form new relationships; (6) create parenting coalition; (7) accept continual shifts of membership in the family; and (8) risk involvement of parent-child relationship despite little societal support' (Visher & Visher, 1988, pp. 24-25). When looking at these tasks and the major areas of difficulty (Appendix 4), it is easy to detect that the achievement of the tasks rests heavily on the shoulders of the parents in the stepfamily. There are many issues arising from the parent-child relationship and parenting responsibilities. It should be noted that the major areas of difficulty in five out of the eight tasks (task #1, #3, #5, #6 & #7) are caused by unrealistic belief systems. According to Visher & Visher, successful achievement of these tasks and overcoming the difficulties will help the stepfamily develop realistic expectations of each member's roles and functions, and create a satisfying family life. However, Visher & Visher (1979) noted that stepparents' expectations of themselves are usually unrealistically high. These would affect their parenting behaviours which may incline them to be overly anxious whilst not obtaining the expected outcomes.

Where gender difference in stepparenting roles and responsibilities is concerned an examination of the concepts about housework and the division of labour in a family will help us to appreciate the duties and tasks taken up by parents in stepfamilies. Ann Oakley was the British writer and groundbreaker who acknowledged that housework was work and she learnt from housewives that the tasks they performed were 'monotonous, neverending, and lonely' (Oakley, 1974). Coverman (1989) examined six famous studies on the division of housework in families in the United States which were conducted from the late 1960s to the early 1980s and concluded that wives performed about three or four times as many tasks as do husbands. Some authors have found that there have been some changes in recent years towards increased equality in the division of housework between the couples, but Aulette (1994) found that the change is slow. Pleck (1983) argued that as more women have entered the labour force, they do fewer hours of housework whilst the amount of housework done by husbands remained about the same: the proportion of men's participation in housework seemed to increase because of the alteration in the proportion, which created the appearance that men were contributing more.

With reference to the above discussion, women in general have taken up heavy housework responsibilities, no matter whether they are full-time housewives or employees with a full-time job. When women become parents in stepfamilies, their loads may be even heavier because two broken families have merged into one and the family relationships have become more complicated, thus making division of labour difficult. It is unlikely that the mothers in stepfamilies are able to excuse themselves from playing the major role of housekeeper and care-givers. The findings of a study illustrates this situation: Ishii-Kuntz & Coltrane, using data from a nationally representative sample in the United States, found that wives in stepparent families worked more hours, had less conventional beliefs, and contributed more to family

24

earnings. They also contributed more to overall household labour if their stepfamilies were with stepchildren (Ishii-Kuntz & Coltrane, 1992, pp.229-231).

These findings suggest that wives in dual-income stepfamilies with stepchildren work hard both in the family and at work outside the family. They have to face not only the emotional difficulties arising from the process of adjustment to the family, but also have to shoulder a considerable proportion of housework, which can be stress-producing. But what are the implications of heavy responsibilities in a stepfamily on the role perception and role performance of stepmothers? Why is heavy labour particularly demanded of stepmothers in the stepfamilies, and why do they feel their role as stepmother is particularly difficult? There are mothers in other types of family where the family is large, with complicated family relationships, who also work hard and find it difficult to meet the demands by child care and house work as well, so why are stepmothers special? It is suspected that it is the social expectation of women taking up housework and child care duties, and the overwhelming feelings of stress and strain, rather than the actual housework and child care duties, that have made it difficult for stepmothers to play their roles. Feeling burdened, rather than actually being burdened, seems to be the key factor. This will be uncovered in the examination of data collected in Chapters 5 and 6.

Parent-child relationships in stepfamilies: Difficulties caused by myths, social expectations and gender differences   In the minds of some people, stepfamilies are instant families. Stepfamily relationships are 'glued' together very often without sufficient time and consideration of readiness. Prosen & Farmer (1982) pointed out that the couples in remarried families have had no chance to form a bond, nor to prepare for the arrival of children. Moreover, some experienced clinicians also found that instant families expect instant love of new family members.

In reality, it is rather rare for stepparents not to have met their stepchildren before stepfamilies are formed. Many divorced individuals have entered into another relationship by cohabitation, if not legal marriage. Stepchildren may be taken as one of the conditions of the 'stepfamily package', and they may have been 'parented' by the couples who live together in their trial marriage. In fact 'sufficient time for building relationships' and 'readiness to live together as a family' are subject to debate. How much time is regarded as necessary and sufficient in building a parent-child relationship? How 'ready' is ready? Sometimes the parents may be very ready to make the decision to stay together, but the children may not be ready to do so; it is difficult to have both parents and children ready at the same time. Moreover, it is different meeting the stepchild on social occasions than to having the child living with the couple while experiencing trial cohabitation. Commitment is not necessarily strong for all parties concerned and parents may not play a 'full role' as parents to the stepchild and may not set limits in disciplining as they may do with their own child. When they actually commit themselves to a permanent relationship and form a family, they may raise their standards in limit-setting for their stepchild and set house rules which their stepchild may find it difficult to accept. When stepparent and stepchild are living under the same roof, they interact much more frequently and at times assert their expectations of the relationship. The stepparent and stepchild each bring their past experiences into the stepfamily, and they still need to come to terms with what has not been dealt with in the past, they may be sceptical about the present relationship. Stepparents may feel that their investment is not rewarded and disappointed stepchildren may displace anger with their biological parent onto stepparents, or may feel he or she cannot live up to their expectations. If the biological parent feels guilty that they are not able to fill the part played by the departed parent, he/she may compensate his/her child by inappropriate means; the child may play one parent against the other and this may make building of the stepparent-stepchild relationship more difficult.

Many researchers have studied the difficulties confronting parents and stepparents of different gender when making adjustments to the new family. Fine & Schwebel (1991) suggested that stepmothers have more adjustment difficulties than stepfathers (Clingempeel, Brand & Ievoli, 1984; Santrock & Sitterle, 1987; and Visher & Visher, 1988). Ahrons & Wallisch (1987) noted that when compared with stepfathers, stepmothers are less likely to be satisfied with their relationships with stepchildren. It may be related to the observations that some stepmothers are very eager to play their role well and win the love of their stepchildren. This unrealistic belief would affect stepmothering behaviours which would in turn affect a stepmother's relationship with the stepchild. Research findings suggest that 'of all the step-relationships, the stepmother-stepchild relationship is more problematic' (Pasley, Ihinger-Tallman & Lofquist, 1994, p.7). Clingempeel et al (1984), Hetherington (1987), and Santrock & Sitterle (1987) found that stepmothers display more negative behaviours towards stepchildren. Kupisch (1987) also noted that some stepmothers said that the attributed 'wicked stepmother' characteristics tended to be incorporated into their self-concept.

To examine further the factors leading to the difficulties of stepmothers and an undesirable stepmother-stepchild relationship, Fine & Schwebel (1991) noted the following: (1) stepmothers have fewer socially accepted role prescriptions than stepfathers; they are seen negatively in playing their mothering role and they may live up to their negative image; (2) stepchildren have split loyalty problems when relating to their own mother and their stepmother; (3) as women are traditionally and socially expected to assume responsibility in child care and household tasks, they have greater expectations to do well but they may be frustrated when they fail to develop attachments with their stepchildren. Moreover, Fine & Kurdek (1992) noted that fathers are given custody of their daughters only in exceptional cases such as father-daughter close relationships or conflictual mother-daughter relationships; such situations may make building of stepmother-stepdaughter relationships difficult. However, Guisinger, Cowan & Schuldberg (1989) added that adjustment in stepmother families can be improved if there is a biological father who helps with household and child care tasks. These findings are from observations in stepfamilies in the Western societies. From the Chinese cultural perspective, parents and stepparents may have greater difficulties because of the traditional values upheld by their family members. For example, stepmothers not only have fewer socially accepted role prescriptions, but it is questionable whether they are socially accepted at all as yet. In addition, role expectations in child care and the household tasks of women in Chinese families may adhere to traditional gender-role expectations more strongly than for their Western counterparts. According to the findings of a local study about contemporary Hong Kong families, the researchers noted that 'in families with working wives/mothers, there is a certain increase in the father's share of housework, although this is incomparable to the share of the mothers. There is still a long way to go before the equal division of labour in the family between men and women is achieved' (Law et al, 1995, p.92). This will be explored from the cultural aspects and discussed in the subsequent chapters.

Parent-child relationships may be affected by gender of the children. In general, girls experience more difficulty than boys (Amato & Keith, 1991; Aquilino, 1991; Bray, 1988; Hetherington et al, 1985; Vuchinich, Hetherington, Vuchinich, & Clingempeel, 1991). Stepfathers may be perceived as lax in sexual taboo. Mead (1970) suggested that 'current beliefs about incest as embodied in law and social norms, fail to provide adequate security and protection for children in households of remarriage' (Cherlin, 1978, p.644). Again, the Chinese may have different social attitudes compared with Westerners, towards remarried women bringing their own daughters into the stepfamily. From the figures for remarriages gathered by the Census and Statistics Department, there were 552 cases in 1986 in which both couples had been married before, and in 1997, the figure had more than doubled (1,334 cases) (Hong Kong Census and Statistics Department, Demographic Statistics, April, 1998). Remarriage may be more common now than two decades ago but remarried women may not be accepted to the same extent as their Western counterparts. Mass media and old Chinese movies have portrayed remarried women and stepmothers negatively. They show that when remarried women and their daughters are brought into stepfather families, they are not to be congratulated or discussed socially; stepfathers carry a negative image of men who may take advantage of their stepdaughters sexually. Evidences of social attitudes which cause difficulties in parent-child relationship will be presented and discussed in Chapters 5 & 6.

Child management in stepfamilies: Choice of parenting style affecting parent-child relationship   When examining child management in stepfamilies, we should also look at the two critical determinants commonly believed to be important to children's development. The two domains of parenting are 'support' (including warmth, acceptance, and nurture) and 'control' (including supervision and discipline) as suggested by Barber & Rollins (1990) and Peterson & Rollins (1987). As pointed out by Crosbie-Burnett & Giles-Sims (1994), studies of stepfamilies with children and adolescents have consistently shown that stepparents are less active in both the control and the support dimensions than are parents in nuclear families (Amato, 1987; Astone & McLanahan, 1991; Fine et al, 1993; Kurdek & Fine, 1993; Thomson et al, 1992). Crosbie-Burnett & Giles-Sims (1994) suggested that stepparent support is more important than control in promoting adolescent adjustment, and a disengaged style was associated with the worst adolescent adjustment. These researchers are inclined to use behaviours observed in nuclear families as 'standards' and compare them with those in stepfamilies, resulting in stepfamilies being viewed as less desirable. Moreover, conditions for the children's adjustment prior to the formation of the stepfamily, and their relationships with their natural parents should also be considered.

Other factors such as consistency in parenting in stepfamilies are considered important in child management. According to Ganong & Coleman (1994), generally speaking, stepparents tend to believe that the natural parent is too lenient with the children while the natural parent, in turn, believes the stepparent is too harsh and does not understand the children well. Kupisch (1987), Maddox (1975), McClenahan (1978), Messinger (1976), and Visher & Visher (1979) noted that conflicts over discipline and child rearing are first on the list of problems in stepfamilies. In child management, Capaldi & McRae (1979), and Skeen, Covi & Robinson (1985) noted that three approaches are often used by stepparents but these strategies have not been successful: inattentive and disengaged; actively involved and overly restrictive; and tentative as if 'walking on eggshells'. Stepparents have to be sensitive to their stepchildren's needs and to those of their own children in order to set a comfortable pace for building trusting relationship.

'Parenting' has many diverse aspects and it differs considerably between families. It is too simple to follow a dichotomized paradigm which suggests only the two extremes of the pole -- 'support' and 'control'. Intact, 'normal' families cannot be analyzed by only using the criteria of 'support' or 'control', and this is also true for the complicated family system of stepfamily which has parenting styles developed in the past and are mixed with what is developing in the new family. It should also be pointed out that in Chinese culture, many parents expect obedience from their children. Fathers, in particular, are perceived as harsher disciplinarians and father-child affectional distance is noted (Ho, 1986, pp.35-36) and they do not express love and concern too openly. There are common sayings 'spare the rod, spoil the child' (棒下出孝兒) and 'don't openly praise a child or he/she may be spoilt' (唔好讚，會讚壞). Parental aspirations based on cultural beliefs will be examined further in the next chapter, and the observations of these aspects in stepfamilies will be described and analyzed in Chapters 5 and 6.

Parenting Behaviours in Stepfamilies

Stepfamilies are complicated family systems which are formed after the dissolution of a previous one. In the process of re-building the family, members need to cope with the losses and changes arising from changing structure and relationships. The couple in the stepfamily not only have to establish bonding in their relationship, they also have to play the role of

29

parent or stepparent which demands understanding between parents and children before trusting parent-child relationships can be built. There are dynamics arising from the roles and tasks taken up by parents in stepfamilies which warrant close examination.

Dealing with Losses and Changes

Concepts of losses and changes   During the course of life people will encounter losses at different stages. Some people have difficulties in dealing with those losses, whilst others survive them and have developed coping strategies which have helped them to face on-going, inevitable changes. Before examining the dynamics of losses and changes in stepfamilies, we have to understand firstly why people have difficulties in dealing with losses. As noted by Marris (1974), men are 'all profoundly conservative, and feel immediately threatened if their basic assumptions and emotional attachments are challenged. The threat is real, for these attachments are the principles of regularity on which our ability to predict our own behaviour and the behaviours of others depends' (pp.9-10); 'loss is usually threatening; the victims recognize that unless they learn to understand the situation and cope with it, they will be helpless to secure a tolerable future' (p.149). When a family is dissolved, the members are thrown into situations which are disorganized, chaotic and confused. Members cannot follow the routine in which they once felt secure because no structure was provided. Adults and children alike are confronted with uncertainties which threaten their identity and lower their confidence to cope. In order to deal with these unpleasant experiences, Marris pointed out that people use the 'impulses of conservatism', the purpose being to 'ignore or avoid events which do not match our understanding, to control deviation from expected behaviour, to isolate innovation and sustain the segregation of different aspects of life, which are all means to defend our ability to make sense of life' (p.11).

But losses should not only be seen as negative. As pointed out in crisis theory (Golan,1974), a feeling of loss is one reaction when one is in a crisis situation. The crisis may provide a double opportunity both to solve the present condition and to resolve problems from the past. In Marris' opinion, when confronted with losses, one may try to preserve the status quo, but there are inevitable changes taking place. Changes can be incremental or substitutional; changes can represent growth; and changes may represent loss (pp.20-21). For family members undergoing the dissolution of a family and entering another one, they are indeed experiencing a crisis of discontinuity or the termination of relationship which requires coming to terms with their separation, anxiety and grief; at the same time they are facing changes in reconstituting a family to fill in what has been lost. As pointed out by Marris, these changes 'may generate great anxiety, because they make the future suddenly less secure...they evoke latent impulses of attachment...' (p.148). Therefore it is important to note that 'recovery from grief depends on restoring a sense that the lost attachment can still give meaning to the present, not to finding a substitute' (p.149). By gradually accepting losses as a reality and the fact that the new can never replace the old, it is possible for one to see new light in the new relationships in which one is now involved.

Losses and changes in stepfamilies   Visher & Visher (1979) stated that in general 'stepfamilies experience more psychological stress than do intact families' (p.49). Some of the stresses confronting members of a stepfamily are caused by changing relationships. The change of relationships result mainly from the losses of the spouse and parent due to divorce or the death of the spouse. The impact of these two situations differs between families and the reactions of family members will differ.

Losses and changes as a result of the death of a spouse and parent   The loss of a spouse will affect a person in various ways. The spouse is no longer physically present and the remaining spouse cannot share intimate moments with the deceased and so will be deprived emotionally, psychologically, socially and sexually. In practical terms, the person has lost a work partner who used to share the parenting and household chores, and brought in income for family expenditure. The person is likely to move through the five stages of mourning described by Kubler Ross (1970), i.e., withdrawal, denial, bargaining, depression and acceptance. At the same time, the person has strong feelings of 'numbed disbelief', 'bursts of intense distress or anger', 'feeling disorganized', and 'despair' as depicted by Bowlby (1980) and Murray Parkes (1986).

When examining the mourning of a marital partner in a family, Robinson & Smith (1993) pointed out that 'although the experience of loss for adults is well known to be immensely distressing, the experience of such loss for children is none the less intense, though it is experienced somewhat differently from adults' (Robinson & Smith, 1993, p.51). Children usually have mixed feelings of sorrow and guilt. Some of them take the death of their parents as if it were their fault. Experiences of clinicians reveal that different children react differently to the death of their parents. For example, Combrinck-Graham (1989) explained that the existence of a supportive network, the degree of closeness children have with their parents, and the childrens' ages at the time of death are significant factors in examining how children cope with the death of their parents. Moreover, there are other factors to be considered which may also affect how children cope. If children have experienced the death of their family members before the death of their parents, their ability to cope with losses may have been strengthened. In cases of the death of a parent who has been abusive and rejecting, the loss of that parent may be a relief to the family and the children may not be as stressed as expected. Furthermore, the death of a parent may foster the re-defining of the child's relationship with the surviving parent. In some cases, if the 'children are seen as like the deceased parent and how the surviving parent feels about the lost parent will also affect how the children and the surviving parent redefine their relationships' (Combrinck-Graham, 1989, p.303).

The feeling of loss is likely to be greater if the deceased parent is the mother to which a young child is strongly bonded. As pointed out by Robinson & Smith (1993), the loss of a mother in the early years would be more significant because a child usually clings close to mother when he/she is young. Developmental psychology documents well the maternal influence on children during their formative years. For example, Bowlby (1953) stressed the emotional aspects of the mother-child relationship. He argued that the child needed to experience a warm, loving and continuous relationship with the mother, in which both found satisfaction. Winnicott (1964) declared that 'the foundation of the health of the human being is laid by its mother in the baby's first weeks and months' (p.16). Therefore, the loss of a mother may make children feel unloved, uncared for and abandoned. The loss of a father who has had a close and significant relationship to a child, may arouse profound feelings of loss in the child, as in the case of a young boy who enters the stage of adolescence and needs to identify with the parent of the same gender. Thus, when looking at the impact of gender difference of parents, 'to lose the parent of the same sex means the loss of someone on whom one can choose to model oneself, whereas the loss of the parent of the opposite sex has implications for one's close relationships with all men or all women' (Robinson & Smith, 1993, p.57).

However, although mothering may be stronger than other bonds, Rutter (1982) pointed out that 'mothering has frequently been too mechanical in equating separation with bond disruption, too restricted in regarding the mother as the only person important in a child's life, and too narrow in considering love as the only important element in maternal care' (p.53). He suggested that children may develop several bonds, and that the mother may not be the only or the most significant figure in a child's life. The multiple mothering practice in stepfamilies and multi-generation family groups relating to the understanding of the dynamics in stepfamilies will be further discussed in Chapter 3, and analyzed in Chapters 5 and 6 as they are not uncommon in Chinese culture and Hong Kong Chinese families.

Losses and changes as a result of parental divorce 'Losing a parent through parental divorce is not an absolute loss if given sufficient contact and support from the non-resident parent' (Robinson & Smith, 1993, p.57). Different stepfamilies have different ways of dealing with the issue of the involvement of a non-resident parent after divorce. Some parents feel very bitter and hurt, and will not allow the non-custodial, non-resident parent to come into sight again; while other non-custodial, non-resident parents want to forget their unhappy marriage by cutting off ties completely despite the fact that the Court has granted them visiting rights to their children. When a new relationship is formed and there is the prospect of forming a new family, the divorcees have to come to terms with the losses in their last relationship and changes in the new relationship. Sometimes, a parent not only feels defeated and frustrated after battling with his/her former spouse in order to dissolve a once devoted and loving relationship, but he/she also has a deep feeling of loss if the child born from the last relationship is not allowed to live with him/her due to child custody decided by the Court. The feeling of loss will be felt greater when he/she remarries, his/her spouse has a child and he/she has to live with a child who is not his/her own in a stepfamily.

It will be more difficult if there are extended kin, either living in or living away, who have not resolved their feelings of grief in respect of their losses and separation before the stepfamily is formed. Their reactions may have an impact on the development of relationships in the newly formed stepfamily. In order to understand losses and changes in a stepfamily after parental divorce, we need to consider how parents, children and significant kin cope with losses and changes.

From the developmental perspective, there are seven stages in the stepfamily cycle: the new beginnings, assimilation, awareness, restructuring, action phase, integration, and ultimate acceptance (Robinson & Smith, 1993). At the 'new beginnings' stage, when a stepfamily is formed, family members have wishful thinking about stepfamily life and relationships. Stepparents wish to establish relationships with their stepchildren quickly whilst stepchildren fantasize about their reunion with their lost or departed parents. But losses and changes are life tasks which parents must undergo before they can help their children to adjust to the stepfamily life. Most adults who enter into another marriage should confront their fears of another failure and a stage in which they are 'swimming' at the same time as 'sinking' (Papernow, 1993). They also have to deal with the unresolved grief about the loss of the previous family. They need to help their children and stepchildren to handle their feelings of loss for the deceased parent, and the loyalty conflicts between each of their parent (Robinson & Smith, 1993). They should allow themselves to be challenged by the blending of the family culture and life style of the past with the present, and to feel fulfilled, disappointed and frustrated at the same time. Some parents are reminded of their failure because they are custodial parents of their children from their past marital relationship. The presence of these children and the resident parents will make their painful past difficult to forget and also make it hard to concentrate on the present tasks they need to fulfil. They need to come to terms with feelings of loss before they can 'map the territory' and begin to set individual tasks and share family tasks in the stepfamily in the 'awareness stage' (Papernow, 1993; Robinson & Smith, 1993).

Different family members may have different reactions to cope with the pain and the losses at different stages. Adults have a difficult time going through an emotional divorce after they have legally divorced their spouses, and children whose parents have divorced have different ways of dealing with loss. There are underlying conflicts of split loyalty which, again, may arouse intense feelings with which they must deal with. Wallerstein & Kelly (1980) noted that 'young children would predominately express feelings of sadness and abandonment. They found it difficult to express their anger towards their departed father [parent], and they entertain fantasy, often in secret, that their parents would reconcile' (Robinson, 1993, p.164). Their wishes may be unspoken, but they are influential or even powerful in preventing them from becoming close to their stepparents: although 'it is now known that, given sufficient contact with the parent who lives in another household, after a period of distress the children of divorce can recover and resume their developmental path' (Robinson & Smith, 1993, p.57). In some cases, they are not given chances to meet their non-custodial biological parents and deal with their feelings of loss, anger, hurt and abandonment. In the family where they live, they are not allowed to talk about the past because of the pain and the shame the divorce brings. The reactions to losses and changes in stepfamilies will be further examined in the chapters which use data from the empirical study.

Building Couple Bond

The importance of couple bonding   When a remarried family is built, the architects of the family -- the couple -- have to face many losses and changes and they need time to recover from emotional divorce at the beginning stage. These persons have fantasies and 'they yearn to heal the pain created by divorce or death. Biological parents hope for a new spouse who will not only a better partner, but a better parent than the previous spouse. Stepparents hope to provide what had been missing' (Papernow, 1993, p.13). But in reality, they need to build a couple bond before they can cope better in the various roles and tasks. Why is building a couple bond so important?

Building a couple bond is 'conceptualized as establishing a boundary around the marital dyad' (Ganong & Coleman, 1994, p.63). In Minuchin's (1974) explanation, the concept of boundaries refers to rules in the family system. The rules not only define the membership and position, but also the tasks and functions required in those roles. Visher (1994) noted that 'the couple relationship is crucial to any family... it is the relationship on which all the others depend for stability...couple bonding is vital; it is the "glue" that makes it possible for a stepfamily household to stay together long enough to work through the process necessary for the other relationships to develop' (p.335). Her notions are also supported by Mills (1984) and Visher & Visher (1988): 'a strong bond between adult partners is helpful in facilitating the development of positive stepparent-stepchild relationships and serves as a buffer when other family relationships are stressful' (Ganong & Coleman, 1994, p.63). Ganong & Coleman recalled that Cissna, Cox & Bochner (1990) had noted two important tasks for relationship development in newly formed stepfamilies, i.e. '(1) the remarried couple needs to establish the solidarity of the marriage in the minds of the stepchildren; and (2) they also need to establish parental authority, particularly the credibility of the stepparent' (Ganong & Coleman, 1994, p.64).

Thus bonding of the couple is essential for development of parent-child relationship in stepfamilies. They can commit themselves to the role of parenting because mutual support is available. However, the development of couple bonding takes time and it is not unusual to learn that many stepparents have to take up the parenting role before they are ready and before marital relationship is solidified. For working parents time is always limited. These parents may not have any private time away from the children for consolidating their relationship; parental duties may have to be taken up in a task-oriented way. These are all factors which contribute to difficulties in marital relationship, which in turn affect parent-child relationship in stepfamilies. These considerations will be discussed in the subsequent chapters in the context of the expectations of marriage in a changing society.

The Negotiation of Different Developmental Needs of Family Members

Duvall & Miller and Carter & McGolderick based their work on the development of a family life at various stages, from the marriage of the couple to the dissolution of the family through death. As the divorce rate rises, individual and family needs cannot be understood from a single normative perspective; there is variation of needs due to differences in family structure, which require additional perspectives in order to identify the needs and difficulties of these persons and families. From clinical observations, Visher (1994) noted that 'the pain expressed by stepfamily members occurs because human emotional needs of a very basic nature are, at least initially, not being met by stepfamily structure. Among these deep human needs are: to be accepted, cared about, and loved; to maintain secure attachments to special individuals; to belong to a group and not be a stranger; and, to have personal autonomy and control' (Visher, 1994, p.339). In addition, and more specifically, from the developmental stage perspective, Carter & McGolderick included additional stages to their theoretical frame for 'those associated with divorce, single parenthood and remarriage -- which they consider are necessary in order to allow the family to restablise and proceed developmentally' (Robinson, 1993, p.44).

In the patterns of development in remarried families described by Robinson & Smith (1993), it is at the early stages of family formation that the parents and children get to know each other and it is when they start to explore the needs of family members. In the 'Awareness Stage' family members begin to define the boundaries and the tasks for individuals. For outsider stepparents, the individual task in this stage involves naming the feelings evoked by their outsider position (jealousy, resentment, inadequacy) with less shame and more clarity ...by the end of the Awareness Stage, stepparents can name some of their needs for changes that would make them more comfortable in the foreign territory they are curious about; and unthreatened by their deepening awareness...' (Papernow, 1993, pp.120-121). At this time the stepparents may have learnt about the likes and dislikes of their stepchildren, their friends, and the kinds of activities they enjoy. Papernow further noted that 'as self-acceptance and clarity grow, the final individual task of the Awareness Stage for stepparents is to form a few definitive statements about their needs' (Papernow, 1993, p.127).

The place and function of biological parents in a stepfamily is crucial for they are the ones who share their knowledge with the stepparent about the needs of their children and act as the facilitator between stepparent and stepchild in expressing their needs. Papernow pointed out that 'just as it is the stepparent's task to name his or her needs of change, it is the biological parents' task to be able to articulate how much change his or her children can tolerate...the trick is to find the right balance between overprotecting children, and asking too much of them' (Papernow, 1993, p.134). It is important for parents in stepfamilies to understand their children's needs by encouraging them to share their anxieties caused by the changes and feelings of split loyalty between the parents living with them and those who are living away from their families.

Stepchildren have needs like other children of their age. Because children's needs differ when they are at different life stage, their needs can be understood from a normative life stage point of view; for example, Erikson's developmental theory (1950) and Pringle's needs of children (1980). In a stepfamily, as noted by Robinson (1993), 'the younger the children were at time of the remarriage, the more likely they were to be absorbed into the remarried family' (p.249). Older children also need to be parented but also need to negotiate their developmental needs; at this stage they would need guidance from their parents but strive for independence. The complicated family structure and relationships of a stepfamily may arouse conflicts especially during the early stage of family formation. It was noted by Visher & Visher (1979) that 'the new stepfamily is attempting to establish a sense of family cohesiveness, and the adolescent is asked to be a participating member of that family at the stage of personal development that requires the loosening of emotional ties with the family' (p.176). Therefore, while noting that the child has to deal with conflicts arising in the course of development, parents in stepfamilies have to recognize the needs of the teenage stepchild from two aspects. One aspect is that difficulties may arise when the stepchild is coping with the demands upon him/her while he/she is adjusting to the stepfamily; the other aspect is that the stepchild has to fulfil the developmental tasks which are required by the particular life stage he/she is going through, which may also cause problems.

Another area of concern are gender-related problems of parent-child relationships affected by parental divorce and remarriage. Studies have generally found that opposite sex parent-child relationships are more difficult in stepfamilies (Hetherington, Cox & Cox, 1978; Margolin & Patterson, 1975; Santrock & Warshak, 1979). Boys have difficulties in accepting parental divorce and the mother-son relationship after divorce is often more problematic than the mother-daughter relationship (Hetherington, Cox & Cox, 1978). Boys may welcome the same sex parent figure and they have less difficulties relating to stepfathers than girls (Santrock, et al, 1982; Clingempeel, Brand & Ievoli, 1984). They need to re-establish the relationship with their mothers and to define their relationship with their fathers and stepfathers. On the other hand, girls have more difficulties accepting their mother's remarriage, fearing that a stepfather will disrupt the mother-daughter bond (Clingempeel, Brand & Ievoli, 1984; Santrock el al, 1982). The needs of daughters who want to maintain a close relationship with their mothers should be recognized and answered. All in all, attention should be given to the feelings arising from children of different genders caused by parental divorce and remarriage and the different needs which may have arisen due to the stage of their development and adjustment in a newly formed stepfamily.

Equity and Authority in Stepfamilies

In stepfamilies the quality of parenting can be affected by the relationships of family members in different sub-systems, namely, marital, parent-child, and wider family subsystems. The parental division of labour in accepting the roles and tasks required to help children grow reflects the social expectations for those roles, parental role enactment, and the relationships between adult-carers in the family. In the following, I will discuss the expectations of parental roles in stepfamilies, how parental roles and tasks are shared, whether children feel that they are being treated equally, and who has obtained more power in decision-making and child management in stepfamilies.

Equity in dividing parental and housekeeping tasks   The major tasks for which parents in stepfamilies are child care and household tasks. Heavy household labour affects the quality of child care. There are three common explanatory models of household labour allocation (Kamo, 1988; Pleck, 1983). Firstly, there is the Relative Resources Model which asserts that housework is seen as a chore that people would tend to avoid and the family member who has the greatest resources and power in decision-making will do less. Secondly, the Ideology Model notes that family members hold certain values and beliefs about how household tasks should be shared between men and women. These values and beliefs would affect the division of labour in a family. Lastly, the Time Availability Model assumes that household chores are allocated to the family member who has the most free time, and in so-doing, resources are utilized to the maximum. In addition to these, 'the size of the household and the presence of younger children is assumed to increase the amount of household labour' (Ishii-Kuntz & Coltrane, 1992, p.220). These notions seem rather simplistic; however, I wanted to find out from this study how this common practice of household labour allocation affects the Chinese stepfamilies in Hong Kong. For example, in dual-earner stepfamilies, neither parent nor stepparent may have free time, so who will be allocated most child care and household chores? In stepfamilies where wives earn more than husbands, would the husbands who have fewer resources and less power do more housework? Would children in stepfamilies be expected to share household tasks with their parent and stepparent? What are the implications and consequences if housework is not divided equitably?

Literature on this subject which concerns stepfamilies is rather confused. For example, Giles-Sims (1984) thought that people would expect stepparents to share more equally in child care duties than natural parents, but in 99 in-depth interviews with the husband or wife in stepfamilies, she found that 'over half of the respondents expected stepparents and natural parents to share the child-rearing duties equally' (1984, p.127). Other sources suggest that although in general members of some stepfamilies are more actively involved in task-sharing, the share of duties in stepfamilies is not equal. Demo & Acock (1993) found that 'mothers in remarried families did not differ from mothers in first marriages in the amount of household

39

work they did, and both groups of women did far more than their husbands' (Ganong & Coleman, 1994, p.65). Guisinger, Cowan & Schuldburg (1989) also noted that many of the stepmothers did not think the amount of work their husbands did was enough (Ganong & Coleman, 1994, p.65). These seem to show that child care duties and household tasks are not equally shared by couples; women have the heavier share as observed in different types of families. In stepfamilies, stepmothers wish that their husbands would share more of their workload and they feel psychologically burdened. One study noted that stepmothers are stressed; the researchers identified two conditions under which adjustment in stepmother families can be improved. One is having a biological father who helps with household and child care tasks (Guisinger, Cowan & Schuldburg, 1989).

It seems likely that women in stepfamilies feel burdened with housework but whether they are more burdened than those in first marriages is not clear. It is, however, clear that in general, attitudes to this work are bound up with assumptions about gender roles and that 'the Ideology model' holds up better than the other two. How couples perceive the situation and whether they regard it as equitable may influence marital satisfaction in such stepfamilies; as Guisinger, Cowan & Schuldbury (1989) point out, remarital satisfaction is related to task-sharing in stepfamilies and the couple's perception on how far child care, household chores and decision-making are divided equally. If the couple is not satisfied maritally, it is likely that their function as parents may also be negatively affected. It is also possible that stepmothers are particularly sensitive in this issue, partly because of past experience, partly because of idealized expectations of the second time and partly because of the stigma which they fear in becoming stepmothers.

Division of parenting duties and parenting a stepchild compared with parenting a biological child   Parenting in stepfamilies is a demanding and complicated duty. Designation of parental tasks and involvement in parental duties reflect beliefs of parenting underlying role enactment. Traditionally the mother's role has been to devote herself to child care, whilst the father's role is that of a breadwinner. Bowlby (1953) pointed out there are implicitly accepted traditional beliefs about the role of women and men within the family. From the feminist point of view, such a division of roles puts women in a subservient position; they are expected to take up the roles cast by cultural and social expectations. When the literature on stepfamilies is reviewed, there is strong evidence to suggest that stepmothers have more adjustment difficulties than do stepfathers and they are less likely to be satisfied with their relationships with stepchildren (Ahrons & Wallisch, 1987; Fine & Schwebel, 1991). Clinicians such as Visher & Visher believed that 'it may be rooted in expectations that women are the ones who are primarily responsible for the ambience of the home and the care of the children, including stepchildren' (Visher & Visher, 1988, p.19). Researchers who studied the lives of stepfamilies in the Sheffield area in England also observed that 'women are also expected and encouraged to imagine themselves as mothers and to anticipate the fulfilment which it is believed motherhood will embody' (Burgoyne & Clark, 1981, p.139). Social expectations then, have made some women to take on the primary role of childcarer and housekeeper in a family, whilst some take on such roles with unrealistic hopes. It is because 'many women still derive much of their self-esteem from their role as parents' (Visher & Visher, 1988, p.19). Many stepmothers also wish to fulfil this expected role and 'begin their new partnership with idealized expectations of their capacity to restore and recreate a satisfying domestic life for their new family' (Burgoyne & Clark, 1981, p.139).

Closer examination into findings of some studies reveals division of parenting duties in stepfamilies is, in fact, unequally shared. Mothers/stepmothers are more actively involved and have taken up a greater share of duties than their spouses. For example, Santrock & Sitterle (1987) pointed out that remarried mothers were more involved in child discipline, arrangement of daily activities and discussion with their child. Further, it was observed that 'stepfather functioned as a more distant and detached observer, and the biological, remarried mother was more responsive to and actively involved with her children' (Santrock, Sitterle & Warshak, 1988, p.159).

Unequal sharing of parenting duties also relate to whether the parenting of one's own child or of the spouse's child. The number of stepchildren, whether the child born from the last marriage is brought into the stepfamily, the gender and age of the children and stepchildren, and so on are all factors affecting the way parenting and parent-child relationships are handled. Stepmother families are known as 'the most likely of all stepfamily types to have conflict and poor adjustment' (Ganong & Coleman, 1994, p.77). It should be also noted that 'intrapersonal characteristic such as values, beliefs, cognitive styles, temperaments, and personality' also affect the stepmother-stepchild relationship (Ganong & Coleman, 1994, p.82). Of these numerous factors, cultural values and parental beliefs are the most significant for understanding difficulties in stepparent-stepchild relationships. This is because in some cultures, such as the Chinese, the blood tie is valued very much, and it affects parenting practice. Parents would normally feel closer to their own children and do not relate as closely to their stepchildren. Children who are taken into a stepfamily as a result of their mother's remarriage may not be accepted by the spouse. This is because the divorced status of a woman carries a social stigma (Yeung & Kwong, 1995, p.51) and her children will also be looked down upon because they do not share the same blood as their stepfathers.

In stepfamilies where members still have to come to terms with the feelings arising from the loss of parents or parental divorce, there are likely to be frictions between the stepsiblings. There may be competition between biological and stepchildren for attention and affection from the parents in the stepfamily, and when a new child is born to the remarriage, children from former marriages may feel left out of the new relationship. It is pointed out by Ganong & Coleman (1993) that some parents who have both biological children and stepchildren may feel closer to their biological children than parents who have biological children and no stepchildren (pp.138-139). The belief in the blood-tie makes the biological parent and child feel that it is natural for them to have closer relationship than that of a stepparent-stepchild relationship, and this belief may affect the child's expectations as to how he/she should be treated as well as the fairness of parenting practice perceived by those excluded from this biological relationship. Demo, Small & Savin-Williams (1987) observed that children are influenced by their perception of parental attitudes and behaviours, rather than actual parental attitudes and behaviours or those reported by their parents. Therefore, it is important to deal with the children's emotions arising from how they feel about being treated by their parents.

Authority in the Stepfamily

Although some researchers such as Coleman & Ganong (1989) and Crosbie-Burnett & Giles-Sims (1991) found that 'decision-making in remarriages tend to be shared fairly equally between partners' (Ganong & Coleman, 1994, p.64), Hobart (1991) noted that remarried men 'gave in' to their wives more when there are disagreements as compared to men in first marriages. But stepfamilies are complicated family systems in which family members have to relate to a sizable number of in-laws and relatives. The multiple sets of expectations and the different values and life-styles may have considerable impact on their daily living. It has pointed out by Henry, Ceglian & Ostrander (1993) that as a stepfamily negotiates and establishes new rules, roles, and responsibilities, the decisions affect, or may be affected by, the grandparents.

Western literature generally portrays kin network as rather supportive to the stepfamilies (Ganong & Coleman, 1983; 1994). At the time when their children end their previous marriages, they experienced emotional difficulties which may be rather intense. 'For older generations, the losses may be particularly difficult since the losses resulted from another's action, allowing less of a sense of control', and they may 'face the task of letting go of the fantasy of a "life-long happy marriage" between the adult-child and the adult-child's former spouse' (Henry, Ceglian & Ostrander, 1993, p.27). During the crisis of their children, grandparents react differently according to their relationships with their children and the resources available. Some grandparents may offer practical help in the forms of child care and financial assistance. They may have good relationships with their grandchildren and from some studies, grandchildren strongly affirmed that their grandparents are an influence on their lives by virtue of their values, behaviour patterns and advice (Kennedy & Kennedy, 1993). Wilks & Melville (1990) cautioned that there would be a paradoxical aspect to such influence. Grandparents can be a great source of support at times of familial re-organization; however, such affiliation may potentially interfere with the building of solidarity in the stepfamily. Henry, Ceglian & Ostrander (1993) also pointed out that there is a developmental challenge presented to grandparents for them to increase contact with, and support for, the adult-child without resuming a parental role. Johnson (1988) suggested that they should provide support at a level of equal power, rather than as a parent resuming control over the adult-child's life.

The above are taken from Western literature with reference to the specific cultural context. Distinctive manifestations of parent-child relationships and role expectations in Chinese families are different. Some manifestations may also appear in Western families but they are more strongly expected in the Chinese families holding traditional values. For example, although the idea of 'raising children for one's old age' is not always realized in practice now, 'children still think that the socially desirable answer is to be responsible for taking care of one's elderly parents' (Law et al, 1995, p.93). Mothers who hold traditional values consider that they lose their sons to their daughters-in-law when their sons marry, whilst former grandparents may still rightfully demand to visit their grandchildren after the dissolution of their child's marriage and this does not have to be authorized by a court. The extent and intensity of grandparents' influence on their grandchildren and parent-child relationships in stepfamilies in Hong Kong are rather different from Western societies. Therefore, the culture specific characteristics affecting hierarchy and authority in Chinese families should be understood. In Chapters 5 & 6, these will be discussed together with an examination of how authority is exercised in stepfamilies.

Communication and Conflict Management

Communication between parents and children   It is through communication that the information required for effective role performance and task accomplishment is exchanged (Brody, 1974; Alexander, 1973). In its content, communication can be affective, instrumental, or neutral (Brody, 1974). Baumrind (1966) and Maccoby & Martin (1983) also noted that 'adequate control, reasonably high demands, warmth, and open communication between parents and children are all necessary for healthy child development' (Thomson, McLanahan & Curtin, 1992, pp.368-9). Many clinicians believe that open and trusting communication may facilitate conflict management. In stepfamilies many stepparents have to deal with their personal problems and work hard on building marital bonds at the adjustment phase and they do not focus on communicating well with their stepchildren in order to establish trusting relationship with them. They may be negatively judged in their parental attributes. From the findings of Amato (1987), Astone & McLanahan (1991), Furstenberg & Nord (1985) and Hetherington, Cox & Cox (1982), 'stepparents provide less warmth and communicate less well with children than do original parents' (Thomson, McLanahan & Curtin, 1992, p.368). This may result in difficulties in role allocation and task accomplishment since the lack of effective communication blocks successful problem-solving and guarantees a perpetuation of tensions (Steinhauer, Santa-Barbara & Skinner, 1984).

Parents differ in their ways of relating to their children through communication. Some stepparents want to relate closely to their stepchildren but they lack experience and skill in interacting with them. Ganong & Coleman (1994) pointed out that clinicians observed that a warm, nurturant stepparent sometimes arouses resistance in stepchildren who fear being disloyal to their deceased/non-residential biological parent if they warm up to the stepparent (p.74). They further noted that stepparents, particularly stepfathers, may be unaware of the need to develop a bond of attachment before disciplining them. Santrock, Sitterle & Warshak (1988) noted that stepfathers function as a more distant and detached observer and the biological, remarried mother is more responsive to and actively involved with her children.

Conflict Management in Parenting

If parents are congruent in their childrearing orientation, they are more likely to be effective in parenting (Tein, Roosa & Michaels, 1994). Minuchin (1985) also noted that incongruent parental behaviours are associated with negative interaction patterns. Re-married people may not have the time or skills to resolve the conflicts and problems from their previous relationship and former family before they form the stepfamily, and they may carry with them the old problem-solving pattern and methods of relating into the family. Others may have the skills to resolve conflicts but are overwhelmed with the tasks and duties required at the beginning phase when the stepfamily is formed, so that they may not be able to respond and cope adequately. According to Bray, Berger, Silverblatt & Hollier (1987) and Larson & Allgood (1987), 'remarried couples have been found to possess poorer conflict resolution and problem-solving skills and to be more coercive toward each other than couples in first marriages' (Ganong & Coleman, 1994, p.66). Maddox (1975), Kupisch (1987), and Visher & Visher (1979) have also noted that 'conflicts over discipline and child rearing rank first on the list of problems in remarriage units' (Walsh, 1992, pp.710-711).

Major parenting conflicts in stepfamilies can be identified as those arising from parental incongruence in expectations and practice, and those between parent, child and extended families. As parent-child relationship problems have already been discussed in earlier sections, the following will focus on conflict management of parenting problems by parents in stepfamilies.

In general, in parenting practice, stepparents tend to believe the biological parent is too lenient with the children, while the biological parent believes the stepparent is too harsh and does not understand the children well (Furstenberg, 1987; Thomson, McLanahan, & Curtin, 1992). This difference in beliefs contributes to difference in parenting practice, which is

45

also a cause of marital conflict and difficulties in establishing stepparent-stepchild relationships. When there are conflicts in child management, parents in stepfamilies may often react by letting the biological parent take care of his/her own child's problems. Ganong & Coleman (1994) suggested that stepchildren are more comfortable in dealing with rules imposed by their parents because of their shared history. The biological parent becomes the 'fixed advocate' of the child, even during those times when he and she is annoyed with the child's behaviour. However, he/she should allow himself/herself to act as an 'alternating advocate' without feeling that he/she must defend the child or be over-involved in disciplining (Browning, 1994).

In addition, child disciplining in a stepfamily may not only be enforced by the parents living in the stepfamily. Non-resident, non-custodial biological parents also have influence on the rules set for child management. In general, it seems that 'there is more competition from the noncustodial parent when the remarriage occurs soon after the divorce' (Walsh, 1992, p.714). Children usually suffer when their custodial parent, non-custodial parent, biological parent and stepparents are unwilling to cooperate to facilitate the arrangement of visits or agree on limit-setting.

Another influential factor is the involvement of relatives, especially grandparents, in child management in stepfamilies. In Western literature, as mentioned earlier, grandparents are seen as supportive figures for their divorced child. They may act as 'volunteer firefighters' or 'watchdogs' as described by Cherlin & Furstenberg (1986). Clingempeel, Colyar, Brand & Hetherington (1992) speculated that the stress of a new remarriage might cause grandparents to remain more involved with the child and grandchildren, at least temporarily. For many Chinese families, the degree of involvement of grandparents in stepfamilies is more than temporary and their influence is far-reaching. Grandparents may actually live in or pay frequent visits to the stepfamily without prior notice, and give suggestions on rule-setting and child disciplining. Conflicts between parents and resident grandparents, as noted by Hanson, McLenahan, & Thomson (1996), may be an important source of disadvantage for children in stepfamilies. This kind of relationship and living arrangement is not uncommon in Chinese families and, therefore, warrants closer examination in the following chapters.

Summary of the Chapter

In this chapter I have first defined stepfamilies and the classification of stepfamilies. I have then examined social attitudes from the cultural stereotyping perspective. The negative attitudes towards stepparenting and stepfamilies were explored in reviewing Western literature and research findings. It was found that although both Western and Chinese societies view stepparenting and stepfamilies negatively, Western societies expressed their views and feelings more openly whilst Chinese societies tended to sweep the issues under the rug.

From the literature review, it seems that social attitudes have affected parental perception and beliefs and in turn, have influenced parenting behaviours. Role expectations, the division of labour in parenting, parent-child relationships, and child management in stepfamilies are influenced. As the main focus of this study is parenting in stepfamilies, concepts relating to parenting behaviours were considered in detail in five aspects.

1. Dealing with losses and changes: I have reviewed and discussed the concepts of loss and change. Stepfamily is a family system in transformation, the unfinished business and the challenges faced by family members at the times of change needed to be understood.
2. Building couple bond: a review of the literature on couple bond was made. The stability of the marital relationship can help facilitate the building of trusting relationships between stepparents and stepchildren. This is an important area which can help us to understand the couples' aspirations for their marriage and the difficulties they may encounter in a stepfamily.
3. Negotiation of different developmental needs of family members: a review of the literature on the needs of stepfamily members was made. It brings to our attention that it is important to note the developmental and gender perspectives when examining parenting behaviours in stepfamilies.
4. Equity and authority in stepfamilies: because the relationships in stepfamilies are complicated, the equity of gender-role tasks, whether the stepchild and biological child are treated equally, and authority conflicts in stepfamilies are important issues to be noted.

5. Communication and conflict management: the concepts of communication and conflict management in parenting were explored. These are components of the theoretical framework for this study which serve as a guide to data analysis in Chapters 5 and 6.

3 Traditional Chinese Beliefs and Current Views in Hong Kong Influencing Family Life and Family Relationships

Introduction

In Chapter 2 major concepts concerning social attitudes, parental perceptions and behaviours in stepfamilies have been reviewed and discussed with reference to Western literature and research findings. Cultural considerations are crucial as this study was conducted in Hong Kong and the respondents were Chinese. In this chapter I shall examine important Chinese concepts and discuss their relevance to this study.

This chapter is divided into three parts. The first part highlights fundamental Chinese beliefs and values which influence family life and relationships. The second part discusses some of the changes in society and values which took place when New China was formed by the Communist Party and also during and after the Cultural Revolution. Such changes have had a tremendous impact on the values upheld by the Chinese and greatly affect the structure and life of families. Many Hong Kong people have relatives living in Mainland China and they pay frequent visits to them. Their contact with each other has sustained and reinforced traditional values and beliefs. The third part discusses current family life and family relationships in Hong Kong. Awareness of these will facilitate an understanding of the social attitudes, as reported by stepmothers, in the subsequent chapter.

Fundamental Beliefs and Values Influencing Chinese Family Life and Family Relationships

There are various beliefs and values which have had an impact on the family life and relationships of the Chinese. Among the more prominent ones are Confucianism, Taoism and Buddhism. The latter two are regarded more as religious beliefs which emphasize ritualistic practice, with Taoism preaching the complementary relationship between men and environment, and Buddhism encouraging the cleansing of one's mind and unloading of one's desire in order to find ultimate happiness and reward after life. Confucianism has a rather different emphasis. Confucius, the master of Chinese philosophy, lived between 551 and 479 B.C. and his disciples are respected as role models. Confucianism has focused on human issues in relation to country, families and their members. It has been a prevailing ideology in Chinese history throughout the centuries and generations. These teachings have contributed to the building of Chinese moral and ethical beliefs, and have had a strong influence on the Chinese family and social relationships. The following discussion will focus upon Confucianism because it continues to be the main influence on Chinese beliefs and values in Hong Kong families.

Highlights of the Basic Beliefs of Confucianism

Harmony through following order and taking position   Confucianism stresses 'ennobling qualities of righteousness, beauty, harmony, and order' and these qualities are diffused into family relationships (Redding, 1993, p.44). In order to achieve harmony, there are orders to which people must comply, and positions for people to take. The aim is to define roles so that behaviours can be explained (King, 1985, p.60). Individuals would be likely to develop the virtues of behaving properly and having beautiful characters if they live in a harmonious environment where ordered relationships are sustained. These beliefs had particular value in Confucian time, when the country was engaged in widespread warfare. The warlords were eager to expand their territory while their people longed for peace and better social order. By introducing a clear, systematic rank and order system to the country and to the paramount social unit in the society -- the family, the position of people in various systems was defined and the behaviour expected from the role would follow. Indeed this suggestion for structured relationships was indeed appealing to the rulers and the ruled at that time.

After two thousand years, Confucianism has been challenged because of the constraints it has imposed on human relationships. Yet its advocacy of developing and sustaining harmony still holds as an ideal to be appreciated in human relationships, as shown in the proverbs used in everyday language. For example, 'harmony is to treasure' (以和為貴) is encouraged in social relationships in general and is used for dealing with relationship conflicts; 'harmony in family brings prosperity to that family' (家和萬事興) is advocated in families and is usually used by the older generation to intervene in conflicts between youngsters; and 'harmonious relationships of the seniors resulting in friendly relationships of the juniors' (上和下睦) is fostered in families, as well as in work places, to sustain better relationships.

Owing to rapid social change, people have to be flexible in the taking up and enacting of their roles. Clear-cut, well-defined and structured behaviours of each role are, therefore, not feasible and practical. For example, the Confucianists' position that the male is the 'Master of his family' (一家之主) is not strictly followed by families at the present time. Some husbands in contemporary Chinese families have greater acceptance of their wives earning higher wages than they do themselves and of their wives taking over their role of making important decisions. Moreover, in atypical family structures, as in single parent families, the single father has to take on dual roles as father and mother to his children who are living with him; alternatively the eldest child may take up the mothering role to care for his/her younger siblings when the parent is out working.

Individuals as relational beings   From the perspective of Confucianism, 'Chinese society is neither individual-based nor society-based, but relation-based' and man is a 'relational being' (King, 1985, p.63). Redding interpreted Ketcham's work (Ketcham, 1987, p.111) and noted that 'the individual is instead a connection...for the Chinese, fulfillment comes from the very structure and dynamics of the relationships and emphasis on belonging' (Redding, 1993, p.44). Family is seen as a familistic group which may consist of extended kin and distant relatives or clan; the boundary in a family is blurred and permeable. It permits open membership and encourages interdependence of the members. It is quite different from Western beliefs that people should develop themselves by individualism. As a result of Confucian thought, people have no privacy because family members in higher 'rank' will intrude into their private matters. From a positive point of view, however, members of a family can get the support and resources they need from a network of relatives and clan. The older generation, who retain traditional Chinese thinking based on Confucian thought, would prefer large families living under the same roof. In feudal families before the industrial revolution, the idea was a practical one. More family members living nearby would provide more hands at work and generate greater productivity of the family business. An elder member who had more offspring had greater power in decisions. That person would be seen as more influential and powerful if he/she had more male offsprings. Although families where the older generation still hold the belief that they have the ultimate power in the family may not require their adult children to sustain the family business, they may nevertheless penetrate the life of their children by telephoning them at odd hours, demanding that they visit them, or arriving at their home without being invited. The extreme situations are those where older generations are living with adult children. Some of them are not aware that interference with child management and the disciplining of grandchildren may make the parents of the children feel that their parental rights are being taken away.

In contemporary Chinese families, relationships between family members living together and relatives living away from them are regarded as equally important. Chinese would lend support to them when the need arises. They would rely upon the immediate family members for support before reaching out to those outside their family system. A hierarchy of help is formed from the intimately-related to the distantly-related. Although requests for help are not always answered or may be conditionally entertained, the existence of a relationship pool means connections which have functional purposes are sustained. The larger one connection circle the person has, the greater support he/she feels he/she has from these resource persons. Sometimes the connections may include people who do not have blood ties with the person as in the case of an 'adopted sibling' (誼或契兄弟姊妹). People create intimate relationships with others by taking their name and by acting as if they are their biological siblings. They widen their relational network for support and utilitarian purposes. For example, when one makes it known to the public that an intimate relationship built with a business partner would help advance his/her business. An understanding of this network of relationships is necessary in order to examine the source of support or strain in stepfamilies, which will be considered later.

A wide relative network has its advantages. If members do not want to take up certain responsibilities in their family, they can make use of the various relationships they have enjoyed in a big family. Sometimes they may be quite happy to retreat into a submissive position. Individuals may not wish to be free from the relationships with other people, because they may feel secure and contented by positioning themselves in a network of relationships and indulge in an submissive role in certain circumstances. A network of complex relationships allows them to have the choice and the convenience of making use of those connections as they see fit.

Individuals and their families According to King (1985), from the structural point of view Confucians classify the human community into three categories: 'chi' (自), the individual; 'chia' (家), the family; and 'ch'un' (群), the group. For a Confucian, 'the emphasis is on the family, Confucian ethics have developed an elaborate role system on the family level' (p. 61). Individuals do not relate only to immediate family members and a family should be understood as 'familistic group' because sometimes a family may include all members of a lineage or a clan (King, 1985, p. 61). Individuals are not regarded as an individual member of a family, but are assigned a particular position in the family in relation to another family member's position. For example, a man is not regarded as just a member of his family, but he is the second son of his father, and the third grandson to his paternal grandfather, etc. This tradition has its roots in Confucius' time. The practice has continued until today that Chinese not only address their parents and grandparents by their rank and order respectfully, but also address relatives by their rank and order rather than using their first name. For example, it would be offensive to address one's mother's younger sister by her first name, she should be addressed as 'aunt Ling' (玲姨) even though she may be younger than oneself in age. This idea can be taken further in relation to another important concept 'shame'. Family members know their place and should behave properly. They should not bring shame to themselves, which means bringing shame to the family group.

Positioning oneself in the structure of a family through abide by rectification of name, the hierarchy of family members is ranked, role and task are defined. Structure brings order and order helps to stabilize relationships and foster harmony within a family. As pointed out in Hanfeizi, the subject must serve the ruler, the child must serve his/her father, and the woman must serve her husband. 'If these three rules are observed, the world will be in order, but if they are acted against, the world will be in chaos' (Roetz, 1993, p.55). A well-defined family structure is, therefore, the prerequisite to family harmony.

Within the structure of a family, individuals relate to each other in a rather complex system. The ideal family relationship is harmony in the family. In order to achieve this, there are expected behaviour standards to follow when relating to family members. It is by means of an examination of family process that the dynamics of family relationships can be understood.

The essential relationships within a family are parent-child, husband-wife, and those between in-laws. Parent-child and in-law relationships are relationships of superior-subordinate, and the moral foundation for these relationships is basically 'Hsiao' (filial piety). In Confucius' teachings, there are three degrees of filial piety: the highest is to respect one's parents; the second highest is not to bring disgrace to them; and the next is to take care of them. Therefore, the top priority of a child's responsibility is to observe these behavioral expectations and to be seen as filial. As in-laws are clan being related to one after his/her marriage, children are expected to follow the principle of order because it is understood that 'blood is thicker than water', and there is a difference in degree in the implementation of the principles of respect, not to bring disgrace and taking care of one's parents. Respecting one's parents should always come before respecting in-laws or other members of the clan, although in male-centred families women are expected to respect their parents-in-law more than their own parents once they have married into the family of their husbands. Sons are expected to choose an obedient and gentle wife who can preferably bear sons. It will be seen as unfilial if a son has a wife who is capable of provoking family disputes, although it is usually the woman who will be blamed for causing disharmony in the family.

The relationship between husband and wife also related to the practice of filial piety. 'Among the duties, marriage is the most fundamental. It is the starting point of the family -- the procreation of legitimate children. No man or woman can satisfy his or her filial piety without marriage' (Chao, 1983, p.42). The marital relationship has to be understood, therefore, from the point of its function to carry on a mission of the family. The wife is not an equal partner in the marital relationship and she is incorporated into her husband's family to fulfil some presumed roles and tasks. The wife's functions are to assist her husband to be filial and to expand the family line, which means that she can justifiably be replaced if she fails to fulfil the expected roles and functions. A husband may have several wives, but the wife is expected to stay within the family she married into for the rest of her life. This is regarded as practice of filial piety by a married woman. In contemporary Chinese families, the parents of adult children hope that they would bear offspring after marriage. It is still the usual practice for a woman to give up her maiden surname once married; a widow would continue to use the surname of her deceased husband and take care of his parents as far as she can.

Discussion of the Concepts of Confucianism for Understanding the Family Relationships to be Presented in the Findings

Virtues and moral concepts influencing family relationships in families To begin the discussion, there are four basic concepts which help to understand relationships in a stepfamily. They are: 'Jen' (仁), 'Shu' (恕), 'Hua' (和) and 'Hsiao' (孝).

'Jen' can be translated as kind and loving. According to the classical Chinese philosophy, The Four Books, 'Jen' is defined as 'not to do to others as you would not wish done to yourself' (Louie, 1980, p.121). When this is viewed in a family context, older family members are expected to be kind and loving to their younger generations. This can also be seen as the expected behaviours of grandparents and parents who should teach their offspring with patience and affection. This seems to stress the ideal behaviours of parenting, but it fails to recognize those in a parenting role may sometimes be unkind and unloving to children as a result of stress or when children behave defiantly.

The next concept is 'Shu' which means forgiving. When a family member has done something wrong, he/she is pardoned by other family members. The older generations, as role models of younger generations, are looked up to for possessing this quality. Again, this is easier in theory than in parenting practice.

The third concept is 'Hua' which means harmonious. 'Before the feelings of pleasure, anger, sorrow, and joy are aroused it is called equilibrium ("chung", centrality, mean). When these feelings are aroused and each and all attain due measure and degree, it is called harmony...when equilibrium and harmony are realized to the highest degree, heaven and earth will attain their proper order and all things will flourish' (Koller & Koller, 1991, p.433). Confucius' illustration of equilibrium is contained in his discussion of the Doctrine of the Mean. To Confucius, 'Perfect' is the 'Mean', equilibrium is the great foundation of the world, and harmony its universal path (Chan,

1963). In a family, if each member has a proper title, proper position and he/she behaves accordingly, which is known as 'cheng-ming' (正名), the family will be in a harmonious state because everyone knows their place and how to relate according to expected behaviours. It is assured that they would not be likely to behave wrongly and they would relate to others kindly and with forgiveness. From the positive point of view, this can certainly help to stabilize the structure and relationships in a family. However, 'because harmonious interpersonal relationships are so highly valued, direct confrontation is avoided whenever possible' (Shon & Davis, 1982, p.216). In a family, disagreements among members are discouraged and conflicts are suppressed. Family members fail to see that disagreement and conflict are at times necessary for development of new order or better relationships. Moreover, one is expected not to cause a bad atmosphere in the family, and to suppress negative feelings at all times.

The fourth concept is 'Hsiao' or filial piety. This is the most important virtue expected of members of Chinese families. As pointed out by Redding (1993), 'the basic building block of the stable Confucian order is the family, and within that, the crucial stabilizing feature is filial piety' (p.49). According to Munro (1985), 'the basic social roles come in sets of two…one role carrying the duty of exercising authority and the other obedience…the principle that ties them (the roles) together is "Jen"…love ties parents to children and children to parents…therefore, Confucius said "Filial piety and fraternal love are the root of all humaneness"' (p.266). The older generation provide a family in which youngsters live and satisfy their basic needs; in return they would expect them to practise filial piety. According to Wu (1981), 'No matter how unreasonable parents' demands, or how harsh the treatment inflicted by parents, children must obey, endure and make sure that the parents' wishes are fulfilled' (O'Brian & Lau, 1995, p.40). Especially for younger child, complete compliance with the instructions of the older generation is expected; older children are expected to help with housework, contribute to the family income and take care of their parents when they become old. A person may be regarded as having ethical, moral and behavioral defects if he/she does not treat his/her parents 'well' and the judgment would carry further to make the generation conclude that he/she is 'not a very well-behaved person'. In extreme situations, there are greater expectations that the eldest son, no matter whether he is married or not, will take care of his aging parents, than for the youngest daughter who has married. Sons are normally expected to be responsible for the health and maintenance of their parents. This is seen as a form of practising filial piety. However, although the sons in Chinese families adopt the theory of filial piety, in practice, it is usually their wives who are asked to carry out these moral obligations on behalf of their husbands.

Following the brief introduction above to the four concepts, there will be an examination and discussion of how these moral ideals have affected parent-child relationships in stepfamilies.

As depicted earlier, Chinese parents who hold traditional Chinese values are likely practitioners of 'Jen' (kindness and lovingness to younger generations), 'Shu' (forgiveness to younger generations), 'Hua' (avoidance of direct confrontation in order to foster harmony in family relationships), and 'Hsiao' (filial piety largely through obedience to older generations and taking care of them). Parents in stepfamilies face tremendous changes in family structure and relationships when the stepfamily is formed. The situation becomes more complicated because of the introduction of another daughter-in-law into the family. As pointed out by Freedman, the affection between mother and son is threatened when the son marries; the difficulties which arise between a mother-in-law and daughter-in-law are possibly due to the mother's jealousy of her son's wife (Baker, 1979). In a stepfamily where the son's former wife has either died or left the family as a result of divorce, she is remembered with painful and/or negative feelings by members of her husband's family. The new daughter-in-law may elicit the feelings once felt following the death or departure of the former daughter-in-law. It is difficult for the new daughter-in-law to live up to the expectations of the extended family members of the stepchild. It is even more difficult if the three generations are living under the same roof. She is possibly criticized for not practising 'Jen' and 'Shu' and is capable of bringing disruption to the family by introducing new rules and routines -- failure to foster 'Hua' and is not able to live up to the expectations of the parents-in-law for being a 'Hsiao' -- a filial daughter-in-law.

Chinese values influencing the methods used in child management
According to O'Brian & Lau (1995), 'in general, two mechanisms to train the child in filiality are stressed: the inducement of both physical and emotional closeness so that a lifelong bond is assured; and the maintenance of parental authority and children's obedience through harsh discipline' (p. 40). Hsu & Tseng (1974) also noted that 'this quest for filiality gives justification to the absolute authority of parents over their children' (O'Brian

& Lau, 1995, p. 40). According to the research findings of a social work agency in Hong Kong, close to half of the respondents claimed that their styles of parenting were either authoritative (27.7%) or authoritarian (15%) (The Boys' & Girls' Clubs Association of Hong Kong, 1994). With reference to the clusters of behaviours identified by Baumrind (1966, 1971, 1991) regarding these two parenting styles and the indicators proposed by the BGCA's study, Chinese parents seem to adopt the following child management tactics: having an expectation of standards higher than the age-appropriate level of the child; firm enforcement of rules and standard; using commands and sanctions in social situations; attempting to shape, control and evaluate the behaviours and attitudes of their children in accordance with an absolute set of standards; emphasizing obedience, respect for authority, work, tradition, and the preservation of order (The Boys' and Girls' Clubs Association of Hong Kong, 1994, p.7). Chinese parents who adopt a traditional moral and ethical stance in their parenting practice would expect compliance with their instructions from their children; they would be inclined to use negative reinforcement methods, e.g. shaming, in order to stop or change their child's undesirable behaviour.

Child management is linked with consideration of the child's age. As noted by Ho (1986), Chinese parents would focus upon rearing more than education for children below six years of age. They are rather lenient in disciplining and pre-school age children are usually pardoned for their behaviour because they are regarded to be of an age where they do not know any better. Once they have reached six years old and have entered primary school, they are expected to be 'growing up properly' and to be less dependent upon their parents for supervision. They are assumed to know better and behave better. Parental attitudes and practices are quite different. When the child has left pre-school education to enter primary school, he/she is expected to learn more adult-like manners and behaviours, but in fact, the rise of expectations comes quite suddenly at an arbitrary division by age; the child is pushed to become a 'little adult' because of the unrealistic expectations of his/her parents who may not consider the developmental needs of the individual child. In Western theories, the development of a person is divided into stages, whereas in the minds of Chinese parents, human development seems to have only two stages, i.e. child and adult. When young, a child may be expected to act in an adult manner as a result of desirable social behaviours; but when the child has grown into an adult, parents wish he/she were a child and for him/her to continue to be dependent and obedient to his/her parents. Indeed, Chinese parents are ambivalent with regard to their expectations and their roles of their children.

When will parents stop being 'Jen' and 'Shu', i.e. kind and forgiving, parents? When parents 'lose face' in front of other people as a result of their children's behaviour in social situations, they are more likely to give up these traditional virtues. Bond & Hwang (1986) 'describe "face work" as a subtle type of interpersonal encounter calculated to avoid embarrassment or loss of poise and to maintain for others an impression of self-respect' (O'Brian & Lau, 1995, p.41). As pointed out by Hsu (1971), although 'face' is universally aspired by human beings, 'the result for Chinese is that loss of face becomes as a real dread affecting the nervous system more strongly than physical fear' (Redding, 1993, p.63). A parent who has ordered his/her son to stop misbehaving in a social gathering would feel that they had 'lost face' if he/she repeats the instructions several times without being able to make his/her son comply in front of a group of on-lookers. A grandmother who has no adult child taking care of her when she needs it may suffer a similar feeling. She 'loses face' when her relatives gossip about her son's unfilial behaviour. This example shows that there is relationship between practice of filial behaviour and shaming. By not bringing disgrace to one's parents, one is doing less than one's best to practise filial piety (Roetz, 1993, p.54). If the child makes his/her parents 'lose face', unkind and unloving behaviour by parents is a justified response to the child's unfilial behaviour.

'Shame and loss of face are frequently used to reinforce adherence to prescribed sets of obligations' (Shon & Davis, 1982, p.213). In Chinese families, it is not unusual to observe parents using shaming as a technique in child management. When a child behaves in a way not acceptable to his/her parent, his/her parent may shame him/her in front of other people in order to stop that behaviour from recurring. The purpose is not only to stop the behaviour, but to evoke internal shameful feelings so that the child will not exhibit undesirable behaviour for fearing of being shamed again in public. This technique may not be effective because the undesirable behaviour may not be curbed easily, but nonetheless this has a profound effect. It should be noted that it is not only parents who would use this method for shaming children whose behaviour is not appropriate for their age. In families where there are live-in members of older generation, the elderly may use this method on their adult children and their spouses, as well as on their grandchildren. This can be seen as a tool of asserting authority and power in a family.

The above leads us to a reflection on how parent-child relationships in stepfamilies may be affected.

Filial piety is expected to be practised by younger generations in Chinese families in which parents and children are related and linked by blood ties. They share a common family history and development. Although children may not like the ways their parents relate to them or the disciplining methods used by their parents, they have grown accustomed to them. This is the same in a stepfamily. When a stepparent starts living with their stepchildren, he/she does not know the developmental history of the stepchild, and he/she is seen as a newcomer, and/or an intruder. The stepparent has different expectations and child management methods as compared with those of the child's biological parents.

It is a difficult task for a stepparent to deal with a stepchild's behaviour at home and it is even more trying to discipline the stepchild in social situations. Cultural stereotyping may contribute to negative social attitudes. Relatives, friends, and neighbours may accept harsh disciplining of children by their biological parents to a greater extent, but they are less willing to accept the same in the case of stepchildren. The labelling effect of stepparenting may make the 'losing face' problem stand out more distinctively. Social attitudes and a parent's feeling of 'losing face' should be examined together with the shaming method, as these may be contributing to a negative cause and effect cycle of parental perception and child management.

Social and Value Changes brought about by Political Liberation and Cultural Revolution in China

As depicted in earlier sections, a number of traditional Chinese values have been upheld for centuries and serve as guide for the behaviour of Chinese people in family and in social situations. Practitioners of these values were challenged for their beliefs and practices at times of great change in the history of China, i.e. when New China was formed in 1949 and the government was led by the Communist Party, during and after the turbulent Cultural Revolution and at times of rapid economic development from the mid-1980s. The following sections will highlight the changing values which influence family structure and relationships in the context of a changing society.

Since China was 'liberated' in 1949, there have been several important historical milestones which have greatly affected family structure, family life, and family relationships. The first impact came about as a result of the formation of the People's Republic of China which was led by the Communist Party in 1949. The second impact was a result of the Cultural Revolution in the mid-1960s whilst the third was due to the adoption of an open policy and the growth of economy in the 1980s and beyond.

The birth of the New China brought changes in laws and the emergence of the new universalistic ethic. From the perspective of the China Government, the changes made to the laws were in order to attain the social, political and economic objectives of the new state (Conroy, 1987, p.54) and the presence of a universalistic ethic was important to the regime not only because it reduced the threats to political control, but also because it provided a basis for personal relations in a reorganizing society (Vogel, 1965, p.60). From a sociological perspective, the introduction of laws on rural land reform and the Marriage Law had a significant effect on the functions of the family and the relationships of family members. Conroy (1987) noted that the major aims of the laws were to create a new social fabric when new social relationships replaced the old feudal ones and to strike a better balance of power between the sexes within a family and between families. Shum & Yeung (1995) added that the influence of patriarchal family system centred around the father-son relationship was gradually weakened and gave way to the development of a kind of family system which allow marriage by choice, equality of both sexes, separation of marriage from procreation, etc.

On the other hand, the Government introduced a universalistic morality by stressing comradeship over friendship. As pointed out by Vogel (1965), personal relationships in China underwent an important transformation, comradeship was 'an important way in which everyone in the society was related to every other person' and 'it was strongly egalitarian in its underlying ethic' (p.55). This was not only a new way in which fellow citizens were related to each other, but it re-defined family relationships in some families because helpful relationships were expected to be found within collective structures in the society. The influence and supportive functions of blood-tied relationships were weakened. This new regime weakened the power of the family as conceived in traditional values and introduced the basis for social relationships.

The second important period of change was the Cultural Revolution. Officially it was said to take place from 1966 to 1969, but its impact began several years before 1966 and extended to some time in the mid-1970s. If the formative years of Communist China are said to have had a great impact in challenging the traditional Chinese family structure, family life and relationships, the Cultural Revolution bombarded these forms and beliefs through violent social movements which shook many people's lives and destroyed the institution of the family. The concept of group conformity has challenged families mercilessly and shaken the beliefs which had been held by Chinese families for hundreds of years.

Potter & Potter (1993) described the Cultural Revolution as 'essentially a revitalization movement, a kind of millenarian movement designed to purify, intensify, and apotheorsize…[it was hoped that through Cultural Revolution] purity of revolutionary thinking was to be restored by eliminating the feudal and foreign customs which had polluted the minds of the Chinese people…' (pp.83-84). They pointed out that Cultural Revolution was a 'witch hunt' and 'it is not intrinsically inconsistent with traditional Chinese thinking, as expressed in Confucianism, which holds that for a society to be well-ordered, everyone's thinking must be harmonious with the true social doctrine; it is the enactment of the dark side of a belief system which values conformity of social thought…' (p. 84). In attempting to reform the established system and to realize the political ideals of the revolutionists, the traditional family structure and values came under severe attacks. The traditional hierarchical structure was regarded as evil and new structures which were inspired and supported by collectivism, were used to replace traditional lineage. Support from the Government, the collectives, and work units were highly regarded as sources of strength when compared to familial support. In fact, during those times, families were broken up when family members holding different political views and having 'rotton social and personal background' were either imprisoned or sent to different parts of the country to work or to live. The wish to have children take care of ageing parents, which was previously regarded as a common filial act, could hardly be realized. In some families husbands and wives were forced to separate from each other and to live in cities where permission to visit had to be granted by officials. Many couples married in name and failed to consummate their marriages.

People from different social classes and geographical locations were influenced, although this differed in its degree, extent and severity. It was pointed out by Potter & Potter (1993) that 'it was generally believed [that the

Cultural Revolution] has affected China's urban dwellers much more than it did the peasantry' (p. 84). Citizens from rural areas were attacked for their superstitious practices and traditional customs, but urban dwellers, many of whom were educated intellectuals or middle class citizens working for Capitalists or behaving as 'bourgeois', were the main targets for attack. The revolutionists believed that this latter group were the people whose minds needed to be cleansed and their behaviour changed since they had been 'poisoned' by Western culture and traditional beliefs. By sending them away from home and cutting off family ties using the movement of 'up to the mountains and down to the villages', revolutionists hoped to see more re-born Chinese who would follow the true social doctrine. During this time of upheaval, cultural heritage was destroyed, and loyalty to the family and the practice of filial piety were especially challenged. The lives of thousands of individuals were lost and thousands of families were profoundly affected. Some of the wounds could never be healed as is evidenced by much Chinese literature which is known as the 'literature of the wounded' or 'scar literature' (Thurston, 1984; Thurston, 1985) and by the vivid documentation of a damaged family in the popular work of fiction 'Wild Swans' (Chang, 1991).

The third important era was the period of economic growth in the mid-1980s which continued until recent years. Economic development has grown at a fast pace as a result of adopting an open policy. Population control and thriving economic development led to greater opportunities for work for both men and women, and improvement in living standards. The population became mobile and people moved to live in cities where they could earn good money. The market economy based upon socialism has influenced the institution of the family in terms of changes in functions and relationships between its members. Findings of recent studies on families living in the cities of China indicate that the transformation in structure and relationships is prominent. There are more nuclear, dual income families living apart from the older generations. With the introduction of the one child policy, family size has decreased because fewer children are born. The traditional patriarchal, lineage-type families have gradually been replaced by equalitarian families in which marital relationships are centred. Families are respected as being private. Through families, individuals' emotional needs are satisfied. The concept of 'family-centred' has been replaced by 'individual-centred', 'couple-centred' or 'child-centred'. Families are no longer dominated by males and the older generations, whilst many supportive, substitutive functions of families have been taken over by welfare services provided by the state (Shum & Yeung, 1995).

In rural districts, structural and functional changes in peasant families are not so obvious. Many families are still male-dominated in terms of decision-making, the concept of 'men are socially-oriented, women are family-oriented' is still upheld, with the latter accepting their roles in child care and house work as reasonable with little complaint. Many of the traditional rituals have been reinstated and they serve the important function of sustaining traditional values, such as the hierarchy of family roles and authority, showing respect to one's parents and being filial to older generations, mutual support of family members and kin, etc. (Potter and Potter, 1993; Sha, 1995; Shum & Yeung, 1995).

Value Changes Relevant to Families and Family Relationships in the People's Republic of China

Traditional Chinese values and beliefs have been challenged at times when the society is responding to great changes. Values and beliefs cherished by many Chinese families and taken as integral parts of the Chinese culture, were severely attacked for almost a decade during the Cultural Revolution. The practice of many 'old' values and beliefs was banned from daily living; those with the flavour of Confucianism were the main target for destruction. The idea of 'man as a relational being supported by family members and kin' was replaced by 'loyalty upheld in comradeship'. Collective well-being was expected to be given more weight than the well-being of one's family. Many people became socially isolated for fear of betrayal, whilst others were alienated from their family members. In some extreme cases, family members would 'draw a clear line of demarcation' between themselves and relatives under political attack. Revolutionists at that time believed that to destroy old practices and beliefs would lead to a state where true socialist living was practised and they would make use of the creation of conflicts to achieve their aims at the expense of the values on which family relationships are sustained.

During the Cultural Revolution conflicts of values reached its peak. The idea of males as the dominant figure at home was replaced by the worship of Chairman Mao and he was made a living deity. Harmony in families was destroyed as one could no longer trust a family member who may report another family member unfavorably to comrades. Filial piety to parents was

64

transformed into relating intimately and responsibly to Chairman Mao, whilst children were taught a rhyme 'father is close, mother is close, but neither is as close as Chairman Mao'. Kindness, love and forgiveness were rarely practised because support for the collective judgment was proof of one's loyalty to the state. A person should not let their emotions come before a rational, political decision whereby he/she has to accuse his/her family member in open court formed by revolutionists.

Following the turbulent Cultural Revolution, families in rural areas have reinstated many old customs and rituals, which are important in order to sustain traditional values and the functions of the family as an institution. Potter & Potter conducted a study (1993) the findings of which have supported this claim. In urban cities, the values affecting families have been affected by policy changes, and the social and economic developments of the last decade. As there are more educated and gainfully employed women, their social status has been upgraded which, in turn, helps them to become a more equal partner in a marital relationship. Sha's (1995) 'Status of Women in Contemporary China' notes the rising status of women in society, but observes that areas such as the changing of traditional gender-role expectation, the social attitudes towards women getting equal work, pay, and education opportunities, etc. have yet to be addressed and improved.

To summarize, there have been changes in values in the People's Republic of China which are relevant to my study. Firstly, men and women marry more for the satisfaction of emotional and companionship needs than for procreation and the continuation of their family name. The expectations of husbands and wives of the marital relationship have changed and those changes have subsequently affected the couple's relationships with their in-laws and children. They may not tolerate their spouse and remain in the marriage in response to the authority or expectations of the older generations, or in order to rear their children in an intact family. Secondly, although divorce is considered to bring shame on all concerned, more women have sought divorce to end their suffering and are willing to face the social stigma (Conroy, 1987, pp.54-55). We can see that women who were previously disadvantaged have been given legal rights and this together with their rising social status and increasing earning power, mean that women are beginning to no longer be regarded as the weaker sex in a spousal relationship. More divorced women have made themselves available for remarriages. Divorce initiated by women and the remarriage of divorced women is not uncommon in big cities and among intellectuals. This challenges the traditional values that 'a good woman would not marry twice' and 'marry once and that marital relationship should last for life'. Thirdly, the responsibility of childrearing is shared by the state and not solely taken up by the parents supported by their kin. If a couple dissolves their marriage and are having financial difficulties so that there are problems in taking care of the older generations and their children, the state would provide welfare benefits or services for those in need. When there are problems arisen from marital separation and divorce of a family member, relatives may not play such an important helping role as in the past. The above illustrates the faster changes in values in urban areas and big cities in contemporary China, whilst the rural areas and villages have more practitioners of traditional values and beliefs which are still influential in their daily living and family relationships.

Current Prevailing Views on Family Relationships and Parenting in Hong Kong

Social Changes and Changing Family Values

Understanding the changes in values must go hand in hand with understanding recent changes in family structure and dynamics caused by changes in the society of Hong Kong.

Hong Kong has been faced with many social changes in the past decades. These have been brought about by industrialization, urbanization, and economic, political and demographic factors. As one Asian's 'four little dragons', Hong Kong has continued to flourish economically. There has been an increase in the participation of the female labour force. This is particularly significant among women who have ever been married: the figures increased from 487,500 in 1981 to 548,300 in 1990 (Hong Kong Government, Social Welfare White Paper, 1991, p.8). The female labour force participation rate was 46.2% in 1992, which increased to 49.2% in 1996 (Hong Kong Census & Statistics Department, Hong Kong Annual Digest of Statistics, 1997). Married women, especially those with children, have contributed to the increase in family income but also have indicated a need for child care services.

As the result of a flourishing economy, Hong Kong has entered a new phase of population movement. This movement is not from the New Territories to city centres. More land has been reclaimed at the waterfront

66

since the beginning of the 1990s so that more high-priced commercial buildings can be built. As land in city centres is scarce, new towns and satellite cities in suburban areas are being developed, making room for the building of more spacious, quality housing. Since the 1980s, there has been a significant increase in the number of public and private houses built in towns and suburbs away from the city centre. It is a movement of suburbanization. Several decades ago, people who lived in the New Territories moved to Kowloon or Hong Kong in order to live independently from extended families and for work. Since the 1980s, the movement of population has reversed. In 1990, 41% of the population resided in the New Territories and the estimate is that this trend will continue. In 1996, 46.8% of the population resided in the New Territories (Hong Kong 1996 Population By-Census Summary Report, 1996). It has also been observed that the percentage of nuclear families is substantially higher in the new towns than in other parts of Hong Kong (Hong Kong Government, Social Welfare White Paper, 1991). The population movement shows that keeping only two generations in one household is the preferred choice of families, irrespective whether they are living in urban areas or beyond the city centre. The movement to new towns and the preference in family structure leads us to consider their implications to the families. The former may mean that older generations may not want to live with their married children in a district with which they are not familiar. If they have a separate household from their children their power to intervene in family matters may be weakened, but there may be new ways to exert 'remote control' over their children. The latter reflects wishes of the married couples who want to re-define family membership to only two generations. When there are disputes and crisis in the nuclear family, the older generation is no longer present to be the buffer for rival conflicts. In the situation where separation and divorce is in progress, the presence or absence of an older generation in the family may be a source of support or stress for the couple and the children. These points will be examined further in the subsequent chapters from the perspectives of the life experiences of the stepfamily members.

Demographically, the population of Hong Kong has changed in its age structure. The trend alerts us to the needs and problems of the family members who need care, and to those of the carers. Statistics show that there are more elderly people in Hong Kong, i.e. 6.6% of the population were 65 and above in 1981, 9% in 1992, and 10.4% in 1997; and less young people, i.e. 24.8% in 1981, 20.5% in 1992, and 18.5% in 1996 were dependent children aged below 15 (Hong Kong Council of Social Service, 1993, p.3; Hong Kong Census and Statistics Department, Monthly Digest of Statistics, July, 1998). Moreover, average household size has also decreased. In 1971 it was 4.5 persons, in 1992, it had decreased to 3.4 (Hong Kong Council of Social Service, 1993) and in 1996, it had further decreased to 3.3 (Hong Kong 1996 Population By-Census Summary Report, 1996, p.6). Nuclear families constituted 61.6% of the total number of households in 1991 (Hong Kong Council of Social Service, 1993). A more recent reference entitled 'Role of the Family in Community Care' confirmed that nuclear families represent over 60% of all family groupings in Hong Kong (Hong Kong Council of Social Service, 1994, p.1). Government statistics show that there are more domestic households consisting of one unextended nuclear family, that is, a married couple with or without unmarried children or a single parent with one or more children who have never married. Their share was 64% in 1996 (Hong Kong Census & Statistics Department, Monthly Digest of Statistics, Dec., 1996). The nuclear family is the most dominant family type in Hong Kong. In view of the longer life spans of citizens and low birth rates, there would be heavier demands upon carers who may have few siblings or relatives to share the support. What if stepfamilies, the targets of this study, have to care for older generations while busily reorganizing their family and building family relationships? Wives in families are regarded as carers. Would stepmothers be expected to take care of the young and the old? This will be discussed in the following chapters by examining the data collected.

It has always been said that Hong Kong is a place where the culture of the East meets that of the West. Before World War II, traditional Chinese culture still dominated. In the 1950s, the pace of economic growth became faster and society was influenced by American culture because Hong Kong was chosen to be the target for exports and a stepping stone for the trade with Mainland China. In the 1960s, Japan became a competitor of the United States in trade and retail business. From 1970s onwards the economy of Hong Kong continued to flourish and people living in Hong Kong were exposed to a variety of cultures because Hong Kong is considered to be a fascinating place with varied culture and with plenty of opportunities for money-making. Hong Kong has attracted businessmen from all over the world to work and live here. Tourists from developed countries travelled to Hong Kong before touring China. These people brought information and modern values which they imported to local citizens. Over the years, Hong

Kong has absorbed foreign culture into its foundation of Chinese culture. In the last decade, people from Hong Kong have made frequent visits to overseas countries for holidays or for work, whilst others have migrated overseas and returned to Hong Kong after seeking the citizenship of a country of their choice. Wider exposure to different cultures and the enrichment of their life experiences means that they come home with new ideas which change their daily lives and their ideology for family relationships. Moreover, the advance in information technology has provided up to date knowledge and cultural transmissions can easily be made through computer-aided devices and mass media. Choi (1987) summarized the situation as follows: Hong Kong is an international city which has been influenced by different cultures: i.e. England has influenced its educational system and its laws; the United States and Japan have affected the style of living of people in Hong Kong and popular culture; and, with regard to family matters, Hong Kong is still strongly influenced by the Chinese culture. Similarly, Young (1988) echoed that 'Chinese culture has not only survived in Hong Kong, it also played a positive and supportive role in the process of modernization' (p.737). According to him, although Hong Kong people do not adopt Confucianism in totality the Government has made efforts to encourage people to cling to certain aspects of their local culture; this modified practice is in pursuit of a 'folk Confucianism' (p.738); and the Confucian ethos has become linked with Hong Kong's business-industrial performance (p.739). He also supports Wong's (1986) observation of distinctive features in the culture of Hong Kong, i.e. high achievement motivation, familism, and utilitarian discipline. These elements may throw light on understanding the changing values in Hong Kong and how they are influencing families and family relationships. For example, a husband's over-involvement at work, parents' expectations for their children's academic and career achievement, the influence of family-oriented beliefs in family relationships and child management. These are important areas to be examined in the chapters on data analysis.

Hong Kong has been affected by the policies and political climate of its motherland. In 1978, Deng Xiaoping pronounced the policy of 'one country, two systems' which guided China's resumption of sovereignty over Hong Kong and which guarantees that Hong Kong, the Special Administrative Region under Chinese sovereignty, could have separate political and economic systems. This policy is now enshrined in the Basic Law -- Hong Kong's post-1997 constitution -- which states that 'the previous capitalist system and way of life shall remain unchanged for 50 years'.

In the early 1980s, emigration was a quiet current that aroused little public concern. Towards the end of the 1980s, emigration and the brain drain became a focus of public attention (Fan & Skeldon, 1995). Since the Sino-British Joint Declaration which returned sovereignty over Hong Kong to China in 1997 was signed, there have been noticeable movements in the society. Since 1985 there has been increase in the number of citizens emigrating from Hong Kong because of anxieties and uncertainty about the future of Hong Kong. The peak in emigration came after the '1989 June 4 Tiananmen incident' when people in Hong Kong were worried about loss of freedom and democracy. At the same time, the industries of Hong Kong moved their bases from Hong Kong to the north because the owners found the labour costs too expensive. As a result, the unemployment rate rose for several years and peaked at 3.6% in September 1995. For Hong Kong, which had an almost zero percent unemployment rate for many years, this was an alarming situation arousing public concern. When the changeover of Hong Kong to Chinese sovereignty was drawing closer, the new structures for the government of the Hong Kong Special Administrative Region (SAR) were put into place, i.e. the operation of the Preparatory Committee for the Hong Kong SAR; the election of the first Chief Executive of SAR and the 60 members for the provisional legislature, etc. In the final months before the handover, although disagreements existed between the ruling British-Hong Kong government and the Office of the Hong Kong SAR Chief Executive designate, both the officials of the government-to-be and the people of Hong Kong had prepared for the transformation after June 30, 1997. There had been obvious changes in the final months before the handover. For example, the construction of a new airport, a grand convention and exhibition centre at the harbour front, the increase in student numbers in tertiary education, the retention of large number of expatriates who work or trade here and the attraction of some new comers. These changes reflected the fact that Hong Kong was trying hard to build the confidence of its people and the people's panic about 'Hong Kong returning to its motherland' seemed to have waned.

In addition, the local unemployment rate had dropped somewhat and the inflation rate was down to a ten year low in 1996, whilst emigration and reverse-emigration had taken place concomitantly (Nyaw & Li, 1996). An analyst for *Time Magazine* examined whether people in Hong Kong are 'afraid' of the handover, and he reported: 'Not the ones who are still there. Polls show their confidence levels are impressingly high. The locals are not easily intimidated, as anybody who has walked down a crowded Hong Kong sidewalk can attest' (Colmey, 1997, p.116).

Although positive reports such as the one in *Time Magazine* are reassuring, other reports have shown the ambivalence of the people of Hong Kong. As pointed out by the editors of 'The Other Hong Kong Report 1996', 'indeed the late transition period is full of such ironies and paradoxes...the people of Hong Kong, in midst of the immediately changeover, are experiencing an identity crisis although Nationalistic feelings are on the rise' (Nyaw & Li, 1996, p.xxxv). They are ambivalent because they are joyful about 'throwing themselves into the arms of their natural mother' while also struggling to accept the inevitable impacts brought about by the transformation. For example, some people find it difficult to be accommodating towards the Mainland Chinese who have become new immigrants to Hong Kong; they are worried about the insufficient resources especially in school places and health care which will be shared by the immigrants from Mainland China. They are also dubious about the promise made by the late Deng that 'Hong Kong will retain its political status quo for 50 years'. They are alarmed by the growing number of divorces and separations resulting from men working in Mainland China; the crime rate has increased and there is evidence of robberies and break-ins committed by illegal and/or new immigrants from China. There has also been outbreaks of a number of contagious diseases due to the highly populated environment and poor living conditions in areas where most of the new immigrants from China reside. They can sense that the economy of Hong Kong and their daily lives are being greatly influenced by some powerful organizations and people in China, who have intervened in the buying and selling of local stocks and real estate properties, etc.

Tung Chee-hwa was elected the Hong Kong SAR Chief Executive at the end of 1996, and since then his Office had started to prepare for the changeover of the government. He had outlined nine areas in his policy statements. Under the Policy for Education, Mr. Tung is determined to 'promote moral well-being in the society and the quality of Chinese traditional values' (培養公德心和中國優秀傳統價值觀), 'make sure there are equal opportunities for all citizens' (確保全民有平等機會) and 'enhance the quality of social and cultural aspects and the quality of daily living' (提高社會文化和生活質素) (*Express News*, Hong Kong, December 11, 1996, p.3). As demonstrated in his public speeches, Mr. Tung is an advocate of 'smooth and stable transformation' (平穩過渡), continuous economic prosperity（安定繁榮）, filial piety（孝）, harmony（和）, honesty and credibility (誠信), and hardwork (勤奮). He impressed upon people that he aspires to Chinese traditional values based upon Confucianism and he seems to favour the Doctrine of the Mean (中庸之道). On different occasions, Mr. Tung stressed that he would overhaul the local education system, and promote the desired Chinese traditional values through moral and civic education. Will he put this theory into practice in governing Hong Kong after July 1, 1997? This remains to be seen when the new government is in full operation.

As a result of the above factors, families in Hong Kong have changed in their structure, relationships and in the values they uphold. New types of family have evolved. There are a growing number of 'astronaut families' where husbands continue to work in Hong Kong, but the wives and children have emigrated to a developed country in order to fulfill the residency requirement. There are also split families in which one spouse may work in Mainland China or where a man works in Hong Kong but is married a Chinese woman who he visits during weekends and holidays. These families are prone to the development of marital problems and parent-child relationship problems (Law et al, 1995; Young, 1994; Young, 1993).

With the changes to family structure and living patterns, the expectations for family life and family relationships have also changed. As noted by Lee (1991): 'small household size, independent households consisting of married couples and their unmarried children, weakened ties relating members of families to their relatives and immediate kin, weakened emphasis on honouring obligations to kin in need, acceptance of daughter's rights to descent and inheritance, equalitarian husband-wife relationships, and so on' (p.41). Change in family life and relationships goes hand in hand with change in family values. As a reaction to changes, people develop feelings of ambivalence and conflict: 'although the change of family structure to a nuclear family is a reality, people have not entirely given up all traditional family norms and ideals' (Lee, 1991, p.44). As regards those norms and ideals which are still being upheld and which are relevant to this study, Lee (1991) found that family members expect siblings to perform obligations (to their parents); many believe that sons and daughters should be treated the same but they still find it difficult to depart from the traditional sex-role (p.44). Moreover, in terms of household duties, wives are still the principal home-makers, although they may also take up a full-time job. Husbands are rarely involved in housework. If the couples live with the parents or parents-in-law, wives are further removed from the decision-making process in the stem families. In stem families it would be the husbands or the parents and parents-in-law who exercise supervision and control over the children (p.47). The findings of some local research projects on the subject of parenting (The Boys' and Girls' Clubs Association of Hong Kong, 1990; Lit et al, 1991), noted that the concept of shared parenting is developing but that most families are still content with the strong influence of certain traditional beliefs and Chinese culture (Lit et al, 1991, p.66).

Current Prevailing Views relevant to this Study

Views on parent-child relationship   Traditionally, the parent-child relationship has been greatly influenced by Confucianism which emphasizes hierarchical authority in a family and the behaviours expected of family members.

The parent-child relationship in Hong Kong Chinese families has changed. Although families with traditional values continue to respect men as dominant, powerful, authoritative figures, the important traditional values such as 'having (male) descendants to carry on the family name and of raising children in order to provide for old age, have faded' (Law et al, 1995, p.12). As a result of a decrease in the numbers of children in families, it is not practical to expect only the sons to take care of aging parents; both sons and daughters may have to do so when the need arises. The findings of a recent research study show that although sons have taken up the carer's role (72.9%) compared with daughters (38%) in caring for their elderly parents, the 24% of daughters-in-law who act as carers outnumbers the sons-in-law who do so (Hong Kong Council of Social Service, 1994, p.91). A closer examination of whether the sons take up the role in theory or in practice should be made. As discussed earlier, men in Hong Kong are heavily involved at work and can spare little time at home, it is doubtful, therefore, whether sons can take up the role of carer as they have claimed, and it may be that their responsibilities have in fact been discharged by daughters and daughters-in-law. The true situation will be relevant to family relationships when we consider the overloading of stepparents' roles and tasks.

Another recent report relating to parent-child relationships has noted changes in the ideas of the younger generation, from patriarchal to more gender equalitarian. The changes are indicated by disagreement with the following: 'the father is the master in the family, and he is responsible for all the decision-making'; 'men are society-oriented, whilst women are family-oriented'; 'it is not the responsibility of men to be involved with household work nor with caring for the children' (Law et al, 1995, p.90). On the other hand, the following values have experienced the least change: 'sexual relationships outside of marriage are unacceptable'; 'children should first get permission from their parents when considering choices of occupation or education'; 'family scandal should not be exposed'; 'marital relationships should be permanent'; and 'during festivals, family members should come back home and have supper together' (Law et al, 1995, p.90). The above observations suggest the weakening of patriarchal dominance over the younger generations. Both parents are not rigidly fixed in gender-role division of household and child care work and there are aspirations to a partnership between spouses in parenting. Parents' roles are 'no longer as the dominators' but that of 'consultants' (Law et al, 1995, p.90). Moreover, some values regarding fidelity, permanency in marital relationship, and family scandal are still upheld. These views will require scrutiny of the data collected for this study.

Views on marital relationships   Although traditional Chinese families previously allowed husbands to have several wives and concubines, polygamy was made illegal in Hong Kong 1972. The status of women in society has greatly improved in terms of obtaining protection in marriage, equality between the sexes, increased education opportunities and higher status in employment. They are also eligible for public assistance during separation and divorce. Some local studies have found that there have been changes in the degree of commitment of couples to their marriages and in the social attitudes towards extra-marital affairs (Law et al, 1995; Yeung and Kwong, 1995; Caritas and the University of Hong Kong, 1995).

Traditional Chinese marriages have embodied the major characteristics of 'procreation of male heirs; permanency; harmony; complementary conjugal roles; male dominance; and fidelity for women' (Yeung and Kwong, 1995, p.8). Marriages are expected to continue even if the couple are not satisfied with their relationship. Family stability is emphasized and divorce is discouraged. Married women would endure their marriages rather than seek a divorce because of the social stigma attached to divorced women and the disgrace to the family. In modern marriages, which promote companionship, personal satisfaction and affect, there is greater acceptance of separation if a marriage is found unfulfilling. From the findings of a recent local survey on the attitudes of 952 local secondary school students, 'the discrepancy in personal costs of divorce between men and women is narrower than was the case in the past' (Yeung and Kwong, 1995, p.51), and 'life-long marriage is no longer a dominant view in the society' (Yeung & Kwong, 1995, p.61). These findings have shown that in Hong Kong young people believe that women are more willing to seek an end of an unsatisfying marital relationship; marriage is not a permanent commitment and people may opt out in order to develop a more satisfying relationship. Law et al (1995) also noted a change in social attitude which supports the findings of the above-mentioned study. They noted that the respondents disagreed with the following statements: 'married people should not have friends of the opposite sex'; 'cohabitation is unacceptable even though the couple consider it appropriate' (p.90). The findings discussed above illustrate the trend towards the relaxation of moral standards in order to obtain personal satisfaction, and to develop relationships with friends of the opposite sex after marriage.

There are other characteristics of modern marriages. For example, couples not only aspire to personal fulfillment and affective communication between the couple, but they also believe that a good marriage is based on love, happiness and good communication. Childbearing is a choice of life style rather than commitment in marriage. In Hong Kong many of these beliefs are increasingly held by young people and families, which is evident in the findings of the study conducted by Yeung & Kwong (1995).

Current practice of parenting   As noted by Ho (1974), Lee (1991), and Pearson (1990), 'there has been a weakening of the traditional parent-role differentiation between fathers and mothers' (O'Brian & Lau, 1995, p.42). It was argued by O'Brian & Lau that 'the families in Hong Kong rely more on their own resources to live by rather than depending on their parents for maintenance and support. As a result, parents do not possess absolute authority as before and younger generations do not practise filial piety to the extent of complete compliance and submission' (p. 42).

Although couples in Hong Kong do not depend upon their parents for maintenance and support for the reasons explained by the above authors, the findings of a research project for the International Year of the Family indicate another perspective. In dual-income families where fathers are heavily involved in their work and can spare little time caring for their young children, working mothers rely on grandparents of their children as a vital source of support in child care. Grandparents and paid maids are playing significant roles as primary helpers by escorting children to and from kindergarden/nurseries, and in bathing (Hong Kong Council of Social Service, 1994, pp.146-7). It can be speculated, therefore, that adult children in Hong Kong prefer living by themselves after being married and are financially independent. Also, high inflation rates, a lack of earning power and the unavailability of retirement pensions mean that few aging parents are in fact able to support or maintain their adult children financially. They may offer help in terms of child care services as a kind of support to their married children. This can become dis-service, however, as conflicts may arise when the parents and grandparents have different views and methods of child management. The intervention in child management in stepfamilies will be prone to provoking conflicts between the older generation and the stepparent. Since the parenting views and methods of the current stepparent are different to those of the previous one, the grandparents will find it confusing and may tend to impose their own ways. These may be a source of conflict, which will be examined in the chapters on data analysis.

With regard to the styles of parenting adopted by parents in Hong Kong, findings of recent studies have noted the following: Cheung et al (1990) found that parents in more modern families would allow their children to be more assertive and independent and would use fewer control techniques. However, parents are still concerned with the control of impulsive behaviour and expressions of aggression by their children. This is consistent with the traditional beliefs that individuals should develop self-control in order to hide their negative feelings and to bring harmony to their family. Moreover, today parents in local families emphasize care, as well as supervision, in parenting. In a recent research report it was found that authoritative parenting style is the most favoured style. Parents adopting such style would show care and concern for their children. They would also set clear rules and demands and have open communication with their children (The Boys' and Girls Clubs Association of Hong Kong, 1994, p.39).

As regards the gender-role division of labour in parenting, it is to be noted that more fathers are beginning to participate in parenting in Hong Kong (Lam, 1982; the Boys' and Girls' Clubs Association of Hong Kong, 1990; Lit et al, 1991). In a study of the involvement of fathers in family tasks which was conducted by the Boys' and Girls' Clubs Association of Hong Kong (1990), the researchers confirmed the relationship between a father's involvement and the parent-child relationship. Due to the demands of work, fathers may not have time to be involved in all the family tasks. The degree of their participation is comparable to that of fathers in the United States, but is lower than that of fathers in Taiwan (p.56). Mothers expected their spouses to take a stronger role in disciplining their child. When children behave inappropriately and deliberately misbehaved, half of the fathers would use scolding and spanking to discipline. If they feel that their child behaves badly but not intentionally, they would use explanation, persuasion and counselling methods (p.58).

With regard to children's perceived parenting styles and the relationship between parenting styles and adolescent behaviour, a recent research report released by the Boys' and Girls' Clubs Association of Hong Kong found that 27.7% of senior primary school and secondary school students believe that their parents have adopted an authoritative parenting style; 15% believed that they adopted an authoritarian style; 13.4% an indulgent style; and 43.9% were neglectful. The authoritative parenting style seems to benefit adolescents most and it is the most favoured parenting style (1994, p.9). Adolescents whose parents adopt such style benefit in that they build up self-esteem, strive for better academic achievement, acquire healthier psychosocial functioning, and develop a strong sense of social responsibility (p.39).

I have no intention of drawing any conclusions from the findings of the studies mentioned above, except that the information has helped me to note some salient features of current parenting practice in Hong Kong. It is obvious that fathers do not have much time for sharing child care and housekeeping responsibilities with their wives. Mothers wish that their husbands could be more involved in child disciplining. As far as parenting styles and the resulting child behaviour are concerned, authoritative parenting, which is characterized by firmness and care, seems to be more effective as compared with other methods. These salient features will be examined more closely from the information provided by the informants of this study in Chapters 5 and 6.

Social attitudes and perceptions of stepfamilies and stepparenting   The attitudes of people towards stepfamilies and stepparenting differ from those they have towards families in general. Due to very limited written work about stepfamilies, I gather impressions from talking to professionals and friends, reviewing Chinese poems and folk tales, watching old Chinese movies, and reading newspapers. During the initial phase of this study, I talked to about 30 people in Hong Kong whom I knew from work and others who were my friends. Most people had noticed that the number of broken families as a result of divorce was on the increase, and they suggested that divorce was a fact to be accepted (except by those who are Catholics). Catholics said divorce was forbidden by their Church, but were aware that there are empty shell families in which marital partners have been estranged for years and live quite a different life of their choice. As far as remarriage is concerned, the most common answers were: 'it is alright if the person finds someone who loves him/her' and 'if the future spouse can accept the person's children from his/her former union'. However, when asked to introduce possible informants for this study, they became sensitive and reluctant to help. Almost all refused my request giving as their reasons that the stepparents they knew would not like being identified as a stepparent, or that they would not like talking about family matters. One person did try to assist but the interview was refused by the mother-in-law before the stepmother was able to consider the request. The above responses indicate stepfamilies are a sensitive topic in the minds of some intellectuals and middle-class people in Hong Kong.

I conclude that these responses are influenced by the Chinese culture, which is quite gender-biased. Stepfamilies were portrayed by novelists as an ordinary type of family. They were legalized structures in family life and men were allowed to have more than one wife with bi-families (families with concubines) living under the same roof. Classic novels, such as *Dreams of the Red Chamber* depicted complicated relationships and power struggles in extended families. Men were permitted to have a second wife and concubine, and they were regarded as 'fung lau' (風流), which means that their behaviour was not only accepted by the public, but glorified and romanticized as memorable incidents of handsome, talented men attracted by women. As regards women, only those who were faithful to their husbands by remaining in widowhood after the death of their spouses would be recognized. Those who had thoughts of remarriage would be condemned as 'shui sing yeung fa' (水性楊花), which means 'flowers which grow near water will follow the flow of water without their own direction'.

As time goes by, the males in contemporary Hong Kong families may no longer be absolute authoritarian figures, but many women continue to be suppressed and scapegoated. Stepmothers are convenient targets to be labelled and made scapegoats. Old Chinese movies, television, and newspapers seem to be the most powerful forms of mass media. Many movies were made in Hong Kong in the 1950s and 1960s which portrayed abusive stepfamilies. Stories told on the 'silver screen' reflected the hardships of life for many working class people. In those years Hong Kong had an influx of refugees from Mainland China, and many people who had been once rich had to compete with the labourers for a job. Life was hard at that time. Some women had to survive by becoming concubines or mistresses of rich men and children whose basic needs could not be satisfied were given up by their parents to relatives who could support them. Movies depicted many sad stories of women competing for survival. For example, the child movie star Fung Bo Bo (馮寶寶) frequently acted as a pitifully abused child with Lee Heung Kam (李香琴) as the cruel and wicked stepmother. Grandmothers, neighbours and the biological mother would often say to children: 'Dear child, now that you don't live with your own mother, you will be treated of as no value, and you must behave yourself and not irritate your stepmother'. Stepparenting was, therefore, portrayed negatively. Moreover, in Hong Kong, children have accepted Western culture as they grow and most of them have seen cartoons of Snow White and Cinderella in books or in movies. The impression of children having difficult times with their stepmothers has been formed at an early age through this powerful media.

Why are stepmothers especially being regarded as negative figures in stepfamilies? The following are possible factors: (1) where men have power and authority over women in Chinese families which hold traditional Chinese values, the misdeeds of women are magnified; (2) in a paternalistic society, blaming and oppressing women is common practice; (3) social expectations of mothers as providers of unconditional care and love for their children raise the expectations on stepparenting to an unrealistic level; (4) polygamy was legally permitted until 1950 in the People's Republic of China and until 1971 in Hong Kong and wives and concubines living under the same roof were competitors in a power struggle. Stepmothers who had competitions might be negatively labelled as wicked women. In Hong Kong today, therefore, even stepfathers who may be perceived as an abuser who may sexually harass their stepdaughters, they are called 'hau foo' (後父) or 'kai foo' (繼父), which is a more neutral way to address them. 'Step' (hau) has two possible translations in Chinese language: 'hau' means 'behind' or 'later', 'kai' means 'continue'; and 'foo' means 'father'. Stepfathers are referred to neutrally as 'fathers who come after' or 'fathers who continue fathering'. Stepmothers are called 'hau mo' (後母) or 'kai mo' (繼母) with 'mo' (母)

meaning 'mother'. But they are also called 'hau dey la' (後底嫲), which is a very disrespectful way to address a stepmother and means 'female beast who comes after', the equivalent to 'cow' in the English language. Stepchildren are also given disrespectful names when they are brought into the stepfamily because of remarriage of their mother. They are called 'yau ping chai' (油瓶仔) for boy and 'yau ping nui' (油瓶女) for girl. Thus means literally 'boy/girl of a greasy oil bottle', which means the offspring carries grease which will never be washed away because the shame and filth of the remarried mother will cast on her child forever.

Summary of the Chapter

At the beginning of this chapter, fundamental values and beliefs based upon Confucianism were examined. It is noted that members of Chinese families are not seen as individuals, but as relational beings who hold their positions in relation to others in a group. Their positions linked to expected behaviours, and they are morally judged according to values such as filial piety, harmony, kindness and forgiveness. These traditional values have been aspired to and practised for hundreds of years in Chinese families and this continued until 40 years ago when great changes were brought about by the new ethos which was promoted by the People's Republic of China (PRC). The new regime and political reform have had an impact on the changes in values relating to families and family relationships. As there are quite a number of residents in Hong Kong who came from the PRC and they continue to pay frequent visits to their relatives there, Chinese traditional values are reinforced by their contacts. The values held by them have affected the way they behave as parents. Moreover, an examination and discussion has also been made of the economic prosperity of Hong Kong during the last 30 years, as well as the impacts of the rapid social changes approaching the change-over of sovereignty of Hong Kong on July 1, 1997. The impact of imported goods and Western thoughts, in addition to the changing social and political climate, have influenced family life and the values held by family members. Stepfamilies, however, are still negatively stereotyped by the strong cultural values transmitted from the past to the present. An understanding of these will assist us in the analysis of social attitude, parental perceptions and the parenting behaviours of Hong Kong Chinese stepfamilies in Chapters 5 and 6.

4 Research Methodology

Introduction

In this chapter, the key research questions for the empirical study are first outlined; secondly, the four key aspects of methodology are discussed: the choice of research method, sampling, data collection and data analysis.

Key Research Questions

The key research questions were developed based upon the objectives of this study which are set out in Chapter 1, i.e. to explore social attitudes towards stepfamilies and stepparenting by interviewing local informants who have personal experiences or who have worked with stepfamily members; to examine parental perceptions and beliefs about stepparenting in the local stepfamilies whose members are willing to be interviewed; and to identify the difficulties of parenting in these stepfamilies. The research questions were:

1. how do informants, i.e. the stepmothers and certain professionals (social workers and teachers), perceive stepfamilies and parenting in stepfamilies?
2. how do stepmothers in Hong Kong perceive their position, role and the difficulties faced by stepparents in Hong Kong? and

3. what help/services do informants regard as important in supporting stepfamilies?

The Choice of the Research Methodology

My study uses qualitative methods. Quantitative studies emphasize 'the measurement and analysis of causal relationships between variables, not processes' (Denzin & Lincoln, 1994, p.4). Although it sometimes does perform the function of exploratory study, its main purpose is to test theories through scientific modes of inquiry. The belief behind the inquiry is that scientific theories can be tested, confirmed, or falsified. Explicit, standardized experimental or interview procedures are designed and used predominantly to reveal the causal relationships and for affirming reliability and credibility. A sizable sample of respondents should be recruited in order to draw sound conclusions and make findings generalizable. Quantitative research would be useful in Hong Kong because we lack basic information about numbers and characteristics. I made searches of local literature and research project findings on this topic; there was none available, except for literature and findings on the dissolution of marriages and broken families as a result of divorce. Statistics on stepfamilies are also scarce. For example, the Government has not collected data on the number of re-married persons or families. Only since 1991 has the Hong Kong Council of Social Service started to collect very limited information by asking only one question about stepfamilies in their Central Information Survey form. The question asks whether or not the family seeking help from the social work agency is a stepfamily. There was no adequate local data available for me to draw on at the planning stage of this study. Thus if a number of stepfamilies are identified in Hong Kong, quantitative methods could be used to gather information for the development of a profile of these families. This would form a useful data base.

However, in view of the lack of background information, I was not in a position to undertake a quantitative study. Moreover, my own particular interests lead me in the direction of qualitative research. The major objectives of this study were to examine the structure and dynamics of stepfamilies and to understand more about the values held by parents in stepfamilies about stepparenting and stepfamilies. It was important, therefore, to choose a research method which would help to capture perceptions, beliefs, the ways in which the meanings or thoughts are interpreted and the feelings experienced. Qualitative research does not place the major focus on the examination of causal relationships, but seeks to discover the nature of phenomena as humanly experienced (Minichiello et al., 1990). Strauss & Corbin (1990) pointed out that the qualitative research method is designed for use in 'uncovering and understanding what lies behind any phenomenon about which little is yet known' (p.19). It is used for exploring the intricate details of phenomena that cannot be gathered by quantitative methods. Denzin & Lincoln (1994) suggested that 'qualitative researchers stress the socially constructed nature of reality, the intimate relationship between the researcher and what is studied, and the situational constraints that shape inquiry...they seek answers to questions that stress how social experience is created and given meaning' (p.4). As the subject matter of the study is to investigate the complex family systems with the objectives of exploring the perceptions of the informants, uncovering value issues, facilitating the expression of feelings and stimulating reflection, I thought the study would best be conducted by the qualitative research method.

Research Method Should Be Chosen with Careful Consideration of the Nature of the Subject Matter to Be Studied

The subject matter of inquiry was culturally highly sensitive. From reading Western literature (Fine, 1986; Gannon & Coleman, 1983; Ganong, Coleman, & Kennedy, 1990), the word 'step' carries a negative connotation and social attitudes tend to negatively stereotype those who have this role. It seemed likely that similar attitudes might be held by people in Hong Kong, which is a place where the cultures of East and West mix but where there is also a traditional base in Confucianism which continues to influence the values and behaviours of family members. These impressions were reinforced by casual discussion with friends and relatives as to whether they knew any prospective subjects for the study. Their polite refusal to make introductions, even if they knew someone who was a stepparent, impressed upon me the fact that this subject is a very sensitive topic in my society. People did not want to act as a liaison person for fear that they would offend those who bear the name 'stepparent'.

This experience reinforced the decision to use a particular aspect of qualitative methodology -- the face to face interview, which would be more likely to elicit frank and open responses than a less personal method, such as mailed questionnaires.

The Tools for Data Collection Have to Match the Nature of the Inquiry

The use of interviews is not the only tool in qualitative methodology. Possible alternatives include participant observation and the analysis of records. Neither of these was available to me: for obvious and practical reasons, participation observation was impossible, whilst the agency records of social workers would have been available but were likely to be sketchy and would probably have thrown little light on my main interest -- the perceptions of the social workers and their clients.

Interviews in qualitative research attempt to produce sufficient structure to enable the data to be collected systematically by means of an open and flexible dialogue with the informants. This type of interview is labour intensive and time-consuming. It is 'best when topics are complex and demand open-ended answers, much clarification, and contingency probes' (Powers et al, 1985, p.127). In-depth interviews allows the interviewer to 'initiate a dialogue with a real person and engages the interviewee as a human being, not as a study subject' (Kaufman, 1994, p.123). In addition, through interviews I was able to search for themes from the stepparents' experience in order to 'identify recurrent statements of behaviours that are then labelled, described, and summarized to portray the person's most frequent, that is, most important, experiences of actions' (Luborsky, 1994, 189).

A disadvantage of the decision adopt this method was that there would be little triangulation, in the conventional sense. I was inspired by Denzin's (1970) concept on 'triangulation' and decided to generate further data by interviewing two additional kinds of research subject, i.e. social workers and teachers. These professionals were the most likely to have contact with stepfamily members and were able to provide supplementary information particularly on their perception of social attitudes towards stepfamilies. By interviewing these informants, it was hoped that data from the stepmothers would be confirmed or modified. By collecting three sets of data, I intended to triangulate the data provided by the informants by bringing different kinds of material to bear upon the same question or event, because 'looking at an object from more than one standpoint provides researchers and theorists with more comprehensive knowledge about the object' (Miller, 1997, p.25). Thus the purpose of using these groups of informants was not to present an authoritative picture of each profession's views and opinions, but to use the material as a kind of balance or check to the interviews with stepmothers, which are the core of the empirical research.

The Plan for Data Collection

The main informants for this study were the stepmothers. I was well aware that other members of the stepfamily would have an important contribution to make to the understanding of the dynamics and processes within these families: they would strengthen the reliability and validity of the data collected and analysed by producing data from other sources, so that a more rounded and credible overall picture about the parenting in local stepfamilies could be painted. Realistically, however, stepmothers were the only members of the family whose opinions I was likely to obtain for my sample. There were two main reasons for this. Firstly, it was more likely that stepmothers would give their consent to being interviewed. Secondly, as revealed by a consumer survey conducted by the Hong Kong Council of Social Service, 75.1% of the principal clients of its member agencies which provide family counselling/casework services were female (Hong Kong Council of Social Service, 1995); social workers informed me that there were more known stepmothers than stepfathers in their caseloads. However, this provided some advantages. As revealed in the literature, stepmothers have greater needs and problems compared with stepfathers. They may reach out for help from social work agencies more than stepfathers. In addition, since the researcher is a female who is trained in social work, stepmothers may be facilitated to speak more openly, while they may find it easier to confide in someone of the same gender.

It was planned to recruit stepmothers from two sources: those seeking help from social work agencies and a small number who were not known to social work agencies. The first reason for including the latter was to gather information from interviewees who were not regarded as problematic because they were seeking professional help. The second reason was that to increase the number of stepmothers in Hong Kong who were willing to be interviewed, I planned to take as many stepmothers as would come if they met my simple criteria. This criteria was that the stepmothers were either married or cohabiting with a remarried man who had children under 18 who were living with them.

I planned to interview the stepmothers three times. The stepmothers were interviewed more times than the professionals because they were main informants, and also because a relationship needs to be built before sensitive information will be shared. Disclosure of information requires a trusting relationship. There was the risk that my interviewees would drop out of their commitment after the first or second interview; in fact, they did not.

After interviewing the stepmothers, I planned to interview the professionals, i.e. the social workers and teachers, for the next phase of data collection. Social workers are more likely to have come into contact with stepfamilies because of the needs and problems of the latter. They were to be recruited from family service centres, either from the governmental Social Welfare Department or from a non-governmental social work agency. The criteria for recruitment was that they had experience of working with stepfamilies. They were interviewed once.

Walsh (1992) noted that the school system in Western countries also fails to respond sensitively, and regards stepfamilies as no different from intact, nuclear families (p.713). Crosbie-Burnett (1994) also advocated changes in school policy and the introduction of school-based interventions for stepchildren. In Hong Kong no written references are made to these observations. In addition, there is no documented information regarding local teachers' awareness of the needs and problems of students coming from stepfamilies. Children spend a large part of their day time in school, and they respect their teachers as role models. I decided, therefore, to use teachers as my informants because they have significant influences upon the children's lives. School teachers were recruited from primary or secondary schools. They were expected to have experience in relating to students coming from stepfamilies. They were interviewed once.

In summary, I planned to recruit the following informants for my sample: eight stepmothers, eight social workers (four from the governmental Social Welfare Department and four from non-governmental organizations handling family cases), and eight teachers (four from primary schools and four from secondary schools).

Tools for Data Collection

I decided to use a mixture of data collection strategies within qualitative research methods in order to enhance the richness of the information and to ensure the validity of the data collected. I planned to interview the three kinds of informants, and during the interviews, I planned to use different strategies for data collection. When data for a study is collected by using a variety of data sources, 'data triangulation' is used for data analysis (Denzin, 1978b). Triangulation of data sources is particularly useful for 'comparing and cross-checking the consistency of information derived at different times and by different means within qualitative methods' (Patton, 1990, p.467). This method enables the analyst to understand the reasons for the differences captured by the different data collected. At the same time, 'consistency in overall patterns of data from different sources and reasonable explanations for differences in data from divergent sources contribute significantly to the overall credibility of findings' (Patton, 1990, pp.467-468).

It was planned that the in-depth interviews would last between one and a half and two hours. The interview guide is appended (Appendix 5A for the stepmothers and Appendix 5B for the professionals). Stepmothers were interviewed more times than were the professionals because they were main informants and relationship had to be established before sensitive information would be shared. In addition to question guide for the in-depth interview, supporting tools were used to facilitate the free expression of feelings and opinions, they are summarized and illustrated below.

Free Association Technique

All the informants were asked about their feelings when cards on which the Chinese characters 'step', 'stepmother', 'stepfather', 'stepchild', and 'stepfamilies' are shown. These cards were used as tools in order to warm them up and begin a conversation with the researcher.

Triggering Cards

Emotive statements which were extracted from Western literature on the subject of the feelings of stepmothers were translated into Chinese and shown to the local stepmothers at the beginning of the first session. For example, they were encouraged to share their feelings with the researcher when they saw the statement 'some people are embarrassed when I mention that I am a stepparent. It has connotations of failure...'. It was hoped that they would empathize with what was written on the cards and that they would consequently be more willing to express their feelings and opinions on being a stepmother.

Vignettes

Vignettes showing the cases of local stepfamilies were written in Chinese and shown to the stepmothers. Some of the vignettes were problems faced by stepfathers. I wanted their views not simply on stepmothering and by showing these cards, I hoped to make them consider some of the difficulties that stepfathers might face.

Stepmothers were shown eight vignettes corresponding to the tasks of stepfamilies noted by Visher & Visher (1988). Free flow of opinions and feelings were expected to follow reading. If the stepmothers had difficulties in responding, they were asked: how do you feel when you read this case? What are the problems in this family? Are there any problems in parenting? Who is the key person responsible for causing the problems in parenting and why?

The social workers and teachers were shown five vignettes. Three of these were chosen from the eight vignettes shown to the stepmothers. Those three vignettes had triggered the strongest responses from the stepmothers and they were, therefore, used to test out the responses of the professionals. The other two vignettes were newly introduced and were based upon the case situations reported by the stepmothers. The themes of these two vignettes were 'power and equity' and 'communication and conflict management', which were issues repeatedly raised in the interviews with the stepmothers.

The Use of Questions in the Interview

The questions asked in the in-depth interviews were mostly semi-structured which gave informants the chance to express their feelings and points of view. Since the information gathered from the professionals was intended to enhance the richness and validity of the data collected from the stepmothers, and the professionals would be seen only once, fewer questions were asked and they were more focused (see Appendix 5B).

In order to achieve the first objective of the 'exploration of social attitudes towards stepfamilies and stepparenting from informants having personal experiences or having worked with stepfamily members', stepmothers were asked, for example: 'What were your expectations of the role of a parent in a stepfamily before it was formed?'; 'How were those expectations formed?'; 'Was there anybody who influenced you in developing those expectations? Who were they?' The stepmothers were asked the same questions about the views of their spouse.

The social workers and the teachers were asked about their perceptions of and attitudes towards stepfamilies and stepparenting. The following are some examples: 'Should people remarry after the death of their spouse?'; 'Should people remarry after divorce?'; 'Should people remarry if they have children from their previous marital relationship?'; 'What are your expectations of the roles of parents and stepparents in a stepfamily?'; etc.

In order to achieve the second objective, i.e. 'the examination of parental perceptions and beliefs about stepparenting in the stepfamilies in Hong Kong', stepmothers were asked questions such as, 'What are your expectations of the role of a parent in a stepfamily now?'; 'How are those expectations formed?'; 'Do you think those expectations have affected the ways in which you and your spouse parent?'; 'If you have difficulties in parenting, what may have caused these difficulties?'; etc. They were also asked the same questions about the views of their spouse.

The views of social workers and teachers on parental perceptions and beliefs about stepparenting were explored. They were asked questions such as: 'What are your expectations of the roles of parents and stepparents in a stepfamily?'; 'What are your expectations of stepmothers in their parenting role?'; 'Would there be any difference in their needs and problems depending upon whether the stepparent is male or female? What are these differences and why?'; etc.

As regards the third objective on 'identification of the difficulties of parenting in the stepfamilies under study', stepmothers were asked: 'What are the parenting tasks undertaken by you and your spouse in your family?'; 'Do you and your spouse have any difficulties when carrying out your roles and tasks? If so, what are they?'; 'In your view, what may have caused the difficulties?'; etc. The above questions were asked in order to identify the parenting responsibilities and difficulties in parenting in stepfamilies, as reported by the stepmothers.

Social workers and teachers were asked: 'In your view, what are the needs and difficulties of the members of a stepfamily, i.e. the stepparent, parent, stepchild, child?'; 'Would there be any difference in the needs and problems depending upon whether the stepchild is a boy or girl? What are the differences and why?'; etc. The answers to these questions were intended to enrich the understanding of the difficulties of parenting children and stepchildren in stepfamilies.

Information with Secondary Gains

After the information was collected using the techniques described above, additional information will be generated from the answers to the key research questions. The following can be said to be 'information with secondary gains'.

Firstly, it is expected that the information will be confirmed or contradicted by the three kinds of informants. This is the result of 'triangulation' of the three sets of data. 'The data should be sufficiently rich to reflect the plurality of perspectives' (Walker, 1985, p.160) and this will be reflected in the discussion of the findings and the conclusion to this study.

Secondly, there will be information for discussion based upon the implications that the findings of this study will have for policy and service development of the social services in Hong Kong, as perceived by the informants. For example, stepmothers were asked: 'What kinds of help do you think you would need to solve the problems? Are you getting any help now? If not, would you like some?'; 'What kind of help do you think your spouse may need?'; 'Whether you are reaching out for some help or have decided not to reach out, what made you decide whether or not to seek help? Has this decision anything to do with the way you perceive yourself, your family, or your encounters with others who know you are from a stepfamily?'; etc. These questions will help the policy-makers and practitioners understand the needs and difficulties of the parents in the local stepfamilies, based upon the reports of some stepmothers.

Social workers and teachers were asked to reflect upon the kinds of help they are able to offer stepfamilies, in order to identify the service gap. For example, they were asked questions such as: 'In your role as a social worker/teacher, what kind of help do you think you can offer to the stepparent, parent, stepchild or child in a stepfamily?'; 'Is there anything you think your school/agency can do to help them?'; 'Is there anything the Government can do to help them?'; etc.

It should be noted that the questions asked in the interviews did not need to follow a pre-determined sequence. Informants were asked for some personal and confidential information for data needed for the facesheet which they may have felt uncomfortable providing, for example, details of their family income, the full name of their spouses and extended kins. I usually scheduled this for the last session of the interview, unless I felt that rapport had been built between myself and the interviewee. In addition, the researcher welcomed information and responses which had not been exhaustively included in the question guide, provided that they were relevant to this study. Such voluntary information may contribute to a fuller picture of the subject matter.

Method and Tools for Data Analysis: Ways of Handling Raw Data to Ensure Authenticity and Consistency

I considered using a computer-aided data analysis program, such as 'NUDIST'. I decided, however, that I would not feel comfortable using it, as it might restrict my creativity and sensitivity in 'seeing' and 'exploring' the raw material. I wished to explore the untold information from the interviewees and make meanings out of what I had been told. As I was the sole interviewer and transcriber for all the interviews, I knew the factual information well and I remembered the non-verbal expressions from my observations during the interviews; I could easily refer to the notes and remember the non-verbal cues shown during the interviews.

A full transcription of the content of interviews from audio-tapes by the researcher him/herself has the following advantages. The researcher will go through the process of the interview again and pick up the important messages he/she may have missed during the interview. In addition, colloquial language and special expressions were put down in written words or in phonetic expressions. This was done in order to note the idiosyncratic use of the words by a particular family to understand its culture.

The Process of Data Collection and Data Analysis

At the recruitment phase of this study, I had great difficulty in finding stepparents who were willing to be interviewed. My plan to find them through my acquaintances at work and through relatives and friends was a failure. I had approached the governmental Social Welfare Department for referral of informants but my request was not successful. The non-governmental family service agencies I had made contacts responded with understanding and supportive attitude.

My original design for the number of stepmothers to be interviewed was eight. Ten stepmothers were finally recruited. Seven of the stepmothers were referred to me by different family services centres belonging to one of the largest social work agencies in Hong Kong and by one agency specializing in the handling of child protection cases. The remaining three were referred by para-professional counsellors who were 'friends' of the stepmothers. All of these stepmothers had at least one stepchild under 18 years of age living with them.

During the data collection process, stepmothers were interviewed three times. The first session aimed at building up an initial working relationship with the stepmothers before they could talk comfortably with me on this sensitive topic of stepfamily and stepparenting. In the same session I also gathered the background information of the stepmothers and their families and explored their perception on stepparenting and difficulties of parenting in their families by using cards and vignettes to trigger feelings and free association (see Appendix 5A). If the stepmothers needed more time to warm up before sharing their feelings, I did not restrict them by following the interview sequence but encouraged them freely talk about their immediate concerns. In the second session I continued to explore the stepmothers' perception on stepparenting, needs and difficulties in parenting. I also explored the gender-role division of parenting responsibilities and the feelings underlying parental perceptions which had affected their parenting behaviours and feelings of their children. In the final session, semi-structured questions were used to further explore the parental tasks undertaken by the stepmothers and their spouses, the difficulties of the parental tasks taken by the stepmothers and their spouses and the causes of those difficulties. I also explored the kinds of help needed by the stepmothers and their families.

After interviewing the first informant, I used the information I had collected and my observations from the interview to refine the tools for data collection.

I made slight changes to the language on the triggering cards in order to make them clearer. Thereafter, there was a period during which I had to wait patiently while at the same time sustaining my working relationships with the professionals to whom I had sent requests.

After interviewing the stepmothers and subsequently reviewing the data, slight modifications in the informants to be targeted in the next phase were made. I had decided to interview all eight social workers from non-governmental organizations. I dropped my plan to include stepmothers from the Social Welfare Department of the Government of Hong Kong. It was also decided that it was important to look at gender differences in both groups of professionals. I, therefore, decided to interview equal numbers of male and female social workers and teachers -- four of each in both of the two groups. There was no problem in recruiting them.

After informants were recruited, I started collecting data from the teachers and, at the same time, analyzing the data from the stepfamilies. I interviewed eight full-time teachers from Hong Kong who were studying summer courses at the University of Nottingham. The University was chosen because it has a large population of students who are full-time teachers enrolling in part-time B.Ed. or M.Ed. studies. Informants recruited are likely to come from different types of schools and from different districts in Hong Kong. After interviews with the teachers were completed, social worker informants were recruited in Hong Kong.

The teachers and social workers were interviewed once. Information collected was supplementary to those gathered from the stepmothers with the intention to enhance the richness and validity. Cards and vignettes for warming up were used in smaller number than those employed in interviewing the stepmothers. Semi-structured questions were selected from those used for interviewing stepmothers to bring a better focus for answering questions on perceptions of stepfamilies, stepparenting, the roles they had played or would like to play in helping stepfamilies (see Appendix 5B).

During the data collection and analysis period, all the audio-taped interviews were transcribed by me. The 30 sessions with the stepmothers produced 992 pages of verbatim-manuscripts. The transcribed manuscripts ranged from 22 to 51 pages. The 16 sessions with social workers and teachers produced 189 pages of verbatim-manuscripts. The transcribed manuscripts ranged from 9 to 16 pages. In total, I produced 1,181 pages, or 375,166 words of transcriptions for this study. The reliability and consistency were reinforced. I then began to analyse the information I had collected and to write the draft report of this study.

In the following I shall describe my methods of analysis by using information gathered from the stepmothers as an example. Firstly, I read the transcribed manuscripts of each interview carefully. I detected repeated wordings which seemingly were the subjective concerns of the informants. It was also important to identify feelings underlying expressions. Coloured stickers were used to pick out what the informants had said about the three major areas I studied, i.e. I used green stickers for remarks on 'social attitudes', red stickers for 'parental perceptions' and blue stickers for 'parenting behaviours'. On each sticker I put down key words to note the theme under the area, e.g. on a green sticker on social attitude I wrote 'rejection by in-laws', or 'labelled by neighbours', or 'negative attitudes of teachers', etc. These coloured stickers helped me to trace the information I needed at one glance and for more refined categorization.

I repeated the same procedure on the manuscripts of the second and the third interview I conducted with the same informant. By careful examination of the coloured stickers of the three interviews, I was able to form a more complete picture of what the informant told me about social attitudes, parental perceptions and parenting behaviours from his/her subjective perspective. By cross examination of the manuscripts of the three interviews I gradually made sense out of my observations.

When the ten sets of manuscripts (three manuscripts for each informant) were labelled by coloured stickers, I went on to identify common concerns across information supplied by different informants; it was easy to find the commonality because they were highlighted by the same coloured stickers. For information which were other than the three major area of study, different coloured stickers were used, e.g. yellow stickers to note 'help needed by stepfamily', orange stickers to note 'help offered by social workers/teachers', etc. For very significant information, the key words written on the stickers were highlighted with red ink, e.g. Mrs. Lau (M09)[1] told me the biological mother of her stepson suddenly disappeared from his life, her stepson could not accept that he was deserted by his mother and rejected his stepmother. This had tremendous negative impact on the relationship between the stepmother and the stepson and the stepmother and her own daughter. I marked on the blue sticker 'sudden loss of bio.M. affect stepM-stepS & M-D relationships' in red ink.

Reflections on the Process

As pointed out by Fontana & Frey (in Denzin & Lincoln, 1994, pp.373-4), 'interviewing is currently undergoing not only a methodological change but a much deeper one, related to self and other... as we treat the other as a human being, we can no longer remain objective, faceless interviewers, but become human beings and must disclose ourselves, learning about ourselves as we try to learn about the other'. Indeed, the exploration into the needs and difficulties of the informants evoked in me feelings of helpfulness and helplessness which were followed by a need to reflect on my role function and affirm my role in this study. The following examples illustrate my struggle between my roles as a researcher and as a social worker.

I was a social worker before taking up my position as a social work educator in Hong Kong. During my years of teaching social work, I also rendered voluntary services by counselling a small number of clients. Due to my training and profession, I found it difficult to separate my role as a helper from that of a researcher. When I saw my informants crying, I had to 'control' myself so as not to become involved in the helping process. On one occasion, a stepmother left an urgent message for me on my answering machine, which said in a distressed tone, 'Please, please help me. I need your help. Please phone'. Since I was away from my office for two weeks, I did not know when the message had been left and I wondered whether or not my informant had survived the trauma. I wanted to telephone immediately in order to show my concern but, after careful thinking, I wrote a comforting letter containing empowering words to remind my informant that she had the strength to cope. I also xeroxed a copy of the letter to her social worker at once to enable her to follow up the case.

Another situation arose which had to be handled carefully in order to avoid hurting the feelings of my informant. During a second interview, my informant said she would like to give me her wedding photograph and would like me to bring her my photograph in the final interview, as a keepsake. My social work training reminded me that I had to deal with her separation anxiety and feeling of helplessness when the professional relationship came to an end. I was not in the position, however, to give help or foster the false hope of on-going friendship. Therefore, I considered possible solutions and came up with the following: I went to a bookstore and found a bookmark which had written words of encouragement. It said: 'Accept what you are and have confidence in yourself, live happy everyday...'. In the final session, she gave me a beautiful wedding photograph and I guiltily handed her just a bookmark and explained to her sincerely, 'This is what I would like you to remember me by'. I informed her social worker of what I did so that she could follow up on the separation issue which had arisen from our short, but trusting, relationship.

The two incidents described above illustrate that the use of personal interviewing is a very sensitive area which often raises ethical dilemmas. The feelings of the researcher about the difficulties and distress which informants may be experiencing must be managed, but it is also important to keep lines of communication open to those who are in a position to offer support or help.

The Limitations of This Study

My original design for the number of stepmothers to be interviewed was eight. To my relief, and after overcoming initial difficulties, I was able to recruit ten. I included the first informant of the pilot run in my sample. I found from my first interview that the tools for data collection served this purpose well. I only had to make slight changes to the language on the triggering cards in order to make their meaning clearer. Some changes had to be made to the wording of the cards showing 'voices of the stepmothers' because they had been translated from Western literature and the translation needed refinement.

This study, then, is based on small samples of stepmothers who were mostly the clients of family service centres and samples of social workers and teachers. Nonetheless, the three batches of informants provided very rich information from 46 interviews (each stepmother having been interviewed three times and each social worker and teacher once). This has enabled me to draw attention to highly significant experiences and difficulties in the lives of stepfamilies in contemporary Hong Kong as reported by the stepmothers I interviewed. It is to be hoped that this can be further explored by eliciting the perceptions of other parties to the situation. In particular, and in addition to the obvious value of fathers' and children's perceptions, the perceptions of extended family members would be very valuable. It is my impression that the influences of mothers-in-law and paternal kin were powerful in the families I studied. I foresee difficulties, however, in the fact that older people are not used to being interviewed and questioned about their difficulties.

Culturally they believe that 'it is shameful to disclose the problems in a family'.

In future studies of stepfamilies, the marital relationship of the couples in stepfamilies might be further explored. In this study most of the stepmothers were disappointed in their marital relationships and reported that this had affected the development of stepmother-stepchild relationships. The quality and consequences of the marital relationships were not the focus of this study, but it would be worth making an effort to examine their marital life, including sexual relationships, in greater detail.

It would be valuable if more stepmothers not associated with social work agencies were recruited as interviewees. If I had been able to find willing informants of this kind, I would have included them in my sample.

When the data was analysed, I was careful in analysis, interpretation and drawing conclusions. Firstly, I reminded myself the limitations of the sample, i.e. the information I gathered was mainly from the reports of a small number of stepmothers; I did not have the opportunities to collect the first-hand information on marital, parent-child and family relationships from the spouses, children and in-laws of the stepmothers. Moreover, I am woman and I had to be careful not to over-identify with the informants of the same sex and thus affect the objectivity of this study. Furthermore, I was careful not to interpret it as if it was exclusive to stepfamilies. I did not have a group of families to compare with the stepfamilies I interviewed; some of the problems of stepparents and stepfamilies which I noted may well also be difficulties shared by parents and families.

When conclusions were drawn, it was pointed out that the source of information was mainly from reports of the stepmothers, the conclusions were supported by evidence, relevant quotations from the authentic remarks of the stepmothers. In addition to my awareness of the limitations of the sample. I was also aware of the possibility that the chosen data-collection method might predispose the emergence of certain particular conclusions or areas of concern, at the expense of other possibilities. For example, I might have been influenced by many Western literature I read and unconsciously adopted a deficit-comparison paradigm to view stepfamilies and stepmothers negatively and focus on their difficulties. Furthermore, most of the informants I successfully recruited were clients of social work agencies. The reports I obtained from the interviews with them might further reinforce that negativity because most of them were stressed and felt inadequate as parents. As I was aware of the effect of biased views, I had encouraged my informants to share with me in the interviews their success in parenting and I recognized their strengths. For example, stepmothers M04, M07 and M09 had positive experiences. I had affirmed their efforts in overcoming their difficulties in parenting. Moreover, the literature I had read was only a map for me to explore the untold stories of my informants. I was aware of the cultural uniqueness and the values affecting this highly sensitive topic I had chosen to study.

However, the conclusions in this study echoed what had been unveiled in the Western literature about difficulties confronting stepfamilies and stepmothers. Remembering that the sample of this study was small, I did not attempt to generalize the conclusions to the larger population except to note the influence of Chinese culture and values which had emphasized the problems of stepfamilies --- the stepmothers in Hong Kong were further weakened in their position in the stepfamily because they had more dominating and powerful mothers-in-law than their Western counterparts.

Lastly, it should be pointed out that two of the teachers and one social worker were children of stepfamilies and one teacher and two of the social workers had experienced parental divorce. As mentioned earlier, their personal experiences will have coloured their views when they were asked about stepparenting and stepfamilies. On the positive side, it is good to have a good proportion of empathetic informants who could provide information for this study; on the disadvantage side, they might over-identify with the situations presented during discussion and consequently the information collected could be biased and represent only the views of a group of overly interested informants.

Conceptual Framework and Themes for Data Analysis

The Conceptual Framework for Data Analysis

With reference to the literature reviewed earlier, their relationship can be understood from the diagram below.

Figure 4.1
The Relationship Between Social Attitudes,
Parental Perceptions and Parenting Practice of Stepparents

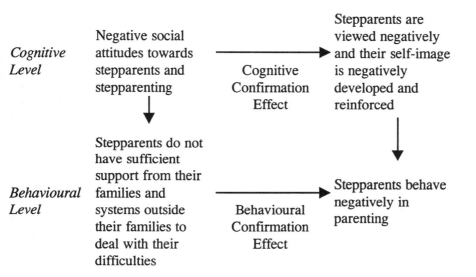

I shall explain the concepts drawn for use in the above diagram. Visher (1994) stated that social attitudes towards stepparents and stepparenting are like a 'mirror of negativity which can lead to a self-fulfilling prophecy: stepparents are bound to fail'. Social attitudes affect a person's perception and the support available to him/her, 'parental cognition affects parental behaviours' (Sigel and others, 1992). In the case of stepparents, negative stereotyping has the cognitive confirmation effect which would result in behavioural confirmation effect (Coleman & Ganong, 1987a). Stepfamilies are labelled by the public and people around them and seen as an 'incomplete institution' (Cherlin, 1978); thus stigma results in less social support (Strong & DeVault, 1993). Stepparents feel that no matter how hard they try, their hard work is not recognized. Some of them, such as stepmothers M03 and M06, appear to have behaved negatively in parenting and and to have lived up to their poor self-image.

The diagram on the previous page was meant to show a conceptual framework developed from literature review to guide my thinking.

Themes for Data Analysis

The themes are drawn from the Western literature which has been reviewed, but they have been modified to taken into account the specific aspects of the Chinese culture which have affected perceptions of stepfamilies. The three major themes are: social attitudes on stepparenting and stepfamilies; parental perceptions of stepparenting and stepfamilies; and parenting behaviours in stepfamilies. In developing the themes, the significance of Chinese terms and metaphors used to describe stepfamilies and their family members are utilized; for example, 'worn shoes' and 'children of a greasy oil bottle' are metaphors which reflect the bitterness of social attitudes and the humiliation felt by the stepfamily members and are Chinese culture-specific. There are other themes, such as 'flow of a rough river' which is metaphor vividly symbolizing one's life as a running river; however, it can be seen as related to the developmental stage concept in Western literature. Some of the themes used in this study are taken from Western literature because there are no equivalents in Chinese or Hong Kong literature about the dynamics of stepfamilies from which I can draw. These themes include, for example, 'dealing with losses and changes', 'the negotiation of different developmental needs of family members,' etc. The following is an overview of these themes developed after their adaptation for the reasons discussed.

Social Attitudes and Parental Perceptions on Stepparenting and Stepfamilies in Hong Kong

'Broken Mirror': aspirations and the reality of marriage and family life in stepfamilies.

'Worn Shoes' and 'Children of a Greasy Oil Bottle': social attitudes and parental perceptions of stepparents and stepchildren.

'Harmonious Music Out of Tune': traditional values are challenged which leads to intergenerational conflicts.

'Outsiders Looking in Through Glasses': the influence of mass media and popular culture; helpers' perceptions of stepparenting, stepfamilies, and help needed by stepfamilies.

'Flow of a Rough River': a general description of the changes in stepfamilies and the difficulties in parenting from a family life cycle perspective.

Dealing with Losses and Changes: the wish to bury past history; family and social relationships when a stepfamily is newly formed; the forms of support available and the coping strategies employed by stepfamilies.

Building Couple Bond: developing marital relationships whilst at the same time coping with the challenges of in-law relationships and the demands of children in stepfamilies; the stepmother competing with the stepchild for the love and attention of her husband.

Negotiation of Different Developmental Needs of Family Members: the stepmother is expected to care for the stepchild but she wishes to be loved as a wife by her husband; the stepchild has ambivalent feelings towards maintaining tie with his/her biological mother; the husband wishes to have a happy and harmonious family.

Equity and Authority in Stepfamily: paternal grandparents take care of their grandchildren during their son's divorce, and they expect to continue having authority over child management and decision-making in the stepfamily; grandparents and the husband want to be exclusively responsible for the parenting, without the involvement of the biological mother from the former marriage.

Communication and Conflict Management: the husband of the stepmother is caught in the middle of conflicts between parents, siblings or his wife; the stepmother feels that the 'insiders' are against her, as an 'outsider' because of an alliance exists between her husband, stepchild and paternal relatives.

Summary of the Chapter

In this chapter I have outlined the research questions. I have also discussed the reasons for my choice of methodology, the issues which needed to be considered in the use of the interview, and the research process including data analysis. I have also reflected upon some of the sensitive matters which arise in this kind of process. Finally, I have presented my framework for data analysis which leads us to the analysis of the information gathered in the subsequent chapters.

Note

1   Informants are assigned codes. For personal particulars of stepmothers please refer to Chapter 6 pp. 148-9.

5 Social Attitudes and Parental Perceptions of Stepparenting in Stepfamilies in Hong Kong: Findings and Discussion

Introduction

In the previous two chapters I have reviewed the literature and research findings of Western and Chinese scholars and researchers. This has provided me with a map which will help me to discover many stories which were previously unknown and to deduce the meaning of the knowledge and data I have gathered. The stepfamily is an institution which has been deliberately shunned by society but it is beginning to be understood as a result of the information collected for this study by the in-depth, personal interviews with ten stepmothers, eight teachers and eight social workers. In this chapter let us first look at the social attitudes and parental perceptions of stepparenting in Hong Kong.

'Broken Mirror' – Aspirations and the Reality of Marriage and Family Life

From the point of view of the older generation in Chinese families, marriage is a family mission with its primary goal being to produce offspring who will continue the family name. Therefore, a son's marriage, especially that of the eldest son, is the fulfilment of a family duty to achieve this goal. It is explained by the notion that 'the son, once he has become a major, is under the obligation of fulfilling the innumerable duties of piety which affiliate him to his father. Among the duties, marriage is the most fundamental' (Chao, 1983, p.42). Children are expected to demonstrate filial piety to their parents by fulfilling their duty to get married (Chapter 3, p.54). It is important for the son to choose the 'right' wife. She should preferably be younger than her husband and possess a good and gentle character. Whether the woman is educated or not is not crucial as being a capable housekeeper, helpful wife and obedient daughter-in-law. The alternate Chinese description of the word 'wife' is 'yin loi jaw' (賢內助), which suggests that the duties of a good-charactered wife should focus upon functional roles which would bring prosperity and harmony to the family into which she has married.

As discussed in Chapter 3 (pp.51, 55-56), harmony in Chinese families is greatly aspired to by family members. When couples marry they hope to acquire the kind of family life which will bring them harmony and well-being. These wishes can be traced to what the Chinese say about a perfect marriage, that is, a marriage that promotes family harmony and perfection in relationships can be described as 'may moon' (美滿). 'May' (美) literally means 'beautiful' and 'moon' (美滿) means fulfilled and rich. When placed together, these two words have a symbolic meaning: marriage is expected to be as beautiful as flowers, to be rounded with no edge or flaw, and to have a surface as smooth as a silvery moon or mirror. In ancient Chinese poems, the moon and a mirror were alternately used to describe the same picture and on some occasions, they were used together to emphasize the idea of perfection.

When a marital relationship dissolves due to the death of one spouse, or when a marital relationship 'goes sour' and the couple becomes estranged, the silvery moon is over-shadowed by black clouds and the mirror drops to the floor and is broken. Cracks appear on its surface which scar the mirror permanently and it can no longer reflect the perfect image it once gave to the person who looks into it. The relationship which was once seen as harmonious and perfect, now appears distorted and the cracked lines add the 'ugly' side of the relationship to the image. The broken mirror can never revert to its once perfect condition. This is the same for marriage and family life after separation, divorce, and remarriage. Those who have been involved in these traumatic experiences would hope to see beautiful, harmonious images in the mirror, but they also see the cracks which are constant reminders of their unpleasant or even painful past. Some would simply not look into the mirror again so as to avoid confronting the feelings aroused by their past experiences. Others may buy another mirror which is even nicer in order to replace the broken one. These are the possible reactions of people emerging from their last marriages and entering into new ones. They may buy as many new mirrors as they want, but it is the image they see when looking into the mirror that matters. What kinds of image do these people see? In fact, it is not only the person himself who looks at his reflection in the mirror; it is also important to consider how the other members of stepfamilies and the people around them see separation, divorce and remarriage. Their attitudes and views have a profound influence upon the marital relationship and family life. The following are illustrations of social attitudes and parental perceptions of remarriage and stepparenting in Hong Kong.

Case Illustrations

Mrs. Lau's Case: Stepmother Who Was Married for the First Time and Was Chasing after Romance, but the Dream Was Broken

Mrs. Lau's husband had married his first wife after dating her for a few months when both of them were quite young. His first wife met another man and had an extra-marital affair with him while her husband was away on business overseas. The marriage ended when the siblings of Mrs. Lau's husband told him about his wife's infidelity. The latter left shamefully and guiltily and let her husband decide the terms of the divorce. The husband was angry about his wife's behaviour, but felt more hurt than anger after the marriage legally ended. The anger of the husband's parents, especially that of his mother, had never subsided. She swore about the shameful behaviour of her daughter-in-law from time to time and did so indiscreetly on social occasions. The shame of the family had been perpetuated from the past to the present and negative feelings were reinforced by discussions about the unfaithful former daughter-in-law.

Mrs. Lau was only 28 years old when she married. What made her decided to marry a divorced man against her parents' wishes? In the interview she told me about the strong feelings she had for her husband. She said:

I loved my husband very much, and had to marry him. At that time, I did not mind being a stepmother. Despite the views of others and the objections of my parents, I still insisted that I would marry my husband. It was not for any other reason than that I loved him. If I had not been motivated by love, or if he was not seen by me as the perfect mate, I would not have considered a man of his background. I regard him as perfect. (M09(3),37)[1]

Mrs. Lau also had put her feelings into words in a two-page write-up which I have translated into English in full (see Appendix 6). What she had written reflected her unfulfilled wishes and her despairs in her marriage:

Every one hopes that their marriage will be happy and perfect. When they are newly married, they hope to spend some sweet moments alone together, which will leave them with beautiful memories.

Soon after the marriage, however, Mrs. Lau was struck hard by the fact that she had to take up the role of stepparent and be a housewife who attended to the various needs of a sizable group of in-laws. She soon came to realize that:

...if the two people are stepparents, their married life is, from the beginning, a 'three people's world', or a 'multi-people world', and in this 'three people's world' many problems are certain to arise. (M09(2), 11)

From Mrs. Lau's remarks, we can see that she perceived her husband's expectations of marriage were quite different from her own. She said:

To me, it is very clear. I wanted to marry him to be his wife, not to be his son's mother. They are two different matters. So he should have thought clearly: do I want this woman to walk with me on the life path, or do I want her to be the mother of my son? If he just wanted to marry a woman who could take care of his son, he should have spelt out his expectations to me beforehand. He should not have married me expecting me to be a good wife, and to build up a good relationship with his son. That is too ideal and perfect. (M09(2),11)

Although her husband would listen to her during times of need, Mrs. Lau wished for more love and affection. Mr. Lau had difficulty facing the past and he had not yet dealt with the scars left from his last marriage. He had still not told his colleagues about his divorce even though he had been remarried for ten years.

Mrs. Chui's Case: A Remarried Stepmother Who Was Striving for Love but Was Given Household Tasks

Mrs. Chui had a daughter from her first marriage. Her remarried family included her husband, her daughter, her husband's son from his first marriage, and two sons from her current marriage. In a blended family such as this one, relationships were complicated and difficult. Mrs. Chui treasured her relationship with the man she loved and told me her hopes concerning this important person in her life:

> The children are as important as my husband, but let me talk about my husband first...I hope that my husband will not marry a third time, and won't separate from me. (M02(3),1)

According to Mrs. Chui, her first marriage had been hard and she had once worked as a dance hostess, so she had had a strong desire to start a new life. She remarried against the will of her mother and she recalled:

> She [her mother] talked to me a lot about the consequences of remarriage; she warned me that one could be an 'outsider' in a group of people, and never be included as an 'insider'. So I thought carefully before marrying him. That's how I decided. If I was asked whether it [remarriage] was 'ideal' or 'a dream', I think that one should not care about other people's opinions, and one should decide himself/herself what the relationship means to him/her. (M02(2),2)

Mrs. Chui's hopes for her remarriage were built upon love and the desire for a new life. She soon discovered, however, that her second husband expected her to be a traditional wife and mother. She said:

> He is very old-fashioned in what he wants from his family. It is like the women in old Chinese movies who, when their husbands come

home, give them their slippers, pour them a cup of tea or a glass of beer, give them a face towel to wipe their faces and tidy up the home; they (the husbands) then sit down for a while and eat their supper and, afterwards, their wives would take care of the children, clean the table, sit down and watch television. When the work was done, they could talk to their husbands at leisure. The wives would share their troubles with their husbands and, if there was joyful news, they would share the joy with their husbands as well...This is very old-fashioned. (M02(3),2)

In everyday family life, Mrs. Chui reported that her husband clearly expected her to take care of him and his children, and he assumed that those were her responsibilities. She explained that those were the wishes which had not been fulfilled in his last marriage. She told me:

He was eager to see that happened. In his first marriage, he could not have that. In the second marriage, he wished to see that happen: 'I'm in power, I can make the woman beside me work for me that way.' (M02(3),4)

In this case, Mrs. Chui had unhealed the scars from her last marriage. She felt that her roles had not been fulfilled in the past and she wanted to prove that she could do as expected or even improve upon her past performance. Her husband wanted to compensate for what he had not had in his previous union and expected his current wife to satisfy his unmet needs. Mr. and Mrs. Chui had both suffered in their last relationships and wished to paint a happy and harmonious picture of their current marriage and family life.

Mrs. Ho's Case: Love Built upon Sympathy and Dealing with Her Widower-husband's Ambivalence towards Remarriage

As with the stepmothers described above, Mrs. Ho's parents, and especially her mother, strongly objected to the marriage. Nevertheless, Mrs. Ho, who was marrying for the first time, married Mr. Ho. She recalled:

I did not listen to my mother. I said, 'I am marrying him, not his daughter. If she does wrong, I can teach her to do right' (M01(1), 14).

She further explained that she liked travelling and living independently, but she reasoned:

> ...I never thought of marrying him at that time. I think I began loving him through pity. (M01(1),22)

She felt that he was overwhelmed by child care responsibilities since the death of his wife, and she was sympathetic to his situation. She began to help him with childminding and later, a loving relationship gradually developed.

How did Mr. Ho regard the relationship? Although he needed to marry a woman to act as a mother for his daughter, he was ambivalent about getting married. Mrs. Ho said:

> In fact, my husband did not want to marry again. His wife gave him a lot of trouble...He did not plan to marry me. He was worried about something...a kind of fear. He was afraid that he had to be responsible for many things. (M01(1),6)

She later found out:

> ...he felt he owed his daughter's mother a favour. He felt guilty when he thought about his deceased wife. (M01(1),8)

It seems that Mr. Ho was unable to fully recover from his painful and stressful past. There was unfinished business in relation to the death of his wife that Mr. Ho felt he needed to complete and he was ambivalent about entering into a new marital relationship. The traditional belief that a favour from a loved one could be returned by repaying it to that person's loved one (e.g. that person's children) had prevented Mr. Ho from deciding to marry another woman.

'Worn Shoes' and 'Children of a Greasy Oil Bottle': Image and Role Perceptions of Stepmothers and Their Children

'Worn Shoes' - Views on Remarried Women and Their Spouses

Social attitudes have a profound effect on a person's self-image, role expectations and functions. In Chinese culture, 'Chinese have much respect for womanhood, consider feminine purity as something sacred, comparing the woman to flawless jade' (Chao, 1983, p.51). Women who have previously been married or have married a remarried man, do not have a 'pure' history so they are no longer a 'flawless jade'. As discussed in Chapters 2 and 3, stepmothers commonly receive negative labels in remarried families. To examine the stereotyping more closely, in Chinese culture, remarried women are regarded like as 'worn shoes', which means that they have a low status because they are compared to shoes people wear which have constant contact with the filthy floor. They are described not only as 'shoes', but 'worn shoes', which carries doubly shameful meaning because it implies that they are used and their external appearance is unattractive. Some people condemn remarried woman as 'yee sau for' (二手貨) which means 'used goods'. This also has a negative meaning for the purpose of shaming the woman who has failed in her commitment to a life-long marriage. The following provides some examples of women who married into stepfamilies and how they were regarded by the people around them.

Women who are morally good would not marry men who have married before Mrs. Chui was a divorcee and had a daughter from her previous marriage. She felt that social attitudes were negative towards remarriage, irrespective of whether the woman was married for the first time or had been married more than once. She told me:

> Usually what people in the community see is not that accurate. If the stepmother brings her child from a former relationship into the new family, they would know that she was remarried. If she does not bring her own child into the stepfamily, it looks as if she is single, and has not married before, so people would then say that her husband has been married before and, if this woman is a virgin, they would ask 'why she has married him?' (M02(2),7)

This indicates that the general public would think that women who looked as if they had not been married before but who were marrying a divorced or widowed man were not morally good, because normally 'good' girls would have the choice not to marry previously married men.

Mrs. Lee was a divorcee with a son and she had married a divorced man with a son. She also felt that there was strong social stigma about remarried people. She responded to my question 'what is the general attitude of people towards remarried persons and stepfamilies?' as follows:

> They think they are 'not proper' (唔正經), 'not healthily integrated' (唔健全). (M06(3), 23)

She proceeded to give me an example of how she was prejudiced against and looked down upon differently:

> At the beginning [of my marriage] I felt somewhat embarrassed. My neighbours, whose flats are opposite to where I live, know that we have reformed our families. When we met them in the morning I greeted them, but their responses were not very good. They viewed my husband and I through 'colour glasses' ['Colour-glasses' has a particular meaning in the Chinese language: it means 'being prejudiced against'] ...They reacted coldly (when greeted). (M06(3),23)

Remarriage is not supported by relatives and friends and it should not be discussed openly Only three of the ten stepmothers reported that their parents approved of them marrying a man who had been married before, regardless of whether these women had or had not married before themselves. The negative image of remarried persons also affects men who are regarded as 'second hand', although they are not shamed by names such as those given to women. Many of the women in this study who consulted their parents about marrying a remarried man, met with strong objections. For example, in Mrs. Ho's case, her mother refused to meet her prospective son-in-law when the question of marriage was raised for decision. Mrs. Chui who worked as dance hostess before her remarriage, also received objections from her colleagues who thought that being a concubine would be more acceptable than marrying a divorced man. She recalled what they said:

111

Why pick someone like that [to marry]? They would not think [about my situation in the following way]: she has been married before, and she is in the same situation as her [future] husband. They wouldn't think like this. They would say, 'Pick such a man! You have already worked in an improper place, so why not be someone's concubine? There is no need to choose someone like this.' (M02(2),22)

After the remarriage has taken place, those who had remarried had difficulty in forgetting the past and accepting the remarriage. An example of this was given in an earlier section: Mrs. Lau's husband would not tell his colleagues at work that he had divorced and remarried and the secret had been kept for ten years. In another type of family, the second marriage is shameful even though the wife had not been married before and the husband remarried following the death of his just wife. The stigma of remarriage continues, which is illustrated by the mother-in-law's remarks as reported by Mrs. Chan:

...my mother-in-law always says to him (her grandson), 'Don't tell other people that you have two mothers.' I don't think that matters. If that is so [the fact], why hide it?...The people on that side of the family [paternal] are like that; they think it is something bad, and that such things should not be made public. (M04(1),12)

'Children of a Greasy Oil Bottle' - The Stigma of Remarried Mothers is Passed on to Their Children

It is regarded as socially shameful for both the mother and her child when a biological mother remarries and takes her child(ren) to live with the stepfamily. The label of 'greasy oil bottle' is given to a child whose mother remarries, which means that the shame, like oil, cannot be washed off and will pass onto the next generation. Why are remarried women and their children not accepted by people who hold traditional Chinese values? Firstly, it is thought that mothers should not leave their husbands and their husbands' families, even if this is due to marital discord or the death of the spouse. Secondly, if they have a child or children from their former union, they should remain in their husbands' families to enable the child to carry on the family name of the paternal line. Thirdly, a woman with a child should not remarry because not only does the woman's surname have to be changed, but the child will lose his/her father's surname and take the name of someone who has no blood relationship to him/her. This is the traditional thinking which discourages women from seeking to remarry and from taking their former husbands' child(ren) into a new marriage. This is also why there is a strong social stigma attached to the mother and the child when a remarriage occurs. The child suffers the shame of the remarried mother even though children usually have no say in their parent's marriage. In fact, some children have to follow their mothers into a new family for practical reasons.

The stepmothers I interviewed felt bitter and hurt when they talked about the negative attitudes of the people around them. For example, Mrs. Lee told me:

...in the late T.V. movie show, they showed an old Chinese movie which talked about 'children of a greasy oil bottle' (油瓶仔/女). I was touched. [Mrs. Lee broke down and cried during the interview.] Due to the responses of my husband's paternal relatives, I can feel the word 'stepson' very deeply...they look at it in a very special way...their attitude and the way they look at him show that they don't accept him... a lot of people are like that. Maybe this is due to traditional Chinese thinking. I bring a 'yau ping chai' into the family, and he is seen as 'yau ping chai'. He is regarded as no good. (S06(1), 13)

She wept and continued to tell me that it was not only the older generation, but are also younger relatives who had such an attitude towards her son. She said:

...perhaps it is people who are older in age, or people of that generation who think that way. However, my husband's younger sisters look at my son the same way. They are cold to him, and the way they look at him is different... I think my son is innocent, and it is because of me that he is trapped in such situation... it's so unfair! Sometimes their attitudes towards him (her son) are so bad. (S06(1),14)

113

Mrs. Chui also recalled how she and her daughter were prejudiced against by her in-laws:

> They thought I came from a bad background. His former wife was said to have been a virgin when she married him, but, when I met my husband, I worked as a dance hostess. They still hold the traditional thinking (of wanting the daughter-in-law to have a clean record, they regard me as 'filthy', and I think that I should not enter their family. They also thought that I am used to eating well, and spending a lot of money, and that I could not bear hardship. Since I have a daughter, and I was married before, they do not believe that I could be good. In fact I work twice as hard as other housewives, but they still don't accept me. (S02(1),16)

This stepmother felt strongly that her own background had made her paternal relatives think that both her and her daughter had 'bad genes'.

This view was supported by another stepmother, Mrs. Lau, who had not been married before, but suffered from the same negative views of the people around her:

> They think that because adults made a mistake, the kid also becomes that way [wrong and bad]. If you had heard their tone, and seen their act and their behaviour, you would feel that. (M03(3),18)

According to this stepmother, her child was not only regarded as a 'child of a greasy oil bottle' when he entered the stepfamily with his remarried mother, but he was also perceived socially as coming from 'a family with something wrong'. The stigma of the broken family and remarriage had attached itself to the children of the remarried women.

Prejudiced Social Attitudes Reinforce the Negative Images which Affects Parental Perceptions and Functions

The Views of the Stepmothers on the Attitudes of People Around Them

In everyday life, stepmothers have to face people who are inside and outside their families. Stepmothers reported that they usually tolerated their relatives' negative attitudes, and only shared their feelings with their husbands when they could take them no longer. For example, Mrs. Chui revealed:

> Their attitudes are different. When my husband was not there, they would talk about things from the past, and about how happy they were; when my husband was present, they would talk about daily life in my family. In the past, I did not mention this to my husband; I kept my lips sealed. Later I told him that I was not happy...the whole thing is unfair to me...I am with you now; I don't mind what they say about me and I am not afraid of them.... (M02(1),19)

Almost all of the stepmothers had to resolve the problem of social attitudes by themselves and received little support from their husbands. The exception was Mrs. Chung who told me that her maternal family supported her decision to marry a divorced man and, when she had troubles in the first year of marriage, she consulted her elder sister and felt strength generated from their discussion. She said she was told to be rational because it had been her choice to marry a divorcee. She came to realize:

> I knew it was right. I chose, and I knew about the(troubles caused by marrying into a stepfamily) beforehand. Why did I still choose it? I have to accept the consequences. So this gives me strengths to carry on. (M07(1),14)

Stepmothers also have to deal with the attitudes of people outside their family system. As their stepchildren were of school age, they had to have contact with their school. Many of the stepmothers were discouraged by the attitudes of some teachers who they thought, had reinforced the negative image they had already received. They felt that they were seen by teachers, particularly male ones, as 'not as good as the biological mothers'; 'uninterested in child management'; 'holding the belief that parenting rights should rest with the biological father'; etc. One stepmother, Mrs. Lee, told me how she felt about being seen by two male teachers:

> I feel that men usually think of stepmothers as no good...being of the same gender, other women can understand my situation better. But

men just think that a stepmother is definitely no good. When dealing with me, they spoke bluntly and without compassion. (M06(3),22)

When asked what the teachers said to her, she recalled:

They said, 'Let me talk to the child's father.' She felt the male principal had a similar attitude. (M06(3),23)

She said:

His attitude was, 'You don't have enough patience or love for him; it is not enough to just talk.' His message was that he had listened to what I said, but he looked at the father. I felt that he would not like to look me in the face. (M06(3),23)

Another stepmother Mrs. Lau, who was married for the first time to a remarried man, also felt she received the same treatment from the teachers of her stepson. She felt that the teacher would rather ask to talk to the biological father of the child and bypass her (M0(3),19).

Only two stepmothers out of the ten I interviewed said that the teachers were helpful and recognized their difficulties and hard work in parenting (M01, M09). Social workers were not mentioned negatively; seven out of the ten stepmothers were helped by social workers at the time of the interviews. However, there was one stepmother who went to the extreme and felt that the so-called helping professionals, such as social workers, and church fellows, had negative attitudes. Mrs. Lee said:

Their attitude is: there must be problems, that is a must. You [the stepmother] I must accept the road you have chosen. Nobody forced you to adopt it. (M06(3),21)

'Harmonious Music Out of Tune': Traditional Values are Challenged Leading to Intergenerational Conflicts

The Chinese who cherish Confucianism regard harmony as an ennobled quality which should be diffused into family relationships (Redding, 1993, p.44). They believe that harmony will lead to a happy and peaceful family life. Conflicts are expected to be suppressed for the well-being of all family members. In a traditional Chinese family, members have their title and position and they are expected to fulfil their role duties properly. It is like a well-trained orchestra which play harmonious music if every musician practises his/her part well and follows the lead of the conductor precisely. In contemporary Chinese families, members may know their place and the behaviour expected, but there are many unexpected factors within and outside the family system which may prevent the fostering and maintenance of harmony. For example, the value of 'life-long marriage' which was once upheld has been challenged by the imported idea of 'companionship marriage'. Couples think more about their individual needs than about family well-being as a whole and as a target to cherish. When the marital relationship comes to an end because of the death of one spouse or due to marital discord, it is as if one of the key musicians has left the orchestra so that the music cannot be played harmoniously as it was in the past. When a new spouse joins the stepfamily, it is like a replacement musician rehearsing together with the others. Although he/she may be skilful in playing his/her piece of instrument, he/she needs time to adjust to the tempo and to coordinate with the group. It is this odd-man-out scenario that often triggers intergenerational conflicts.

A Filial Son Should Know Best What to Do During Conflicts between His Parents and His Wife

I remember being told about a man in his late 40s who had to kneel before his ageing mother for her forgiveness for an alleged conflict created by his wife. The man was a respected, mature older person with a successful business. In his family, however, one can see clearly where the authority lies. In a stepfamily, conflicts could easily arise because of its various and complicated membership. The stepfamilies I studied, were mainly stepmother-families. All of the ten families were parented by stepmothers and biological fathers, including two which were parented by stepmothers and stepfathers because these two were blended families. The new parents were mainly females and, therefore, we have to note that if the families had mothers-in-laws, whether or not they were living together with the stepfamily, their involvement and intervention in family affairs could be a reason for conflict. This is because traditionally women are seen as carers in a family, and when an adult son loses his spouse or gets divorced, the mother is likely to want to be reinstated to her role as a carer. The potential for competition is there.

Case Illustrations

Mrs. Ho's Case: A Husband Who Has a Widow-mother is Caught in the Middle

Mrs. Ho's husband had a widowed mother, who had a poor relationship with her husband before he died of illness and, as reported by Mrs. Ho, her mother-in-law had not taken good care of her children, leaving them in the care of her sick husband and the elder children. Her children did not have a close relationship with her and she had had a poor relationship with Mr. Ho's first wife, who had fallen ill and eventually died. She was not welcome among her children, so she spent time living alternately with each of her children. Mr. Ho was the eldest son.

In Chinese culture, the son should bear greatest responsibility in taking care of his parents. Mr. Ho, therefore, had to let his mother stay with his family whenever she wished. Mrs. Ho recalled:

> My mother-in-law did not get along with my husband's deceased wife. She does not get along with other daughters-in-law either...she instigates quarrels with me all the time. I avoid quarrelling with her. She said to my husband: 'You cannot *not* have a wife, and you cannot *not* have a mother. In a family one must have both.' (M01(1),8)

The mother-in-law asserted that her position in the family was equal to that of her daughter-in-law, if not more powerful. She started arguments and wanted to push things to the limit to test how far her authority would go. Mrs. Ho had to tolerate this on different occasions. The mother-in-law continued her power game and as reported by Mrs. Ho, her husband was always the peace-maker. On one occasion the mother-in-law asked her other son to remind the couple that she was the owner of their flat. Mrs. Ho recalled what Mr. Ho said:

> One person is my wife, and you are my mother, everyone who lives in this house can stay, so don't say we are not owners.

118

She went on:

> However, his mother commented that he was 'not filial', and was not treating her well. (M01(1),10)

In this case, as reported by Mrs. Ho, her mother-in-law was demanding and authoritarian. She wanted to test whether her son was on her side or on his wife's side during times of conflict. The daughter-in-law had to listen to the warning of a former tenant of her mother-in-law who said:

> Don't fight with her. People would just see that you are wrong...if something bad happened, you would be the one to blame. (M0(1),9)

The son wanted harmony in the family and pacified his mother by assuring her that she was as important to him as his wife.

Mrs. Lau's Case: A Step-mother Whose Mother-in-law Fears an Invasion by Her Daughter-in-law

Mrs. Lau reported that:

> After the breakdown of my husband's marriage, she [her mother-in-law] naturally wanted him to marry another woman. When that happened, however, she had many worries. She was afraid that her son would leave and would not live with her. She was afraid that I would not treat her and her grandson well. She had many worries. She started to adopt a negative attitude towards me. (M09(1),12)

Mrs. Lau wanted to make peace with her and tolerate her. She explained:

> I was raised in a strictly-disciplined family, a traditional one. My mother said to me, 'After your marriage, you have to treat your mother-in-law, your husband and his son well.' (M09(1),12)

Mrs. Lau worked very hard to build relationships with her mother-in-law and stepson; she was disappointed in not getting the results she expected. Mrs. Lau explained to me why she thought her mother-in-law refused to accept her:

She [her mother-in-law] is a lady who views men as superior to women...she is a stepmother herself...I treat my stepson ten or a hundred times better than she treated my husband's elder brother [not borne by her]. But she can't accept this herself, no, I mean she can't accept me. People are used to just looking at other people's flaws, so she fails to look at hers [her own flaws]. (M09(1),11)

In this case, the mother-in-law had difficulties in accepting her identity and had a poor relationship with her daughter-in-law. The latter's status reminded her that she was also a stepmother, but her daughter-in-law had performed the role better. Although she felt unhappy with her in-law relationship, the daughter-in-law tried to fulfil her duties and follow the traditional values as taught by her own parents. She did not get enough support from her husband, who wanted to return his mother's favour by practising filial piety. Mrs. Ho explained: 'He treats his mother very well. His son was taken care of by her, and he would not want to do things against her will.' (M09(1),16)

Heaven Will Judge How Well Mothers Treat Their Children

One of the cultural beliefs upheld by most traditional Chinese is 'good people will be rewarded for the good deeds they have done' (好人有好報). Stepmothers, who feel they are wrongly labelled as 'bad-hearted', would hope to show that they are good mothers. This wish to be regarded as nice and good is similar to what Visher & Visher (1988) said about the myth of stepparenting: hard work prevents the development of a 'wicked stepmother' (see Chapter 2, p.21). In Chinese culture, a virtuous man is respected because of his ability to be 'Jen' (仁) meaning 'kind' and 'loving', and 'Shu' (恕) meaning 'forgiving'. In stepparent-stepchild relationships, it is not always the stepmother who does not treat her stepchild well. There are also cases where stepchildren misbehave, are defiant, and provoke conflicts. Therefore, some stepmothers have indeed worked hard on building relationships with their stepchildren, but their efforts are in vain. The example below illustrates the fact that practising 'good virtue' may not be rewarded in stepfamilies.

Mrs. Lam's Case: If I treat my stepsons well, I will eventually be rewarded
Mrs. Lam had not been married before she married her divorcee-husband. She held traditional Chinese values and believed in the cause and effect of 'doing good will be rewarded'. Mrs. Lam had to parent two teenage stepsons. According to her, they were defiant teenagers and they gave her a hard time. Mrs. Lam could not bear children and she took these stepsons as her own. She believed that 'if one does good things in life, when one dies, he/she will die peacefully while sleeping. I want it that way. I want to do good things. That's true [believe me]; [that's] cause and effect in the life cycle.' (M010(2),6) She hoped that her two stepsons would stop misbehaving and would recognize her efforts to help them. She told me her wishes:

> When the child grows up and marries one day, on the day of his wedding, [if] he won't pour a cup of tea for his parent [to show his respect and gratitude for what has been done by his parent], how would his parent feel then? If one treats his/her child well, the child would pour a cup of tea for the parent, and the parent would feel that he/she has treated his/her child well all of these years. After he has been married, and he has his own kids, then he will come to realize that his parents have a difficult role. He would know his parents have been good to him. As a parent, one should not be afraid of frustration and hurt. One should act according to one's conscience. One should endure being hurt. (M010(1),29)

Unfortunately, to date, Mrs. Lam's hard work has not been rewarded and, from what she reported, she was manipulated by her stepsons. Her parenting practice, based upon good-will traditional beliefs, had been challenged by their unruly behaviour and parent-child relationship problems had developed.

Women Should be Well-equipped to Play a Mothering Role

Women are usually cast in the roles of childcarer and housekeeper. This is universal but in Chinese families, women are strongly expected to play these roles. The expectation that mothers should be caring in child care and functional in housekeeping is developed in the minds of children. It should also be noted that for the Chinese, love and concern are shown in a different form than in Western culture. A mother in Western society may kiss and hug a child to show love and share feelings with him/her to show her concern, whereas mothers in Chinese families will boil a pot of delicious soup or cook the dishes her child likes to show love and concern. This is totally acceptable to both generations. It should be noted that although pampering children with good food is also practised by mothers in many Western countries to show love and care, in the Chinese culture this practise is commonly used and is more favoured than physical intimacy as a means to show affection and care. The following is an illustration of a stepchild's expectations of his mother. The stepmother failed to meet his basic needs, thus developing parent-child relationship problems.

Mrs. Chan's case: A stepmother who does not know how to cook   Mrs. Chan was an independent career woman before she married her younger sister's husband after her sister had died of cancer. She had had a very good relationship with her sister's two children when she was their aunt. After the children's mother died, Mrs. Chan fulfilled the wish of her deceased sister and her husband by marrying her brother-in-law. The elder daughter seemed to want to distance herself from this new union and she left to study in Canada. The young son, who was 12 years old, had difficulty in accepting his new mother, who did not know how to cook or do housekeeping.

Mrs. Chan had never had to cook before her marriage. When she had time, she ate at her mother's home. Otherwise, she ate out or ate simply. She did not know how to wash dishes or wash clothes in a washing machine. Previously she had taken her washing to the launderette. It became a time of challenge when Mrs. Chan felt that she failed in all the duties expected of a mother. She said that her stepson complained to his maternal grandmother:

> She is old enough, and she is someone's wife now, so why doesn't she know how to cook? She must be able to cook something. (M08(1),38)

In this case, the pressure to act as a good mother and housewife did not come from the husband, but from the 12 year old stepson. Mrs. Chan recalled how her own mother tried to comfort her: 'Your husband has no complaint; and you are not dealing with him for the rest of your life; he is just a kid' (M08(1),21). However, Mrs. Chan was very frustrated and felt pressurized. She said:

> Although it [cooking] is simple, very simple, it is very difficult for me. My son [her stepson] is not appreciative...he would look at me cooking and say, 'why do you do this, or do that?'... If you asked me to work on a computer, play a piano, or write shorthand, I could do it, but if you asked me to cook, I would make a mess.... (M08(1),20)

Mrs. Chan was facing the problem of not meeting her stepson's expectation of her as being a functional mother. The traditional values that 'a mother should be a carer and a capable housekeeper' were challenged, and the demands of her stepson that he be fed with home-cooking provoked disputes between the stepmother and stepchild.

Outsiders Looking in through Their Own Glasses:[2] What They See and the Stepfamilies' Need for Help

'Insiders' are the members of a stepfamily and they experience the everyday joy and pain in that family. Outsiders may see a different view which is coloured by values transmitted from their family of origin, their education, training, and the significant people in their social environments. Therefore, they are not 'seeing' with their eyes, but they are viewing as if through the lenses described. In the following I shall firstly present the profile of the teachers and the social workers interviewed in this study; secondly, I shall describe their perceptions of stepparenting and stepfamilies. Thirdly, I shall report on what they claimed about the formation of their perceptions, and, lastly, I shall present their views on the kinds of difficulties faced by stepfamilies and the help needed.

A Profile of the Teachers and Social Workers Interviewed in This Study

Background information and the personal particulars of the teachers and social workers are appended (see Appendices 7A and 7B). The following is a summary of the information.

The teachers   Four male and four female teachers were interviewed. Three of these eight teachers taught at secondary schools, three taught at primary school, and two at special schools for children who have family or behavioural problems. These teachers were informally contacted on the campus of the University of Nottingham. They came from different schools in Hong Kong and were attending B.Ed. or M.Ed. programmes at the time of interview. Their backgrounds were varied and I knew none of them before I asked to interview them.

Most of these teachers had worked for a number of years, ranging from four to thirteen years. The average teaching experience was 8.2 years. Their ages ranged from late 20s to early 40s. Most of them were in their early or mid 30s. Four of the teachers were single and the others were married. One of the married teachers had two children, whilst another had three children. Six teachers out of the eight had Bachelor degrees in education; the remaining two had obtained diplomas from a College of Education.   Three of these eight teachers were Catholic, two were Protestant, and three did not have any religious affiliation. Five out of the eight teachers came from intact families.   The other three were from broken families: one due to parental divorce and two due to death of one parent. Two of these three teachers were children from a stepfamily.

The profiles of these teachers show that they were mature adults and experienced teachers. They had post-secondary education and most of them had a religious faith. Almost half of these teachers had life experience of parental divorce, death, or remarriage.

The social workers   Four male and four female social workers were interviewed. Six of them were social workers working in family service centres, and they were responsible for family casework and school social work. The other two worked in a child protection agency and their major duties were counselling parents and children.

I knew five of the social workers through my contacts in the social work field or from teaching. The remaining three were introduced to me by the persons in charge of the social work agency.

In Hong Kong, those who have worked in the field for three years or more are recognized as experienced social workers. Half of the social workers I interviewed had worked as social workers for between two and a half years and five years; the remaining four had worked between six and ten years and this included two social workers who had ten years work experience.

The ages of the social workers ranged from late 20s to late 30s. Six of them were in their late 20s. Five of the eight social workers were single; the other three were married and one of them had a child. Three of the social workers had obtained a Bachelor of Social Work degree, and five had completed studies on the Master of Social Work programme or post-graduate studies. Six of the social workers had religious beliefs: two were Catholic, and four were Protestant. Five out of the eight social workers came from intact families. The other three social workers were from broken families: two due to parental divorce and one due to the death of a parent. One of these three social workers had experience of living in a stepfamily.

Thus, almost all of the social workers interviewed were mature and experienced; they were professionally trained and had worked with families and children. Close to half of them were married and three quarters of them had religious beliefs. Three of these eight social workers had experienced parental divorce, separation due to the death of a parent, or the remarriage of their parents.

The Attitudes and Expectations of Marriage, Remarriage and Family Life: The Views of Teachers and Social Workers

I interviewed a total of sixteen teachers and social workers, who were the professionals who had the most contact with stepfamilies. Their views on family, marriage, and remarriage will be presented and discussed.

A Phantom from the Past May Make the Decision to Remarry Difficult

As regards marriage, the informants noted the 'scars' carried from the past. One teacher said:

> If last marriage failed, there must be a 'shadow' [a negative impact], especially for women, who would have more to fear than men. (T03,4)

A social worker also felt that it was difficult not to refer to the past experience. He said:

If the [former] spouse did something wrong and left, that is, because that spouse did not treat his/her spouse well, [then remarriage is acceptable]. If the spouse had treated him/her very well before death, then it is not easy for the widow/widower to decide whether to remarry again. (S04,4)

The Decision to Remarry should be Made Carefully as There is Danger of Repeating the Unhappy Experiences

Their general view about remarriage was that it is 'OK', but all of the social workers said one has to consider remarriage carefully when one has child(ren) from a previous marriage; most of the teachers also agreed on this point. Generally speaking, attitudes of these social workers and teachers were more accepting of remarriage following the death of one's spouse as compared to divorce, although some of the professionals had extreme views, i.e. 'remarriage should only be considered after one's spouse has been dead for a considerable length of time, say, almost five years' (T03; T07; S04); or 'remarriage should only be considered for a "victim of divorce" whose spouse had committed adultery' (T08).

These views have made some of them rather sceptical about the prospect of remarriage. They urged more careful and rational decision-making when considering remarriage. For example:

I think he/she should know the reason why his/her last marriage failed. He/she should evaluate his/her situation, and if they have found someone suitable, I think maybe he/she should start a new life and choose to marry again. But one should not jump into another marriage right after divorce, and expect that marriage will heal the pain or resolve problems. (S05,3)

Some teachers held the same views as stated by the social worker above. The following are two examples:

From my observations, some people treat this as a game of repetition. He/she marries, finds that their spouse is incompatible, separates, and finds another one…it is just a process, and this process goes round in a circle. I don't think this is healthy. (T06,3)

126

Another teacher added that past experiences would affect one's future marriages. She said:

> Broken marriage is painful. When he/she has fully recuperated, he/she learns from the experience, and he/she can overcome the difficulties so that the second marriage can be better. If he/she can't learn from the past experience and he/she has not recovered from the trauma, he/she may just want to find someone so he/she can forget the former partner, and that's dangerous. It may lead to failure in the second marriage. (T05,3)

The hope of a harmonious family and bringing reality to a romanticized fantasy of family relationships and family life As regards family, I got the impression that in general they hoped that families would remain intact and be harmonious. They felt that parents should put their children's needs before their own. Teachers felt this more strongly because they had daily contact with their students and the children were the main focus of their attention. It was also generally felt that it was natural for biological parents to love their own children more than their stepchildren.

As far as marriage and family life are concerned, they felt that the expectations before and after marriage would not be the same because there was a difference between 'fantasy' and 'reality'. Teachers had a vague idea on this subject but it was the social workers who had more elaborate views. For example, some social workers said that when people got married, 'there was no private time for the couple' (S01); and the 'children and relatives were sources of pressure' (S04); and they also thought the expectations of wives and husbands were different, for example, 'women wanted emotional support from their husbands but men didn't know how to express their feelings' (S02); and 'men used excuses to avoid playing with the children and to avoid taking up the parenting role' (S02); etc.

The Associations Made and the Views about Stepparenting and Stepfamilies

The teachers and social workers were asked to make free associations when they thought of 'step', 'stepfamily', 'stepmother', 'stepfather' and 'stepchild' (Appendix 5B). They were also asked about their views on stepparenting and stepfamilies during the interviews. Their responses are summarized below.

'Step': a word which carries negative connotations   The stereotyping of the word 'step' in Western culture has been discussed in Chapter 2. From a review of the information received from the teachers and social workers when they were shown the word 'step' written on a card, I have found that the teachers tended to perceive 'step' more negatively. They thought of 'stepmother', 'ill-treatment', 'hau dey la' (後底乸), 'not good', and 'old Chinese movies' when they were shown the word 'step'. Although some social workers thought of 'step' neutrally as being equivalent to the word 'behind' (後), many social workers and teachers said when they saw the word 'step', they associated it with 'continue' (繼), 'not original', 'something added/supplemented', 'second' and 'second trial'.

'Stepfamilies': they are growing in number and are unhappy and problematic   When the informants were shown the word 'stepfamily' and asked to 'free associate', some said that they thought that stepfamilies 'are unhappy', 'have problems', 'have conflicts', and 'can't be accepted by society'. Specifically, they associated stepfamilies with having the following problems: 'there is a barrier between the mother-in-law and the daughter-in-law'; 'the husband sides with his mother'; 'the maternal grandmother may say bad things about the stepmother to her grandchild'; 'the older generation think stepmother is no good', 'in-law relationships in stepfamilies are difficult'; etc.

Although stepfamilies have grown in number, these respondents felt that social attitudes towards stepfamilies are still ambivalent about accepting them. As one teacher pointed out:

> People do not totally accept these families. They just keep quiet, Hong Kong people are like that. They don't talk about it. They quietly say, 'the people living next door are a remarried family' [as if it is something shameful], but when they see them, they pretend that nothing [bad] happened. I still think that they are not totally accepted in society. I think society takes time to change. (T08,13)

This was echoed by a social worker. She said:

128

I think the traditional thinking about stepfamilies is inclined to be negative: remarriage is not good. It [a second marriage] is not as good as the first marriage. (S08,7)

Another social worker reported that some stepfamilies are aware of the social attitudes and they tended to distance themselves from others. She noticed that:

There are some cases I know about from church...where the stepfamilies distance themselves for some time...may be it is because people in the church are not very keen to eager to communicate with them. I guess they [the stepfamily members] are somewhat distant from other people. (S05,10)

'Wicked stepmother'? -- they are fierce and not good　　From carefully listening to the remarks of the informants on the audio-tapes, the teachers and social workers described stepmothers quite negatively as 'fierce', 'bad', 'female beast who comes after', 'somebody who does not treat kids well', 'an intruder', 'morally bad', 'someone who has problems with their stepchildren and relatives', etc. The teachers had contacts with their students in class on an almost daily basis and they expressed greater concern for the well-being of the children; they said stepmothers should accept the child care role as being their paramount responsibility and should love their stepchildren as they would love their own children. On the other hand, social workers did not see their child clients as often as did the teachers, so they had wider concerns focusing not only upon the children but also upon the parents. For example, they noted the difficulties confronting stepmothers in daily life and did not just talk about their subjective impressions.

The opinions of these professionals were greatly affected by their traditional values and moral stance. For example, one teacher said:

Traditionally we think that those women should not enter a family's door. Stepmothers are unfortunate. They are looked down upon, they feel inferior and see themselves as of no value. (T06,7)

129

In addition to their views of stepmothers as being of low status and having low self-image, they regarded them as morally bad. For example, one social worker said:

> Traditionally women are not expected to marry again. The social stigma is still there -- they are promiscuous, they are 'shui sing yeung fa' [flowers by the water follow the flow of the water] and they can't live without men. (S07,9)

Another social worker felt the same. She said:

> Stepmothers feel more pressure from the public...in Chinese society... Although it is said that the society is advanced in technology and science, people have the impression that those who are remarried have bad character. For example, they are seen as 'ng chung yat yee chung' [which means it is expected that one will stay in one marital relationship until one passes away], and sometimes they do not know how to face their own relatives and friends. (S06,8)

Very few of the teachers and social workers saw the positive side of stepmothers. Only one teacher said that a stepmother impressed her as being a beautiful person (T08). One social worker said that stepmothers used a rational approach to child management, so that they worked hard on tasks but were weak in building emotional bonds with children. She sympathized with them because she saw some stepmothers who were treated not as wives but as housekeepers only (S02).

'Abusive Stepfather?' -- the myth of the stepfather-stepdaughter problem
Many of the teachers and social workers I interviewed had negative impressions of stepfathers. They were regarded as abusive people who would take advantage of their stepdaughters sexually. Only one teacher said that some stepfathers love their stepchildren more than biological fathers do (T01), while none of the social workers thought of stepfathers positively although they expected stepfathers to play various roles to promote or maintain the functioning of their family. The following are some examples showing their negative impressions of stepfathers.

One teacher talked about her concerns that stepdaughters are abused or sexually assaulted by their stepfathers:

There is stereotyping that stepmothers must be wicked people, but very few say the same about stepfathers. There are comments made about them, but those are different [from what is said about stepmothers] ...for example, stepfathers are criticized for acts of abuse and sexual assault, and the like...so if there is a girl and a stepfather in a family, one has to be cautious. (T05,7)

A male teacher felt the same. He said:

I have quite a bad impression of stepfathers. When I compare my impressions of stepmothers with those of stepfathers, the latter are more negative -- they do not treat the children of the biological mothers well, they spank them, scold them, or even sexually assault them. When they are mentioned in newspapers, I usually read 'bad' things about them. (T03,1)

A female social worker told me that her impression of stepfathers was formed by knowing what they had done to their stepchildren:

I don't think stepfathers are as fierce as stepmothers. In the past few years, however, there have been more stepfathers who have sexually abused their kids, which gives people a bad impression. (S01,1)

A male social worker also regarded stepfathers negatively and thought they might take advantage of their stepdaughters sexually. He said:

Stepfathers...if you ask for my spontaneous feeling; then my feeling about them is not very good. If the family has daughters...one wonders whether the stepfather would have immoral intentions towards them. (S04,2)

Another male social worker said the word 'stepfather' made him think of sexual child abuse:

...stepfathers sexually assault their stepdaughters, and have sexual relationships with them. A stepfather's role is difficult to play because people have these negative associations. (S07,1)

The above remarks show that irrespective of whether the informant was a teacher or a social worker, or male or female, they associate stepfathers with the sexual abuse or sexual assault of their stepdaughters. The impressions were quite strongly formed but the informants did not give evidence to support their claims.

'Neglected Stepchildren?' -- they are unhappy and have adjustment problems Both the teachers and the social workers noted difficulties in stepparent-stepchild relationships. Teachers had daily contact with students and they were concerned with their feelings and problems. On the other hand, social workers worked with members of the families and they were concerned with parent-child problems and the individual problems of family members.

There were concerns and problems noted both by the teachers and social workers. Both groups thought that girls found it more difficult than boys to accept a parent's remarriage and their stepmothers; they felt that boys appeared not to take things as seriously when confronted with this situation. The following quotations are some of the examples. One teacher said:

> I think girls would find it more difficult to accept themselves as stepdaughters. If her parent, no matter whether the parent is the father or mother, 'takes' her when her parent remarries [meaning the daughter follows her remarried biological parent to become a member of the stepfamily], I think the daughter, being a female, would find it more difficult to accept this. That is what I think; but in reality that may not be so. (T02,9)

Another teacher said that she felt that girls have more problems for the following reasons:

> Girls' personalities are basically more prone to emotion, especially when the girls have entered secondary school. They are easily troubled and confused by their family and their own problems. I think they need to be cared for more than boys. (T05,9)

One social worker also felt that girls were more sensitive in their feelings and they had difficulties accepting their parents' remarriage. She said:

Girls may be more sensitive towards what their parents do and what has happened in their families. Girls do not forgive easily, they are more sensitive, and they are not able to accept something new. (S01,8)

In the views of these professionals, boys appeared not to take problems seriously and they pretended that they were not affected by what had happened. One teacher said:

Boys have problems but they do not take them too seriously. Boys won't listen to others or share their feelings with people. They pretend that they are not affected by what has happened in their families. (T05,9)

A social worker said that she felt the same. She said:

As regards their feelings about what their parents do and what has happened in their families, boys may not take things seriously. They think: 'The wrong will eventually become right one day by itself.' (S01,8)

A male social worker also thought that boys covered up their feelings and did not like to talk about their problems. He said:

Boys hide things in their hearts, and they won't express themselves. It is more difficult to make boys talk about their feelings...we social workers have to probe and dig, in order to help them reveal their problems. If we ask them about their feelings, they just say 'happy' or 'unhappy', and that's all. They won't say 'I feel ambivalent', 'I feel the sky is falling down', 'I feel unfairly treated'. (S07,10)

Both the teachers and social workers felt that stepchildren had difficulties in adjusting to their stepfamilies, but they thought that younger children accepted stepparents better; older children had more problems in adjusting but they would find friends to whom they could vent their feelings. No matter whether the stepchild is a boy or a girl, younger or older, he/she is victim of a broken family and has to make great adjustments when living in a reconstituted family. A teacher summarized his observations and explained why stepchildren were unhappy and had adjustment problems.

He said:

> The stepchild is the greatest victim. He/she needs to be given more time and patience by his family members. He/she has more difficulty adjusting to a new parent than the new parent has adjusting to him/her. The stepchild is miserable. He/she has no choice. His/her mother remarries so he/she is brought into the stepfamily with her. He/she has no status in the stepfamily, and his/her self-image and self-esteem are low. (T08,6-7)

The Difficulties of Stepparenting and Stepfamilies and the Formation of Perceptions

As pointed out by Fiske & Taylor (1984), people need to cognitively organize their view of the world. While categorizing the input of the information we obtain and by scanning our observations, we are involved in the processes of selection, passing judgment and discrimination. Attitudes are a demonstration of how people perceive things and people. In the following reports, the difficulties in stepparenting and stepfamilies which were perceived by the teachers and social workers will be presented. The formation of their perceptions will also be reported. These will help us understand why certain attitudes are held by those professionals and how these have affected their views of the difficulties in stepfamilies and the kinds of help they need.

Problems affected by loss and change: stepchildren need help to deal with their feelings of loss and they are ambivalent about their identity The teachers and social workers felt that difficulties in stepparenting and stepfamilies were affected by whether stepfamily members had come to terms with feelings arising from their past experiences and whether the biological parents had helped their children in the adjustment to their new families.

A teacher felt that children were not properly told about their parents' divorce and that affected their adjustment into the stepfamily. She said:

> If they are young when they enter a stepfamily, it is difficult for them to accept the reality and to tell their friends -- how do they tell them that 'this is not my mother but she lives with me. That is not my father

but he lives with me!'? How can the child face his/her friends? I think his/her self-esteem will be influenced. The child would think that his/her parents divorced because of him/her. He/she would think that he/she is wrong and he/she caused that. (T01,7)

A male teacher told me that he knew a student who had emotional and behavioural problems because his mother had divorced and remarried and he had had to change his surname more than once:

The surname of the boy's father is Chan, and his mother's is Wong. After his father deserted the family, his mother changed the boy's surname to Wong. Later, his mother lived with a man and not long after that, they married. That man's surname is Lee. The boy's mother changed his surname to Lee. This lady did not have long-lasting relationship with her second husband and he left her. The mother then changed the boy's surname back to Wong again. The boy's surname has been changed so many times that the child is pitiful. (T03,4)

A male social worker also felt that stepchildren who were brought into a stepfamily because of their parents' remarriage were miserable. He said:

They hold the hands of their father or mother and go into a totally strange family; they will have identity problems and be confused. They had a surname from their last family, but, in order not to be seen as 'different' from the other children in the stepfamily, they have to change their surname to that of the new family. (S07,1)

In the opinions of these teachers and social workers, some children had no say in their parents' divorces and they had no choice but to follow their parents to live in a stepfamily; they had difficulties in coming to terms with their feelings. They were ambivalent about their identity and they might act out their feelings by inappropriate behaviour.

Barriers in building stepparent-stepchild relationship: biological parents are glorified and there are problems of split loyalty It is not easy for stepchildren to forget their biological parents who are living away from them. Very often they only remember the good things about their parents. For example, a social worker described his observations:

135

Stepchildren have beautified their own parents, thinking that the absentee parent was very good in the past. In fact the parent in the past may not have treated them well. He/she might have left them when they were very little and may not have shown up again since then...If the stepchild twists the image of the biological parent and thinks that he/she is the best, then the replacement parent cannot be as good. (S04,8)

A male social worker observed attention-seeking behaviour by some stepchildren. He said:

I can see that there are struggles in their hearts. The stepchildren want their biological parents to be happy after their remarriage, but at other times they hope that his/her new marital relationship will not work out. They develop behavioural problems. (S08,7)

If the non-resident biological parents still have contact with their children, it is likely that they will influence their children's views and their relationships with the stepparents. A teacher said she knew two students who were aged 10 and 13:

They can't accept their new mother. They are influenced by their own mother, and she makes them think that the new mother is an outsider. (T02,2)

In such a situation, the biological parent who was with the child should become the 'bridge' between the stepparent and his/her child in order to help them to build their relationship. One teacher said:

The biological parent has to be the middleman to mediate between his/her spouse and his/her kid. That is his/her responsibility. He/she needs energy and time, and to understand his/her child to be a bridge. (T08,6)

A social worker also felt that the biological parents have an important role to play in dealing with the ambivalence of their own children in their relation with their stepparents. He said:

I think biological parents should be sensitive. They should not think: it is OK, things will work out by themselves. They have to be sensitive and to be able to detect whether problems have occurred at home...whether there are conflicts between the stepparent and the stepchild. They have to be supportive to the stepparent. (S04,7)

The problem of inadequate supervision: fathers and stepfathers are not sufficiently involved in child management in stepfamilies The teachers and social workers were concerned that the fathers and stepfathers were often absent from home and, as a result, most children in stepfamilies were managed by the mothers or stepmothers without the support of their husbands. A social worker noted that:

Traditionally men in Chinese society are not actively involved in the day-to-day activities of their families, unlike women who have roles [childcarer and housekeeper] to play. (S05,1)

Another social worker said that the stepchildren he knew mentioned their fathers very little. They would say:

'Nothing particular, he goes out to work everyday.' When probed, they may not be able to say any more. It was discovered later that the father was a stepfather.' (S07,9)

Another teacher could only discuss her student's problem with the stepmother because 'the father is always absent from home, and is away from Hong Kong' (T01,9).

A social worker said she had worked with families in which the children did not accept their fathers:

The father goes to work in the morning until late at night; the man is only at home then. The kid would think: 'He is related to my mother, not to me. They can live together like that without me.' (S05,6)

In families where the fathers are always absent, the responsibility for child management will fall onto the shoulders of the mothers or the stepmothers. One social worker observed the difficulties confronting these women and felt that many of their husbands married them because they wanted them to be childcarers and housekeepers. She said:

> I think women want emotional support. I think males don't know how to express their feelings...they don't embrace their kids or play with them. Men usually use the excuse of work to avoid these. They say that they are tired after work...if the stepmothers tell them about problems of their children, they tend to avoid them: 'Don't tell me, I'm very tired. As long as you fix that for me, that's OK.' (S02,7)

It is very likely that children in these families will have relationship conflicts with their stepmothers because their fathers fail to give their wives support in child management.

Relationship problems between stepmothers and their paternal in-laws: non-acceptance and competition   The teachers and social workers felt that stepmothers were not accepted by the older generation and thus family relationship problems arise, especially when they live with their paternal in-laws. One teacher said:

> Old people usually don't accept stepmothers. They have one weapon that protects them: people sympathize more with them. If they are unreasonable, they win the sympathy of their neighbours or their sons by looking miserable...old people usually don't accept the new stepmother. (T04,3)

One social worker also felt that because the stepmothers were not accepted by their in-laws problems arose in stepfamilies. He said:

> Whether the stepmother is good or not, the old people still criticize her...being a mother is difficult...I don't know whether she can share her feelings with her husband, but I can see that she can't do so with her mother-in-law, or her daughter. If she doesn't have any other good friends with whom she can share her feelings, she will be in a very difficult situation and will not be able to adjust well. (S07,3)

Another social worker pointed out that if the grandparents do not accept the stepmother, the stepparent-stepchild relationship is difficult to build.

She said:

> The grandparents may put pressure on the biological parent and make him/her think that the stepparent will not treat his/her child well. So he/she may suggest that each parent takes care of his/her own child...The stepchild is brain-washed by his/her grandparents, and the relationship between the stepparent and stepchild is affected. (S02,7)

The formation of the perceptions of the teachers and social workers: personal and work experiences, traditional values and the influence of movies and mass media   Out of the sixteen professionals I interviewed, three came from divorced families (T02, S03, S07) and a further three were children from stepfamilies (T05, T08, S04). Their life experiences have inevitably coloured their perceptions and views on stepparenting and stepfamilies although there are other reasons which have also influenced them. One social worker said:

> I think I am influenced by traditional concepts, background and culture...I would look at the expectations I have for any family, and then I would expect the same in a stepfamily. (S03,5)

Mass media also has a powerful influence upon the perceptions of these teachers and social workers. One social worker revealed:

> I am very much influenced by soap opera on television. Stepmother is generally not a good person. She doesn't treat kids with kindness. (S08,5)

When asked how her perceptions about stepparents and stepparenting were formed, one teacher said:

> From watching old Chinese movies; they impressed me deeply. (T05,6)

Some of the teachers and social workers had come from broken families and stepfamilies and their personal experiences had influenced their perceptions. One male social worker told me:

139

Why do I associate a stepfamily with having a lot of problems? It is very easy for me to think this way; what can I say? Maybe I can tell you...it is because my own family is one [a stepfamily]. It is easy for me to think that this kind of family has many problems, and that family members face many difficulties. (S04,1)

One teacher was greatly affected by his own family, which was a stepfamily. He had difficulties in establishing a trusting relationship with a prospective spouse. He revealed:

I have been affected by my personal family experience...I am afraid to get married even though I have been seeing a girl for some time. I dare not marry, I think it is hard to relate to another person for life. I have no confidence in marriage. The next generation will be greatly affected. (T08,14)

This shows that people, and educated ones are no exception, are negatively affected by their life experiences, which have influenced their perceptions and behaviours.

The Help Offered to and Needed by Stepfamilies: The Views of Teachers and Social Workers

From the stepmothers' views on the attitudes of people around them (p.113-115), we can see that stepmothers felt that the principal or teachers of a school were prejudiced against them because they were stepmothers. Quite a number of these stepmothers wanted to be involved but were discouraged by some principals and/or teachers who thought that the fathers should be the parent responsible for the child. They were frustrated and hurt. According to the reports of the professionals, however, the picture is rather different. My general impression from reading the interview transcripts is that the teachers and the social workers with whom I talked were rather sensitive and most of them were aware of the difficulties faced by the stepfamily members. For example, teachers admitted that their major duty was to teach, and they could only be listeners (T01, T02) to parents with problems, but if need arose, they referred the cases to social workers. Almost all of the teachers were aware that if stepparents were addressed carefully, this could help to lessen the

140

labelling effect. In the case of changing the womens' surname after their remarriage, when teachers talked to these parents, they would either ask how they would like to be greeted or address them simply as 'the mother of so-and-so'. The social workers I interviewed also followed this method to deal with the uneasiness felt both by the professional and the parent.

The teachers were child-focused and they were quite sensitive to the feelings of the stepchildren they had identified. Although they were busy teaching, they tried to offer help to these students. Many teachers would act as a listener when they had time. For example, one teacher said:

> I listened to her, and provided a venue for her to ventilate her feelings. (T02,12)

Another teacher said he paid extra attention to his students who came from stepfamilies and showed concern for them:

> I would give them more time, until I saw that they were better [in their behaviour and academic work]... I would pay extra attention to them if I had the chance...if I saw the student during recess, I would go up to him/her and talk to him/her. (T03,10)

Some teachers felt that they were not trained to handle relationship problems in stepfamilies and there was not much that they could do for the parents. However, a few of the teachers thought that they could help the stepchildren to improve by pointing out the child's strengths to his/her parents and stepparents. For example, one teacher said:

> It is easy to say bad things about the kid when talking to his/her parents over the telephone, but we hope to stress his/her strengths. It will help the kid to feel that the teacher does not especially pick on him. (T04,9)

Some teachers also felt that the efforts of stepparents needed to be recognized in order to improve the stepparent-stepchild relationship. One teacher said:

> I have a student who is a stepson and things happened in the past who have contributed to his poor academic performance...his stepfather

cared about him greatly, and he always came for the teacher-parent interviews even though he was very busy at work. He said he wanted to obtain information from the school so he could think of ways to help him improve. I said to him, 'Your [step]son accepts you well, I am not close to him but he still told me that he loves you and accepts you more than he accepts his own daddy.' I told him that to him [stepfather], he was happy. I encouraged him not to give up. (T07,11)

The social workers said that they also cared greatly about the stepchildren when they came to their attention. However, some of the social workers told themselves not to be overly helpful and not to treat the stepchild with greater affection than children from other kinds of family. The reason for this was that they did not want to create dependent relationships. One social worker explained:

I don't want to create dependency. If the child comes from a stepfamily and I pay more attention to him/her, I am encouraging dependency. (S06,9)

Another social worker said there is a difference when treating a child who is a stepchild. He said:

I feel that I want to protect him/her more. That's my feeling. But when I relate to him/her, I will not show this by different attitude and actions. (S08,7)

Many social workers felt that they needed to work with the parents of the stepchild first, otherwise the stepchild's problems could not be solved. However, they noted that fathers and stepfathers in stepfamilies did not want to have contact with professional helpers, even though they had problems. They felt that stepmothers were lacking enough support. For example, one social worker said:

No matter whether the parent is a biological parent or a stepparent, they have equal responsibility in handling the kid's problem...I want to see both of them. (S06,7)

From what the social workers told me, I was impressed by the fact that they knew that they needed to be sensitive when identifying the needs and problems of stepchildren, but they were not very confident about working with them which was due to either a lack of knowledge or a lack of skills. As most of them worked in family service centres, they adhered to the general principle that 'working with the family as a whole is paramount'. In reality, however, it was not easy to see the men in the families because they did not feel they needed to go or they were not cooperative, so ultimately the social workers could only engage the mothers or the stepmothers. The information gathered was mainly from one parent and the accuracy of the case assessment might have been affected.

There were several kinds of help suggested by the teachers and social workers.

For teachers and schools   Teachers should be encouraged to be sensitive to stepchildren and to deal with their feelings by showing an understanding of their needs and difficulties (T06, S07). Female teachers may be the prime targets for attention (T06).

Teachers have a role to play in strengthening parent-child relationships in stepfamilies. Teachers should meet with the parents who are the key persons related to the children's difficulties. The efforts of stepparents in helping their stepchildren should be recognized (T07). Parents should be educated about the needs of their children (T04, T06), and the strengths of their stepchildren should be pointed out to the stepparents (T04).

When relating to the parents and children from stepfamilies in an interview or in the classroom, teachers should be sensitive as to how to address these stepfamily members after the stepfamily is formed. The careful handling of the issue of name changes would help the stepparents and stepchildren to adjust because they would feel they are respected and would be spared embarrassment (T02, T07, T08).

The school principals who set the school policies can help too. As suggested by these teachers, there should be a change to narrow the gap between education policy and practice. It was also suggested that a student's problems should not be regarded and treated in a piece-meal fashion (T08). The administrators of schools should encourage teachers to not only impart knowledge, but to teach the 'whole person' (T04). The school should think of ways to provide channels through which the students from these families could be made to feel of value rather than merely being encouraged to achieve (T05).

For social workers and social work agencies   Almost all of the social worker respondents felt that it is very important to hold group sessions for parents in stepfamilies. The purpose is to create opportunities for the mutual sharing of feelings amongst parents and to generate mutual support.

They also recommended different types of counselling services for parents and children in stepfamilies: pre-marital counselling to help prepare parents before stepfamilies are formed (S05, S08); marital counselling to help develop skills in parenting and stepparenting, and to encourage the husband's involvement in child care and household tasks (S02, S08); family counselling to deal with parent-child issues, and to help members to appreciate each other, and understand each other's needs (S04); and individual counselling for children to help them to adjust in a stepfamily (S02) and to form a realistic picture of their biological parents (S04). One teacher felt that social workers should conduct more home visits to stepfamilies in order to help them (T08).

Social workers were aware of the growing numbers of stepfamilies (S05, S06, S08), but some noted that due to manpower constraints, social work agencies have not placed stepfamilies at the top of their list of service priorities (S06, S07, S08). They saw that there is a need to obtain more statistics and to conduct further studies in order to understand stepfamilies (S05). It is also important to develop skills for working with stepfamilies through training (S03, S04, S07), and to start planning services for stepfamilies (S06, S07, S08).

For the government   The teachers suggested that the Government can help by reducing teaching sessions so that teachers can spare the time to talk privately to students with problems (T01). It should provide funding to set up a special team to help stepfamilies, for example, a counselling team whose members were all formerly full-time teachers in the school; they should be released from teaching to help students with their problems full time (T07).

The Government should provide educational programmes for stepparents to teach them how to take up their roles (T06, S03, S05, S07, S08). Their social images could be enhanced by promotional programmes in the community (T01, S03, S05, S07, S08). One social worker thought that

144

stepfamilies should not be seen as special, but as just another type of family (S06). Two social workers hoped to see changes in the attitudes of the older generation (S02, S08). Stepfamily members should be encouraged to voice their feelings in radio phone-in programmes, so that more people will understand their needs and difficulties (T05). Three social workers suggested that the mass media must make an effort to change the image of stepfamilies from negative to positive in order to compensate for the negative images that have been presented in news headlines (S04, S05, S06). In addition, community education should be provided to help people in society to better understand marriage and sex, so as to decrease the number of broken families and stepfamilies (T08).

From the above, remedial work was suggested to strengthen marital and family relationships in order to help stepmothers and stepchildren. The teachers focused their help upon dealing with the feelings of students coming from stepfamilies, and they hoped social workers would help by working with the parents and conducting more home visits. The social workers suggested many remedial strategies to help family members, but they did not have support from their agencies to provide services to stepfamilies. It seems that the two professions should join hands to help stepfamilies as there are areas of common concern and they can complement each other to fill service gaps.

Summary of the Chapter

At the beginning of this chapter, the aspirations for marriage and family life were explored. It was found that stepfamily members hoped for a happy marriage and harmonious life, but they were troubled by unresolved feelings from the past and unrealistic expectations of the present. Remarried women and their children, and women married to remarried men, were all found to be stigmatized. The older generation, paternal kin, and the mass media were perceived as having negative attitudes to stepparents and stepfamilies. Prejudiced social attitudes had reinforced negative parental perceptions, and this affected the performance of the parental role.

From the reports it was found that conflicts existed between the generations in stepfamilies. Stepmothers were reported to have most conflicts with their mothers-in-law, and their spouses were caught in the middle. There were also conflicts between stepmothers and stepchildren because the former found their 'instant love' was not rewarded, and the latter had difficulties in accepting a new mother who failed to meet their expectations.

The views of the teachers and social workers were examined and discussed. They were sensitive to the feelings of stepfamily members but it was difficult for the teachers to focus their concerns on the children, and for the social workers to focus on the family as a whole. Although most of these professionals had negative impressions of stepparents and stepfamilies, they were eager to help. Several teachers suggested some innovative ideas and some social workers suggested a wide range of services.

Notes

1   Some informants in this study have the same surname. For personal particulars of individual informants please refer to Chapter 6 Table 6.1 (pp. 148-149). The code and numerics at the end of each paragraph of quoted remarks are for reference to a particular informant. For example, M09 is Mrs. Lau, age 40, who is different from Mrs. Lau, age 36, who bears the reference code of M03. The bracketed numeric after the code for the person is the number of the interview, e.g. (3) means the researcher's third interview with the informant. The numeric(s) after the bracketed interview number is/are the page number(s) which the quoted remarks can be traced from the transcribed audio-taped interviews.

2   In Chinese 'Looking in through one's own glasses' means the views and perceptions developed from one's life experiences. The meaning of this saying is neutral, unlike the English expression 'looking through rose tinted spectacles' which carries the meaning of 'being seen more favourably than is true in reality'.

6 Parenting Behaviours in Stepfamilies in Hong Kong: Findings and Discussion

Introduction

In the previous chapter, I presented the social attitudes and parental perceptions of stepparenting and stepfamilies in Hong Kong from the point of view of the stepmothers, teachers and social workers I interviewed. In this chapter I will focus on the parenting behaviours and issues which arise predominantly from stepparenting. The content of this chapter is drawn from the reports given by the ten stepmothers. The sequence of presentation is as follows: firstly, a brief summary of the profiles of the respondents; secondly, the changes and difficulties in the life course experienced by these stepmothers before and after they joined these stepfamilies; and thirdly, the challenges faced by parents in stepfamilies. The discussion will be based upon five themes in parenting behaviours in stepfamilies (Chapter 2 pp.30-46 for concepts discussed).

Profile of the Stpemothers and Their Families

I interviewed ten stepmothers. Seven of these stepmothers were known to non-governmental family service agencies as clients who were currently receiving services or had once received services from them. Two were referred to me by a para-counsellor, and one was introduced to me by one of the informants I interviewed.

Eight of these stepmothers were married for the first time. Two had married once before. All of the husbands of the informants had been married once before. Seven of these husbands dissolved their marriages by divorce, whilst the marriages of three of them ended because of the death of their wives. Seven out of ten of the previous marriages had lasted four years or less. Three had been married for between ten and fourteen years. Most of the stepmothers had been married between five and ten years; two had only been married to their present husbands between three and four years.

Most of the stepmothers were in their mid 30s or mid 40s. The husbands of these stepmothers were also aged mid 30s to mid 40s. Half of these stepmothers had a job, while the others were housewives. All those who worked were professionals or white-collar workers, except one who was blue-collar worker. As regards the employment of their husbands, nine had jobs of with three were in managerial positions, two were owners of small factories, and the remaining four were service workers. One did not work because he would soon be migrating overseas.

Of the stepfamilies in my sample, only two families had monthly incomes between $50,000 and $70,000. Half of the families earned below $30,000 a month, which included two families which earned less than $15,000 a month. With reference to the statistics of the Hong Kong Census, the median household income reported in 1996 was HK$17,500 (Hong Kong Monthly Digest of Statistics, December, 1996). Therefore, most of the stepfamilies in this study had monthly family income in the lower middle range.

Nine of the ten stepfamilies lived in private flats, whilst one lived in a cubicle of a public housing estate. Two stepmothers had mothers-in-law and/or fathers-in-law currently living with their families; the other eight families were nuclear families. However, four stepmothers had at one time lived with their mothers-in-law and/or fathers-in-law.

Two of these families were 'combination stepfamilies' where both parents, who are either divorced or widowed and each with children, remarry and live together with their children from former relationships. The other eight families were 're-assembled stepfamilies' where the stepparents are first time marriers who are childless, and they marry a divorced parent with a child or children.

Eight families had one stepchild, while two had two stepchildren. Of the total number of children living in the stepfamily, six had two children; three had three and one had four. There was a total of eight stepsons and four stepdaughters. The age of the stepsons ranged from late latency to late teenage. The stepdaughters were slightly older, with most of them being teenagers. The personal particulars of these ten stepmothers are highlighted in Table 6.1.

Table 6.1
Personal Particulars of Ten Stepmothers

Code	M01	M02	M03	M04	M05
Name	Ho	Chui	Lau	Chan	Lam
Age	45	32	36	39	43
Position of Work	Accounts Clerk (part-time)	Housewife	Garment Worker (part-time)	Housewife	Teacher
Age of Husband	46	41	37	41	46
Husband's Position of Work	Salesman of Takeaway Chinese Food	Construction Worker	Small Garment Factory Owner	Taxi Driver	Factory Manager
Monthly Family Income	$17,000	$15,000	$13,000 + Husband's Income	$18,000	$20,000
Household Type	Nuclear	Nuclear	Nuclear	Extended	Nuclear
Sex and Age of Child	M/4	F/13 M/7 M/6	M/5	M/3½	M/2½
Sex and Age of Stepchild	F/15½	M/17	M/12	M/9	F/12
Length of Current Marriage	7	10	5	8	4
Reason for Husband's Dissolution of Last Marriage	Wife Died	Wife Divorced	Wife Divorced	Wife Died	Wife Divorced

149

Table 6.1   Personal Particulars of Ten Stepmothers (cont'd.)

Code	M06	M07	M08	M09	M10
Name	Lee	Chung	Chan	Lau	Lam
Age	39	32	46	40	35
Position of Work	Insurance Agent	Insurance Company Team Leader	Legal Secretary	Housewife	Housewife
Age of Husband	35	33	44	44	40
Husband's Position of Work	Insurance Agent	Insurance Company Manager	Retired	Manager	Small Construction Company Owner
Monthly Family Income	$50,000	$70,000	$30,000	$30,000	$30,000
Household Type	Nuclear	Nuclear	Nuclear	Nuclear	Extended
Sex and Age of Child	M/12 F/1 3/4	M/9 M/4	None	F/8 M/4	None
Sex and Age of Stepchild	M/9	F/13	F/19 M/15	M/16	M/14 M/13
Length of Current Marriage	3	13	4	9	5
Reason for Husband's Dissolution of Last Marriage	Wife Divorced	Wife Divorced	Wife Died	Wife Divorced	Wife Divorced

The life situations of these stepmothers can be further understood by a brief description of their families which are much influenced by their family structure and dynamics.

Family of M01   This stepfamily was composed of a stepmother aged 45 and her husband who was 46. The husband remarried after the death of his first wife. The stepdaughter was teenage and the couple had a pre-school age son.

This was a family with lower middle monthly income. The stepmother earned more income from her part-time job than her husband who worked full time. The stepmother claimed that she married her husband for love and wished to help him in child care. She was disappointed in her marital relationship feeling that her mother-in-law was manipulative and her husband sided with her stepdaughter. She had adopted a disciplinarian approach in parenting her stepdaughter and had relationship problems with her.

Family of M02   This stepfamily was large. It was composed of a stepmother aged 32, her husband aged 41, a teenage stepson, a teenage biological daughter of the stepmother from her previous marriage, and two pre-school aged sons from the current marriage. The family was formed after divorce of the husband. This family was financially disadvantaged because the husband worked as a construction worker and his income was unstable. The stepmother felt loaded with household and parenting tasks and she had difficulties in relating to her stepson. She felt a lack of support from her husband in child management and felt that she was looked down upon by her paternal relatives.

Family of M03   In this stepfamily there was a 36 years old stepmother and her husband aged 37. They had two children: one 12 year old boy from the father's marriage and a pre-school aged son from their current marriage. The family was formed after the husband's divorce. The stepson had behavioural problems and the stepmother found it difficult to deal with those problems without support from her husband who spent most of the weekdays working in Mainland China.

Family of M04   This stepfamily was in an extended family household. The middle aged couple lived with the parents of the husband, the nine year old stepson of the stepmother, and the pre-school son born from the current marriage. The husband worked as a taxi driver. He only had two days off from work each month but he was reported to be a caring husband and father. The stepmother had tried very hard to play her roles as parent and daughter-in-law and seemed successful. She felt loved and supported by her husband and reported that her commitment to the marital relationship and parenting had changed the attitudes of her parents-in-law from sceptical to accepting.

Family of M05   This stepfamily was composed of a divorced male new immigrant from Beijing who remarried a middle age music teacher in Hong Kong. The stepmother had employed strict discipline in parenting the teenage stepdaughter. The husband and the stepdaughter seemed submissive to the control of the wife/stepmother. The couple had a pre-school aged son from their current marriage and the stepmother said that she was very lenient in disciplining their son. There were difficulties in their marital and parent-child relationships.

Family of M06   This stepfamily consisted of a man aged 35 and a woman aged 39. Both of them had divorced once and each had one son from the previous relationship. They had an infant daughter from their current marriage. The couple both worked as insurance company agents. The wife was the main breadwinner and felt very loaded financially and emotionally. There were marital and parenting problems. The stepmother had difficulties in relating to her stepson and said that the father was punitive in disciplining his own son.

Family of M07   This was a stepfamily with high family income. The remarried male divorcee, aged 33, worked in insurance company and so did his wife aged 32. The stepmother seemed to relate well to her teenage stepdaughter. The couple had two sons, aged nine and four from their current marriage.

Family of M08   At the time of the interview this stepfamily was undergoing a big change because they were about to emigrate to Canada. The husband remarried his deceased wife's elder sister who said that she lacked parenting skills and she did not know how to play the role of housekeeper. The stepmother, who used to be the aunt of her younger sister's daughter and son, was frustrated in playing the role of parent, felt insecure after resigning from her well-paid job and was anxious to emigrate overseas. She had relationship problems with her teenage stepdaughter and late latency age stepson.

Family of M09   This stepfamily was once a very large extended family because the husband allowed the paternal kin to live in the same house and have meals with the nuclear stepfamily in the evening. The stepmother, aged 40, had difficulties to cope with the demands imposed by the relatives around her. She was rejected by the teenage stepson who could not accept the sudden disappearance of his biological mother who divorced his father. The stepmother focused child management on the daughter from the current marriage and wished that the daughter would excel the stepson in school performance so as to prove that she was an able mother.

Family of M010   The stepmother whose husband was divorced was not accepted by the mother-in-law and the two teenage stepsons living with them. Financially this stepfamily was rather well-to-do but the husband, who owned a small construction company, worked long hours and the stepmother had to take care of his family with loaded tasks without support from her husband. She said that she did not have the skills to manage the behaviours of her stepsons and had difficulties in being accepted by her mother-in-law.

'Flow of a Rough River': Challenges in the Lives of Stepmothers and Their Spouses

An examination of the challenges confronting parents in stepfamilies, as reported by the ten stepmothers, will help to deepen our understanding of the difficulties these stepmothers and their spouses had experienced in their earlier days.

Developmental Perspective and the Metaphor of the River

Life course is defined as 'the major life events and transitions an individual experiences between birth and death' (Schulz & Rau, 1985, p.129). Dallos (1992) stated that there are transitions at different stages of the family life cycle and there are external and internal demands for change. These demands are continuous and become critical at transitional points in a family's life, i.e. courtship; early marriage; the birth of children; middle marriage; leaving home; retirement and old age (p.12). Some people may experience non-normative life events such as acute illness, sudden death, unemployment, separation, divorce, etc. Haley (1981) noted the following stages as critical transitional stages for families: the courtship period; marriage and its consequences; childbirth and dealing with the young; middle marriage difficulties; weaning parents from children; and retirement and old age (Dallos, 1992, p.8).

Consequently, we come to understand that a member of a family inevitably

153

has to face changes. A person brings their history into his/her marriage. There may be unfulfilled developmental tasks and needs which will be carried into this newly formed family. Moreover, individuals have their own developmental life stage and tasks to be accomplished. Difficulties often arise when individual needs come into conflict with those arising from family, or when family tasks are so overwhelmingly demanding that individuals find it difficult to achieve the tasks required by his/her family at the same time, as struggling to achieve his/her own developmental tasks.

Family life cycle and individual development tasks may be alien to the Chinese culture, and a person's life is not structured in stages as the theories suggest. For example, in Chinese families with traditional values, members must abide by the rules and meet the expectations of the older generation. Those demands continue throughout life. Moreover, childhood is not divided into several sub-stages, each with distinct characteristics and tasks to be fulfilled. In Chinese culture, childhood is prolonged to accord with the wishes of the parents to supervise or to care, or to claim reward in old age from their child, as evidenced in the frequently-heard saying of many parents to their middle-aged or retirement-aged children: 'No matter how old you are, you are still a child in my eyes'. Therefore, it is more appropriate to perceive life development of the Chinese as 'the flow of a river' as suggested by Lam (1991).

The use of the metaphor of the river to portray the life of the Chinese, although documented by Lam, has, in fact, been used in many old Chinese movies to describe quick passing of the years or shorten a long story by omitting to describe the events in detail. For example, when describing hardship of a child or personal struggles over a lengthy period, the cameraman may film a scene of river flowing and put subtitles on the screen such as 'AFTER 18 YEARS'; or when there is a scene which shows a man leaving his family to pursue a career or study far away and before returning years later, he is shocked to find his family has undergone great changes; or when a female domestic helper is raped by her wicked master and gives birth to an illegitimate child, the scene of a flowing river tells audiences that the woman has survived the trauma and that the child has grown up. Life course is, therefore, portrayed as a river whose water keeps on running for ever. The Chinese have the attitude that 'no matter what happens, good or bad, life has to go on'.

A Ride on a Rough River: Changes and Difficulties Experienced by Stepmothers and Their Spouses

The stepmothers and their spouses were between the ages of adulthood and middle-age, which is a time when they should have established their families and had advanced in their career. All of the stepmothers had married later than the median age for the first marriage of women, which was 26.9 years old in 1995 (Hong Kong Census & Statistics Department, Dec., 1996); most of them had married in their late 20s or early 30s, with the exception of two who had married in their 40s (M05, M08). The spouses of these stepmothers had also married later than the median age for the first marriage of men which was 30.1 years old in 1995 (Hong Kong Census & Statistics Department, Dec., 1996). These men had all been married before, so their age at the time of their remarriage was mid 30's or older.

These men were at the life stage when they were expected to achieve tasks at home or at work. Life experiences before their marriage and current life situations had affected their functions of their roles. The following sections describe the challenges they had experienced when riding down the river of life.

The Ride of the Stepmothers on the Rough River

The family of origin had financial problems and could not fulfil their needs in their growing years Four out of ten of the stepmothers had had to work hard to contribute to the family income before their marriage. From her early school years, one stepmother had to work during the day and only studied in the evenings. She recalled:

> She [my mother] had many children. She couldn't look after us too well (M01(3),2)...I started work when I was ten. I had six other siblings and I was the eldest. (M01(1),5)...From childhood, I fought with my family about getting an education [for myself]. I could only afford to study in an evening school. My mother was illiterate. She did not allow me to continue my schooling. I begged her to let me study, so from primary one to secondary school, I only studied in the evening. (M01(10),4)

Another stepmother told me that she was adopted by a loving, but poor couple when she was eight days old. As her adoptive mother had to work hard to earn money to pay the family expenses, she was placed in an aunt's family and only returned home for school holidays. She still remembered how much she had missed seeing her mother:

> I remember that when I had to return to my aunt's home after school holidays, my mother had to quietly leave me with my aunt while we went for an outing, [then she left], when I did not see her, I would cry my eyes out. I have vivid memories of that. I was living in an attic room then, there was a window overlooking Victoria harbour...when I knew my mother would come to fetch me, I would lean over the window looking at the ferries wishing my mother would come sooner.

She had fond memories of her adoptive mother and was resentful of her biological mother, she said:

> I won't look for my biological parents, because my mother has never accepted the responsibility of being my mother; even if she comes to look for me, I won't choose her [to be my mother]. (M09(2),27)

Another stepmother started work at the age of 11 and earned money to help her family (M010); another worked as a dance hostess because of the poor financial situation at home. (M02)

Parents, especially mothers, had not taught their daughters life skills nor prepared them for their gender-role   It is important for parents to act as role models for their children and to prepare them for the roles to be taken up in their life. One of the stepmothers over-identified with her mother and was unable to cope with life crises because she always depended on her mother's advice and was not confident enough to make a decision for herself. She admitted: 'My mother imposes a lot of ideas in me, she has changed my life. I follow the life path like her' (M06(2),9). She further described what her mother was like: 'She has a strong character... in our family all members are afraid of her. She ordered us to walk certain pathway, and if we did not comply, she would throw a temper...she wants her kids to be good but she does not know how to express herself' (M06(2),25). The mother of this stepmother had imposed the view of her marrying a remarried man: 'My mother's view was, because I have a son of my own from my previous marriage, if I remarry, my future husband should have one kid too...because we would be equal, the family would then be good. So I married a man according to her wishes'. (M06(1),28)

And this stepmother later regretted the choice of mate that she had made.

Another stepmother was not taught to develop the age-appropriate gender-role. Her mother did everything for her and she was not equipped to do any of the tasks which are traditionally thought to be performed by women. She told me:

> I think I am totally inadequate in my role [as a housewife]. I'm very messy. I don't know how to deal with things. In the past, I did not need to cook (M08(1),28)...I didn't know how to light a stove, until my mother taught me. My mother knows where the things are in my kitchen better than I do. (M08(1), 31)

Stepmothers worked very hard before and after their marriage   All of the stepmothers had worked full-time before their marriage. Half of these stepmothers continued work after their marriage, (M01, M03, M05, M06, M07) while the others finished work after they were married. Four of them worked very hard to earn good money and they earned more than their husbands (M05, M06, M07, M08). The consequences were that these stepmothers could spare little time for housework and developing parent-child relationships.

Those who had become full-time housewives after their marriage had a heavy workload. The following are illustrations of their daily work.

Mrs. Chui's busy routine started early in the morning by helping her children to get ready for school and ended after supper when children went to bed; it was only then that she had a spare moment. She told me about the most difficult time which was:

> When the youngest one was sick [with asthma], I had just returned home from the market. If they had troubles with their emotions and had temper tantrums, that was the most difficult time. The youngest one needed attention, and I was cooking and dealing with the other children's emotional problems at the same time; my hands were working, my ears had to listen to what was happening outside [the kitchen], my mouth had to follow what they said.... (M02(3),7-9)

157

In the case of Mrs. Lam, after she woke up, she swept the floor, boiled water for drinking, prepared food, washed clothes, cooked lunch, and afternoon snacks for her growing stepsons who ate more than once, and cooked supper which had to be ready at different times for her mother-in-law, stepsons, herself, and for her husband, who returned home late from work. She said:

> After supper, I peel off the skin of a pear for my mother-in-law...then I wash the dishes, boil water, pour a cup of tea for her... [when my husband comes home], I re-heat food for him. I don't get to bed until after 1 a.m...my stepsons may be hungry and want to eat again. They have supper at 6 or 8 p.m., I cook noodles again for them after midnight. (M010(2),23-25)

Working stepmothers like Mrs. Chung sometimes had to work late:

> If I return home late, my eldest daughter has already asleep. She usually goes to bed between 11 and 12 p.m. If they are all asleep when I return home, I start doing my own things. (M07(2),22)

Divorce was painful and had left scars on the present relationship   The last marital relationship was not easy to forget. Two of the ten stepmothers had married and divorced once before and they still felt hurt and upset when they thought about it. Mrs. Lee said:

> If someone asks my opinion about divorce, I would say, 'Divorce? No. If there are no kids, it is no problem. If there are kids, one must think very carefully.   If one is financially OK, don't pay attention to the trouble, just tolerate the husband without divorcing him'. (M06(1),29)

Mrs. Lee had initiated the divorce from her husband of 8 years who did not want to end the marriage. She recalled:

> The divorce procedure was very long, because my husband did not want the divorce. So it dragged on...later, I began to see some light. Because I insisted, so he...he did not appear in court though. I was lucky that I was given the [custody of the] child.... (M06(1),6)

She won the battle, but entered another marriage which she regretted very much because her second husband failed to support the family financially, her own son was perceived as the 'child of a greasy oil bottle', and her husband abused his own son.

Another stepmother, Mrs. Chiu had also been married and divorced once before her current marriage. She had two children from her former relationship which had lasted for four years. Her former husband had custody of their son, and she had their daughter. She became upset when talking about her ex-husband who failed to support their daughter:

> He needed to pay $800 a month. The judge ordered him to visit [his daughter] twice a month but he never visits. He does not care about his children, let alone the visits. His son belongs to his parents. The grandmother wants her grandson. (M02(2),38)

Mrs. Chui was not given the chance to visit her biological son and she was upset about this.

There were other difficulties confronting these stepmothers in their daily family life. For example, they were overloaded with child care and housekeeping tasks, two stepmothers had to serve their parents-in-law and relatives by cooking and satisfying their many requests (M02, M09); two stepmothers had to work very late after midnight (M03, M010); and one lacked the skills to handle the many tasks required (M08). Their difficulties were also related to the lack of support and help from their husbands; all but two reported this problem (M01, M02, M03, M05, M06, M08, M09, M010). The final area of difficulty which was identified was related to relationship problems with in-laws. Eight stepmothers reported that their relationships with their parents-in-law were difficult, irrespective of whether they lived with or away from their families (M01, M02, M04, M06, M07, M08, M09, M010).

The Ride of the Spouses of the Stepmothers on the Rough River

The family of origin was distant from their children and their parents failed to provide care and models for behaviours   The stepmothers who reported on their current husbands' background confirmed that their husbands came from working class families. Many did not have close relationships with their parents, either because the latter had failed to provide child care when help was needed, or because they were illiterate and could not give advice on child management or could not be the role models for their adult children. The following are some examples.

Mrs. Ho told me:

> My husband does not like his mother. He said she left him and his siblings and lived elsewhere when they were very young. She did not take care of her husband when he was suffering from cancer. (M01(1),4)

The husband of another stepmother had a poor relationship with his parents. Mrs. Lee reported:

> It is a fact that the relationship between my husband and his mother is not that good. (M06(1),21)

When asked who had influenced her husband the most, this stepmother said:

> His father. He treats his son the same as his father treats him [i.e.physically punitive]. I reminded him of that, but he did not listen to me. (M06(2),27)

She further stressed:

> He has adopted his father's thinking and he deals with his children like his father; they just pay no attention to their kids. (M06(3),19)

She gave an example of how the poor the relationship between father-son had affected the grandparent-grandson relationship:

> He lives very close to us, just above our flat. It is common for a grandfather to take his grandchildren to a tea house; many families do that. He never does. My stepson is their [her parents-in-law's] blood grandson, and he is so close, but they never take him out, or to a tea house. (M06(3),19)

Some of the parents of these men were limited in their intellectual abilities, and could not provide adequate models for their children, which was reported by the stepmothers interviewed. Mrs. Chung told me:

160

One has to look at the background of my husband though. His family did not teach him during his formative years. His family was very poor, and his parents had no education, but they are very nice. They don't know how to teach kids...his parents have not taught him any moral teaching, or living habits...they have not done so because they don't know about these themselves. (M07(2),19)

Dissolution of marriage triggers negative feelings and it is difficult to accept
Seven men divorced their wives and six of these wives had committed adultery which lead to the divorce. Only one divorce was based on mutual consent. One of the husbands of the stepmothers I interviewed felt hurt and shameful and could not accept the fact; he hid the divorce even though he had been remarried for ten years (M09). Another stepmother reported that her husband's former wife left the family suddenly and created emotional turmoil. Mrs. Lee told me:

His wife...when his son was about 2 years old, asked for a divorce. She also had a daughter. She left the children at home and deserted the family...My husband placed the children in his mother's home for about a month, and then their mother appeared and took the daughter away. She said she wanted the daughter but did not want the son. He [the informant's husband] said he did not want to split up the two siblings, but his wife insisted on taking the daughter away.... (M06(1),2)

The impact of the divorce has influenced the father-son relationship:

He relates so badly to his son. I suspect his former wife gave him a lot of problems. He might think because of his son, his wife left him. So the father-son relationship is troublesome. (M06(1),28)

It may be because his son, who now lives with him, reminds him everyday of the pain and anger caused by his last marriage.
Another stepmother told me how her husband's former marriage ended and how the aftermath was reinforced by her mother-in-law. Mrs. Lau reported:

According to my husband, his former marriage lasted about one or two years. It was very short. He said he married his former wife after dating for 3 months, then they married...they didn't know each other that well.

161

His wife met another man... After their son was born, she met another man and she ran away with him... At first the woman didn't want to divorce, but my husband said 'You did such a thing, so we must divorce.' The custody of the child would usually be granted to the mother. She wanted to fight to get custody of her son. My husband had no choice but to charge her with adultery, so that they got divorced quickly. Otherwise they would have had to wait for 2 years [before getting a divorce]. (M03(1),4)

Mr. Lau wanted the custody of his son, and, therefore, he reluctantly had to use 'adultery' as the grounds for divorce. The marriage ended in such a way that the divorce brought him shame and made him angry. Mr. Lau's mother caused further problems by always telling her grandson about the misdeeds of his unfaithful mother, so Mr. Lau was reminded again and again of the unhappy experience. She reported:

My mother-in-law told him [the stepson of the informant] how bad his mother was, how she had improperly had a relationship with another man, and how cruel she was because she didn't visit him. She also told him that this happened not because his father didn't want his mother, but because his mother left their family. (M03(10),6)

These reminders reinforced the humiliation felt by the man as a result of his wife's betrayal.

Three of the husbands of the stepmothers interviewed had wives who had died. Their feelings about their deceased wives were reported by the stepmothers.

One man had tried very hard to find a cure for his dying wife and had stopped work for a whole year (M04(1),10). Mrs. Chan reported:

She [the deceased wife of her husband] was having treatment in Hong Kong for a while, and then she went to Mainland China for a cure. She died there...my husband was with her. He stopped working for a whole year. He did a lot for her! He is the kind of man who loves and cares a lot about his wife. (M04(1),10)

She also told me that her husband was so depressed at that time that 'he wanted to "go" with his son' meaning he wanted to 'pass away with his wife'.

She added:

> Now whenever it is 'Chung Yeung' or 'Ching Ming' [ancestor worship days for the Chinese], he returns to Mainland China to visit his former wife's grave. (M04(1),11)

Men whose wives had died felt badly about their spouse's death and would treat their children very well in order to compensate for the loss. Mrs. Chan reported:

> He loves his daughter very much. He loved his late wife very much. He loves his daughter and spoils her. (M08(3), p.23)

Another stepmother Mrs. Ho also noted that her husband 'feels he owes his daughter's mother a favour. He feels guilty when he thinks of his deceased wife.' (M01(1),8)

Coping with Heavy Demands of Work

Work is very important in a man's life. As the spouses of these stepmothers were in adulthood or middle-age, they needed to work hard either to maintain or enhance the quality of life of their families, or to seek satisfaction from work.

Out of the ten stepmothers, seven of their husbands were very busy at work and could only spend limited time at home. For example, two husbands (M03, M05) had to travel to Mainland China several times a week or stay there for a few days, and returned home for the weekends. Five husbands (M01, M04, M07, M09, M010) worked long hours, including one who worked shifts and only had two days off a month.

Two husbands did not earn enough money to bring home. One was a casual worker in the construction industry and his work was seasonal (M02). Another worked as an insurance agent and his income was variable. His wife was worried about not having enough money to meet family expenses; she became upset when she was telling me about the load which was on her shoulders alone. Mrs. Lee sighed:

I feel embarrassed to tell you this: I am the pillar of the family. I am not exaggerating... I'm heavily loaded...I am very loaded, it is exhausting. I couldn't imagine before how difficult this could be.... (M06(1),28)

One husband had had to retire early because of their impending emigration overseas. He was in his late 40s and used to work long hours but had had to shut down his own business as part of the migration arrangement. He was uncertain about whether he could earn a living because of the language barrier. He was anxious that he had to live on his savings from the past.

Dealing with His Mother's Demands and Her Conflicts with His Wife

Six of the ten stepmothers reported that their husband had a demanding mother (M01, M02, M04, M06, M09, M010). Out of these six mothers, three were widows (M01, M09, M010). These mothers had conflicts with their daughters-in-law. The examples below show how difficult some of the husbands' mothers were reported to be. Mrs. Ho told me:

I refurbished this flat after our marriage; she blamed us. I bought a bed for us, she wanted a new sofa bed too...last time I saw her she complained that we did not give her enough pocket money ...she complains all the time...she would like us to give her money and said we should not use our money on furnishing our home. (M01(1),18)

Another stepmother, Mrs. Lam, reported how she was treated by her mother-in-law and that her husband had to act to protect her from verbal abuse:

After we married, she [her mother-in-law] did not like me; she always scolded me as 'stupid', 'lazy', 'like a pig', 'crazy'...I let her scold me but she still did not accept me. I cried. My husband always said to her, 'Don't scold her'. (M010(1),6)

Dealing with Losses and Changes

As pointed by Marris (1974), loss is usually threatening and changes generate great anxiety (refer to Chapter 2, pp.30-31). Feelings of loss may have been dealt with but could recur at the time of change when a stepfamily is formed. Robinson (1993) noted the unresolved problems following the divorce or death of a biological parent, and said it may take years for the integration of a stepfamily (p.115).

Reactions to the Loss of a Biological Parent

Three stepfamilies had experienced the death of the biological mother. The reactions of the husbands were that they felt they had obligation to their deceased wife which had not been fulfilled and they tried to compensate by giving their children extra care and attention. According to the stepmothers, one husband refused the suggestion of sending his daughter to a boarding school and said he had to treat her well for the sake of his deceased wife (M01). Another husband loved his former wife very much and had thought of committing suicide at the time of her death. He decided to remarry thinking that the adjustment of his son to a new mother would be easier when his son was young (M04). Another husband continued his love for his former wife by marrying her older sister (M08) and because he felt that his children knew their aunt well.

Stepmothers tended to give the matter a 'low profile' and did not show strong feelings. However, there were signs of their ambivalence. Mrs. Ho hid photographs of the deceased mother and said she will let her stepdaughter have them when she grows up (M01). Mrs. Chan disagreed with her parents-in-law telling her stepson not to mention that he had 'two mommys', but she said that because he was pre-school age, he was too young to understand death and, therefore, she would not initiate discussion (M04). Another, Mrs. Chan, took over the role of mother from her deceased younger sister and said she did so to complete her sister's unfinished parenting duties. However, she was angered by her stepdaughter hanging onto the past and by her stepson comparing her to her deceased sister (M08).

The older generation felt sorry for their widower sons and their grandchildren. They provided major support in child care when the biological mother died. There were signs of parents-in-law comparing the past and present daughters-in-law and claiming power in the family. These will be discussed later, in the section on 'Equity and Authority in Stepfamilies' (p.186). Their influence on parent-child relationships and parenting behaviours in stepfamilies cannot be ignored. For example, Mrs. Ho's mother-in-law interfered in child disciplining and provoked conflicts

165

with her daughter-in-law (M01). It is not easy for an older generation to forget the past, especially when they had formed good relationships with the deceased. Mrs. Chan's mother-in-law had been fond of her deceased daughter-in-law. She reacted by hiding her sorrow and asked her grandson not to mention his deceased mother (M04). Mrs. Lau's mother-in-law criticized her inability in child management, and united with the grand-daughter to gossip about their dislike of the stepmother (M08).

When facing the above-mentioned mixed reactions of the adults in the family, what were the reactions of the children? The stepmothers reported that these children reacted mainly by avoidance or confrontation. The following are some examples.

Mrs. Chan's teenage stepdaughter, who was formerly her niece, left her family to study in Canada a year after the death of her mother. She told me how her stepdaughter felt about her:

> She insisted that I am not good, and she will not change her mind. She feels that I have invaded her family. (M08(1),15)

Her 12 year old stepson also had difficulties accepting her. She told me:

> He sat on the floor. He said in the past his mother allowed him to do so...he said his mother was not particularly demanding. (M08(2),3)

Another time he reminded her of the place of his deceased mother:

> This house is mine, my mommy said this house is mine'. (M08(3),20)

He was reminding Mrs. Chan that his mother still had a place in the family which nobody should forget.

Another girl's biological mother died when she was seven or eight years old. Two years later her father dated her stepmother. Mrs. Ho recalled how her stepdaughter reacted to the loss of her mother:

> She deliberately sat between us when we were out dating. She always mentioned her mother in front of her father for fear of her father forgetting his deceased wife. (M01(1),16)

166

She pointed out another example:

> When I went out with her father, she always asked him, 'When are we going to visit mommy's grave?' Every time was like that. She always interrupted our conversation. (M01(1),5)

From the above examples, the stepchildren had difficulties dealing with their feelings of loss and accepting the new mother. They reacted to the losses and changes by physically disappearing from the family; or by reminding their stepmothers of the past to resist the invasion of the newcomer mother.

Reactions to Parental Divorce

As described earlier, seven out of the ten stepfamilies were formed following divorces. Out of these seven divorces, six resulted from the wife's adultery and only one was by mutual consent. In Chinese culture, it is more acceptable for men to divorce their wives if they find their behaviour unsatisfactory. Traditionally, the seven grounds for the unilateral dissolution of a marriage by husband in the old times were: 'unfilial behaviour of the wife to the husband's parents; the wife's barrenness; the wife's adultery; some repulsive disease suffered by the wife; the wife's jealousy; her garrulousness or loquacity; and theft of her husband's goods' (Law Reform Commission of Hong Kong, 1992, p.15). Of all these grounds for divorce, adultery committed by a wife is seen as the most shameful behaviour and is usually hard to tolerate. Bond (1986) noted the observation made by King & Myers (1977): 'the losing of face may bring serious consequences for an individual, especially when he or she loses the so-called "moral face"', (Bond, 1986, p.247). Losing face, according to Bond, may cause an individual to experience an uneasy feeling of emotional arousal which has been labelled embarrassment, shame or shyness. If losing face is caused by a moral judgment imposed by the relatives and public sanction, one can imagine that its impact on the person and his/her family will be much greater. For example, if one is fired by his/her employer, the person feels ashamed and will try to hide the fact from his/her family and friends. If the dismissal is caused by the person having a sexual relationship with his/her boss, that is a situation of 'losing moral face'. It is, therefore, important to observe the influence of the prevailing moral stances on divorce and remarriage, and their impact on people undergoing divorce and remarriage.

Many husbands in this study had difficulties in coping with their feelings when they divorced from their unfaithful wives. As mentioned earlier, one husband kept the divorce and remarriage secret for ten years (M09). He did not allow his former wife to take his son on an outing from his home, but asked his son to meet her in a park on visiting days. Other husbands preferred their former wives not to be involved and were relieved if their ex-wives failed to keep up with their visits to their children (M02, M03, M05, M06, M07, M09, M010). The husbands tended to spoil their children as compensation for the loss of their mother. Mrs. Chui said she had to ask her husband to stop being a 'Santa Claus' (M02); Mrs. Lam noted that her husband had covered up the lies told by his daughter for fear of her being punished by the teacher (M05); Mrs. Chung and Mrs. Lam observed that their husbands often bought gifts for their own children (M07, M010).

Some stepmothers wished that the non-custodial, biological mothers would not appear on the scene so they could build up relationships with their stepchildren (M01, M05, M07). Two felt that their stepchildren needed contact with and concern from their biological mothers, and they did not mind their visits (M09, M010). A number of biological mothers never showed up to visit their children (M03, M06). There are three stories which need elaboration. Mrs. Chung requested that the biological mother of her stepdaughter did not visit as she felt that she had a good relationship with her teenage stepdaughter, and that it was time for the biological mother to stop visiting. According to the stepmother, the biological mother and stepdaughter accepted this without any hard feelings (M07). Another stepmother, Mrs. Lam, told me that the biological mother regretted her divorce and wanted to compensate for her loss by visiting her daughter. This mother resided in Beijing and the stepmother was strongly against the visit after years with no contact, so the stepdaughter suffered emotionally (M05). Another stepmother, Mrs. Lau, reported that the biological mother visited her stepson for several years. She suggested to her that she could increase the frequency of the visits if she wished, but, according to this stepmother, the biological mother seemed to be afraid of this commitment and she never showed up again. This was a blow to the son and he became socially withdrawn (M09).

The reactions of the parents-in-law and relatives were as follows: all seven stepfamilies had parents-in-law and relatives who offered help with child care at the time of their sons' divorce. After the formation of the stepfamilies, two parents-in-law did not actively involve themselves, i.e. one of the parents-in-law lived in the same building as the couple but they did not visit the children or take them out (M06); another of the parents-in-law lived in a village in Hong Kong, and the couple only sent their daughter to stay there during summer holidays (M07). Another two parents-in-law did not involve themselves in child care after the stepfamilies were formed (M03, M05). The remaining three were mothers-in-law. One of them lived with the couple and interfered strongly in child management (M010). The other two did not live with the couple at time of the interview but their influence upon child management was profound: they still dropped in without prior notice or attempted child management by 'remote-control' through telephone orders (M09, M010).

Children reacted by acting out their feelings of separation from their departed parent and their fear of losing the love of the parent who was living with them. They rejected their stepmothers because they had split loyalty, but nevertheless, wanted to be cared for and loved by their new mothers. The worst reaction was that they became withdrawn and were unable to build trusting relationships with people. The following are some illustrations:

Mrs. Lau's ten year old stepson started to run away from home when he was seven or eight years old, not long after the stepfamily was formed. According to the stepmother, he would live on the streets for a week if the family did not look for him and take him home. He began to run away more frequently. Mrs. Lau told me:

He used to run away once a month. Later, twice a month. In the summer, almost every day' (M03(1),18).

This stepson had avoidance-approach conflict which was evident from the report given by his stepmother:

When he runs away, he takes nothing with him, He may take some money. If he had no money, he would run away empty-handed. He is waits for people to look for him. He would go to Wah Fu Estate, he must go there, so that people know where to find him. (M03(1),19)

This stepmother also noted her stepson's emotional need to be mothered, she told me:

In fact he likes to be close to me, like his younger brother, and he wants me to pamper him. Although he wants to be closer, he can't; there seems to be a force which pulls him away from me. Both of us are like that. (M03(2),4)

Both the stepmother and the stepson felt ambivalent in their relationship to each other.

Another stepmother reported the disrespectful and defiant behaviour of her teenage stepsons. Mrs. Lam told me that they were unable to handle the feelings which had resulted from parental divorce:

In my case, they only addressed me as their mother after half a year...if they did not greet, I used my genuine love to move them. There was no other way! My husband said, 'Why it is six months now, and still they don't greet you as "ah ma" [i.e. address mother in a factual manner with no affection], there is no expression of feeling?' I said I have no way to make them otherwise. After six months, they still did not greet me as their mother by addressing me as mommy. (M010(2),12)

They seemed to have difficulties in accepting a new mother figure in their family. Mrs. Lam told me about the defiant behaviour of her stepson:

He said I talked behind his back (to his father). I asked him to do something, and he used a ball to hit me. He threw the basketball at my back. (M010(1),26).

Mrs. Lam was cooking at the kitchen and her hands were burnt by boiling oil when the ball landed in the wok [a Chinese cooking pan].

Another stepmother told me about her stepson's total withdrawal from family life after his biological mother suddenly stopped visiting without saying goodbye to him. Mrs. Lau described how her stepson felt:

His beloved and trusted mommy can't be trusted, can't give love... [after his mother disappeared], he seldom talked, he would not greet his father if he met him on his way out...when we went out, he never went. When we were not at home, he would come out to the living room, and turn on his father's Hi-fi [as reported by the maid]...for example, if others ate fruit after dinner, he would not have any. When everybody was asleep, at about 1 to 2 a.m., he would then come out of his room and eat fruit or cook...he treats the house as if it were rented accommodation.... (M09(1),20-22)

The Impact of Losses and Changes on Parenting Behaviours

The death of a parent is not the same as divorce; the emotional reactions resulting from these life crises are different, but these non-normative life events have an impact on parent-child relationships and parenting behaviours and there are some common themes.

Firstly, loss of a spouse or a parent is irreversible and permanent. As regards divorce, the emotional divorce for family members may take a long time but the parental duties can be filled by a replacement parent. 'The intensity experienced would depend on the quality of the relationship which the individual had had with the lost [and separated] person and how closely intertwined their lives had been' (Robinson & Smith, 1993, p.61). From the information described above, the feelings of those involved were still intense and, if the fathers had difficulties in resolving their feelings and did not make efforts to help their children to deal with theirs, the stepmothers would have difficulties in establishing relationships with their stepchildren.

Secondly, the question of the previous bonding with the natural mother is complex. As pointed out by Rutter, there are six conditions for adequate mothering, i.e. 'loving relationship; attachment; unbroken time of parenting; adequate stimulation; mothering provided by one person; and parenting in the child's own family' (Rutter, 1982, p.26). From an examination of the situations confronting the stepchildren in this study, as reported by their stepmothers, some of these conditions were not met when they were mothered. For example, some mother-child relationships were broken when the mothers left their family during marital separation and did not reappear until the divorce was settled (M03, M05, M06, M09). Moreover, most of the children were taken care of by grandparents or relatives, in addition to their mothers, before and after the stepfamily was formed. For example, Mrs. Chui's stepson was placed in the family of his paternal grandmother and his father's elder sister until he was seven (M02); Mrs. Lau's stepson was placed in her husband's elder brother's family and that continued occasionally after the stepfamily was formed (M03); Mrs. Lam's stepdaughter was taken care of by her husband's mother when his former wife left the family (M05); etc. Mothering was shared by multiple parental figures in the child's life. In the

171

past this was not uncommon in Chinese families, where support from kin was expected. It is also a usual practice in contemporary Chinese families in Hong Kong to have in-laws helping with childminding while parents are out working; some children are even placed in a relatives' family during weekdays and return home only at weekends, when working parents can spare more time to care for them. Therefore, when problems in the stepmother-stepchild relationship are noted, the childminding practice established before the stepmother became a member of the stepfamily should be examined. Children may reject stepmothers not because of her taking over the mothering role, but as a reaction to the changes brought about by the addition of a parenting figure. The focus should be upon the changes, rather than upon the losses.

Thirdly, in view of children's reactions to losses and changes, parents in stepfamilies may want to compensate and give extra attention to their children. However, as shown in the case illustrations above, biological parents may be overly protective or indulgent of their children. Children also wish to be close to their own parents and to exclude the new-comer stepmother. They want their relationship with their remaining parent stay the same at times of change, which is explained as being a natural response by the concept of 'impulses of conservatism' suggested by Marris (1974). An analysis of the data shows that when father-child alliances formed, stepmothers felt insecure and ambivalent. They were anxious that their husbands were too close to their own child and that the latter diverted some of their husband's love away from them. On the other hand, they wanted to build a relationship with their stepchild in order to show that they were not a 'wicked mother' (refer to Chapter 2, p.21 Visher & Visher's myths of stepfamilies). They were ambivalent about their relationships with their stepchildren.

Lastly, signs of negative social attitudes towards remarriage following the adultery of former wife were noted, and those attitudes had affected stepparenting. The older generation in Chinese families regard the divorce of their children as 'shameful' and the adultery of a daughter-in-law is condemned. These feelings are still strong in families in Hong Kong. An observation of the stepfamilies in this study showed that many in-laws had helped with child care, and some had continued to help after the stepfamilies were formed. In some cases the grandmothers told their grandchildren how badly their mothers had behaved. This had affected the children's perceptions of their mothers, and further negatively influenced the development of their trust in their stepmothers. They were afraid to build relationship for fear of losing another mother, as in the case of Mrs. Lau's stepson described earlier (M09).

Building Couple Bond

The quality of parenting is very much affected by the quality of the marital relationship. This is more so in stepfamilies. As noted by Visher & Visher (1988), and Ganong & Coleman (1994), couples in stepfamilies must develop bond which facilitate the building up of positive stepparent-stepchild relationships (refer to Chapter 2, pp.35-36).

Factors Affecting the Building of Couple Bond

Wives romanticize their marriage All the stepmothers said that they had married their husbands for love. Some added that they had felt pity for the man because he had lost his wife or because he had the heavy burden of child care (M01, M04, M05, M08).

One stepmother said she loved her husband very much and adored him because he was 'perfect'. She made the decision to marry him against the advice of her parents and friends. Mrs. Lau recalled:

> Many friends tried to persuade me not to marry my husband. They thought, 'Why marry a man who has married before and has a child?' They did not see me as the third person. They thought they were on my side and suggested that I should not marry such a man. That was my decision, I love him. I did not think about becoming the third person or becoming a stepmother...may be I was emotional. I really love that man (her present husband) very much. I did not mind. I thought I would relate well to his family. I did not feel that it was a difficult task'. (M09(2),2)

After marrying him, she wished her husband would forget the past. She said:

> I did not want my husband to think of things in the past, right!? This was a natural responses. (M09(3),2)

It was quite impossible, however, for her husband not to think about the past, and everyday his son who was living with him would remind him of the past. She noted that and was upset:

> I treated my husband so well, I took him as the centre of everything. When my daughter was born, he still regarded his son as the most important. I felt that. When comparing my status with his son, I was lower. (M09(3),39)

Mrs. Ho married her husband initially because she felt pity for his overbearing child care responsibilities, and later developed a loving relationship. She wished that somebody would care about her feelings. She said:

> Although he knew that I was under great pressure, when he needed to go to bed, he went. He would not comfort me...He doesn't know how to comfort or please his wife. (M01(1),23)

Husbands were seen by wives as having problems in limit-setting and disciplining their biological children Stepmothers felt that their husbands had several ways of limit-setting and disciplining of their own children; i.e. 'indulgent', 'punitive', 'uninvolved and distant', and 'lack skills'. As regards the first type 'indulgent' method, some stepmothers reported that they felt their husbands did not set proper limits for child management. Mrs. Ho said:

> He indulges her. He can't teach her properly and just lets her have her own way. She threw a temper tantrum in the street, she cried and lay on the ground, and he convinced me by saying, 'Let her be, she is just a kid'. (M01(2),9)

Another stepmother, Mrs. Lam, told me how her husband indulged his daughter:

> Sometimes my husband spoils her, and her habit of lying has been formed. When he thought it would disagree with something, he told his daughter: 'Don't let your mother know, she would not be happy about that.' So she tells lies, and the habit has been formed. (M05(1),21)

174

She illustrated this further:

> Sometimes when his daughter answered back, he did not get angry, but he would laugh instead. (M05(3),15)

She went on:

> He spoils her, as a habit. Sometimes he almost wanted to spank her, but he allowed her to carry on. He tolerates her, and spoils her. (M05(1),32)

Second type of method of limit-setting and disciplining is 'punitive'. Mrs. Lee described her husband's parenting method: 'When disciplining his son, my husband nags and picks at his son's weakness...' (M06(2),27).   She added: 'My husband is very strict. He likes rules. I think sometimes he should not be so harsh.' (M06(2),3). She said her husband would discipline his son severely, even on social situations: 'He is very fierce to him. He spanks him without mercy. That is not good' (M06(2),5).   Her husband was allegedly reported as a child abuser by their neighbour and the case was brought to the attention of social workers.

The third type of method is 'uninvolved and distant'. A number of husbands left the management of their children to the stepmothers, either because they worked long hours or because they did not have close relationships with their children. For example, Mrs. Lau's husband had a business in a the border city of Mainland China which is not far away from Hong Kong. He had to manage the business and stayed there several days a week. He usually returned home only for weekends. Mrs. Lau told me:

> He wouldn't discipline or teach his children. When we go out, he wouldn't point out something [interesting] to them [by saying], 'Look, this is fun', he never does. He doesn't talk much to my younger son [from current relationship], but he relates to the younger son a bit better than he relates to his older son [his own son].   (M03(1),14)

Another stepmother, Mrs. Chung, also noted that her husband did not take on active part in child management. She said:

I once told him that I had noticed some changes in our daughter [the husband's own child who had some behavioural problems at school]. He started scolding her, and did not trust her as much. That was the first time. Before that, he had never scolded her or pointed a finger at her. (M07(3),6)

Mrs. Chan's husband was a taxi-driver. He worked shifts and only had two days off a month. He had very limited time at home, let alone time for child management (M04).

The fourth type of child management is 'lacking skills'. Mrs. Chui told me that her husband was unable to handle difficult disciplining situations and he would 'mess up' and leave the scene for her to pick up the pieces. She said:

If neither spanking nor scolding worked, he would just blame anything or anybody. He murmured, 'They are unteachable.' He had no other methods but just blamed endlessly. If spanking and scolding didn't work, he would spank, then scold them again. He shouted at them the whole day, but his method was not effective. (M02(3),23)

Another stepmother felt that her husband did not know how to handle children's problems, Mrs. Chan said:

His personality is like that of his family in that when he sees things going wrong, he won't say a word. He will not confront his kids. He thinks confronting them is a difficult task. He is miserable. (M08(1),7)

Stepchildren were seen by their stepmothers as competitors for the husbands' attentions, and the instigators of conflict When a stepfamily is newly formed, the members struggle to find their place in it and they compete to build relationship. Parent-child relationships which predate the marriage may be seen as a threat or barrier to couple bonding. Mrs. Lau reported:

'I was jealous when I saw his father being nice to him [the stepson of this stepmother], I would wonder whether his father was missing his son's biological mother?' (M09(3),2). She felt that this situation had not changed even after the daughter from their marriage was born. She noted: 'He still treated his son as the most important...when comparing my status to that of his son, I was lower'. (M09(3),39)

176

Another stepmother felt that her husband was too protective of his daughter, and that his daughter also wanted to be close to her father. Mrs. Ho said:

> My husband always thinks that she [the stepdaughter of this stepmother] is a little girl. If this goes on, she will continue to hide things [from me]...she knows her father is on her side; once she hit back at me during a conflict. (M01(2),8)

She further illustrated that not only was her stepdaughter protected by her father, but she was capable of instigating further conflicts between her parents. She told me:

> When I quarrelled with her father, she would irritate me. If we were getting along well with each other, she would not do anything to interrupt. If she knew that we were at odds, she would provoke me and make me angry.... (M01(1),16)

Mrs. Chan was upset when her stepson said that the matrimonial home was his property and that of his deceased mother. She was angry and told him:

> Why yours? This was bought by your father. Your mother was alive then so she shared it. Why only yours? It belongs to everybody in the family. So, I have a share in it too. (M08(3),20)

A home is important to a married woman. The stepmother felt threatened by the challenges made by her stepson, who reminded her that she did not have a 'proper place' in the family. She reported:

> My stepchildren create conflicts between me and my husband. In the past it was not like this. We related to each other peacefully. There was no problem, when there was just me and my husband. (M08(2),22)

In-laws and relatives could help to strengthen a couple's relationships or create stress for them In the formative stage of a stepfamily, support is important to build couple bond. Only one stepmother out of ten had been given help from her family so that she had the space and energy to focus on her marital relationship. She told me how her mother had helped her stepson to understand the marital relationship of his father and his wife. This

177

maternal grandmother said to Mrs. Chan's stepson:

> You can't say things like that...your mom is married to your daddy. She is his wife. When you said that this house is yours, it means that she has no share in it, and she doesn't like that...she is sensitive. She is unhappy, so don't say this any more. (M08(3),21)

Other relatives, especially the paternal parents-in-law and paternal relatives, were regarded as threats to the stepmothers' marital relationships and they created stress in these relationships. For example, Mrs. Chui felt threatened that her paternal kin had the idea of helping her husband's former wife to be reconciled with him. These relatives felt that this stepmother had worked in an 'improper place' [as a dance hostess] before and was not fit to be a wife and a mother. She reported their plan as follows:

> My in-laws give me troubles. They always hope to see my husband get together with his former wife again. This is quite a problem. Although my husband has not done anything to encourage this, the gossip is there...why do they still do something like that? When I was emotionally down, I felt as if I was being stepped on. The feelings were strong then. (M02(1),18)

She reflected:

> My husband's younger sister wants to re-unite my husband and his former wife and re-build their family. There is, therefore, additional force to pull me and my son [stepson] away from each other...when I deal with my son [stepson], I have also to consider his grandfather, his auntie, and my husband'. (M02(1),10)

In another case, Mrs. Ho's mother-in-law had lived with the couple before but was now living elsewhere. Her influence was still there, however, because she would drop by their flat without prior notice, and demanded financial support and gifts. She also intervened in child management. Mrs. Ho recalled:

178

She [her mother-in-law] would not let us discipline my stepdaughter. She would interfere...but because she does not live here any longer, we can discipline her [the stepdaughter] better. (M01 (1),11)

Another stepmother, Mrs. Lau, felt that her in-laws had taken her parenting role away from her. She felt there was an alliance between her paternal kin and her husband. She was isolated and was not given the right to intervene. She reported:

When his paternal grandma was living with us, I would not say a word to confront him [her stepson]. I had no involvement in caring for him or disciplining him. I am his mother in name only. So, when the school needs to contact my stepson's parents, his teachers will contact my husband, not me. I was not even invited to his primary school graduation. (M09(3),7)

The couples rarely have private time to develop or consolidate their relationships   It is important that couples have time to satisfy their needs by sharing their feelings, talking about everyday matters, or having sex. The reports of these stepmothers show that these couples were rather deprived of their marital needs, which is evident from the following examples. Mrs. Lau told me:

I have complained to my husband that there is no arrangement for the 'world for two' (二人世界)... I wished to have such time [to be alone as a couple alone] but now this never happens. Since the day I married, a third person [the stepson] is always there. (M09(2),28)

It was not uncommon for the couples to have very few social outings after the remarried families were formed. This is one of the examples given by Mrs. Lam:

We don't have a 'world for two' since I married. Very rarely. Only when they are asleep. Before we had the maid, and before the baby was born, we took the daughter [the stepdaughter of the informant] with us if we went out...oh, yes, we went to see a movie by ourselves once...but that was the only time. This was two or three years ago. (M05(2),17)

Another stepmother, Mrs. Lam, also had little time to talk to her husband in the evening. He worked and returned home too late:

> After our marriage, there was no 'two people's world', no love story. The children are older now, so it can't be so [she meant there could be no intimate behaviour in front of them]. My husband returns home late from work, so we don't have much time to talk to each other. We just talk about daily things very briefly. (M010(2),14)

Another stepmother, Mrs. Ho, only worked part-time, but had limited time for developing the relationship with her husband. She said:

> No matter whether a woman is married or remarried, when she has children, she has no time to spend with her husband alone. At first I couldn't adjust. My husband always attended to the needs of his daughter, so we had so little time and no space for us to be alone. There was no private time for us as a couple. (M01(2),29)

Mrs. Chui revealed that even her sex life was affected. As they were living in a cubicle of a public housing estate, the small living space created problems for the couple when they wanted to be close to each other:

> Parenting older children is a problem. They go out for a date and return late, and this would affect the time shared by us as a couple. [She was rather covert in expressing herself but from her non-verbal expression and after checking with her, I concluded that she meant the sex life between her and her husband]. (M02(1),15)

The Impact of Factors Affecting Couple Bonding which in Turn Affects Parenting Behaviours

Couple bonding and parenting behaviours are interrelated both in their quality and in how these dynamics influence each other. First, as pointed out by Ganong & Coleman (1994), there is no clear-cut boundary between the marital and parent-child sub-systems in stepfamilies (p.64). Fine & Kurdek (1995) also found that 'the positive and negative experiences that stepparents have in one subsystem are more likely to affect their perceptions in the other subsystem' (Fine & Kurdek, 1995, p.221). We saw earlier (refer to Chapter

2, pp.22-29) how parental perceptions affect the performance of parents. We have now observed further links between parents' marital satisfaction, parental perceptions and parenting behaviours. It is crucial for parents in stepfamilies to find ways to satisfy themselves as married couples and also to let the children know that their parents have their own needs. If couples have satisfying marital relationships, it is more likely that they will function better as parents. The different needs of the family members will be examined in the section on 'the negotiation of different developmental needs for family members' (p.180).

Secondly, Margolin (1981) stated that problems with children often concur at the same time as marital problems: 'when problems arise in the stepparent-stepchild relationship, stepparents may partially attribute these difficulties to action (or inaction) by the biological parent' and 'stepparents are likely to believe that there is a link between marital difficulties and problems in their relationship with their stepchild' (Fine & Kurdek, 1995, p.221). From these findings we should note the influence of the perceptions stepparents have of their spouses' involvement in parenting. If they perceive that their spouses are not involved in the way they expected, they may feel disappointed and their marital relationships may be negatively affected. Moreover, stepchildren may be caught up in the marital conflicts and scapegoated for causing the marital problems. This may result in difficulties in building stepparent-stepchild relationships.

Thirdly, parents or stepparents who had previously been divorced wanted better marital and family lives, and those who were ambivalent about remarriage were fearful of a second failure. Their wishes and fears created tension in their marital relationship which, in turn, affected the performance on their parenting duties. They were anxious that they would not be 'good husbands or wives' and therefore, worked hard to establish couple bonds because they did not want to fail in their marriages again. They could not, however, invest equal energy and time in building parent-child relationships. and, therefore, their parenting behaviours were likely to be affected.

Fourthly, Chinese families are surrounded by networks of relatives which can be a source of support or a cause of stress for the couples in stepfamilies. They may offer help with child care, but they have unresolved feelings from the past which have affected the building of couple bond. The stepparents in this study usually felt isolated from the 'insiders' and some felt that their spouses sided with their kin. This point will be further explored in latter parts of this chapter (pp.186-204).

Lastly, it is important to note the feelings of the children when they witness the couple bond being built. When stepfamilies are newly formed, attention may focus on how the couple resolve their feelings from the past and how they deal with those arising from building new marital and family relationships. Biological children and stepchildren may be ignored because their parents are playing major roles in the family and have themselves taken considerable time to deal with their feelings and changes. When they observe their parents being 'taken over' by their new parents, they may feel upset that their biological parents live away from them and resentful that their biological parents have let their other parent behind. The perceptions of the children that a 'husband and wife should not be split', and the 'parent currently living with me is being disloyal to his/her spouse', may affect couple bonding and the building of stepparent-stepchild relationships if the stepchildren's feelings of 'shared history' are too strong to allow enough room for making a new history.

The Negotiation of Different Developmental Needs for Family Members

Different members of a stepfamily varying needs depending upon their life experiences and age. Their needs may differ depending on what unfulfilled tasks or unsatisfied needs from the past have been brought into the newly formed family. In the following I shall describe the needs of the members of stepfamilies, and the impact that meeting or failing to meet these needs has on parenting behaviours.

The Needs of Family Members in Stepfamilies

The husbands of stepmothers wanted relief from their child care responsibilities   As all the husbands of the ten stepmothers worked, they needed help with child care when their former wives died or departed. This help was offered to them by their paternal kin, mainly their parents. They were concerned that the child care responsibility should not permanently rest upon the shoulders of their ageing parents, and thought about obtaining someone who could take over these duties. They considered remarriage. The stepmothers claimed that the prime reason for their husbands' decision to remarry was this practical consideration of child-care. The following are some examples. Mrs. Ho recalled what her husband said whilst they were on a date:

> While we were talking, I felt sorry for him...he asked me to take her [his daughter] out...he said if I didn't help him, his daughter would have to be sent to his elder sister who was then working as a live-in maid. (M01(1),5)

Another stepmother, Mrs. Chan, also reported:

> Why did he want to marry so soon? His son was small then, and he thought that when he grew older, he would not accept a new mother as easily. (M04(1),10)

Another stepmother, Mrs. Lau, also felt that her husband married her more because he wanted someone to take care of his son than because he wanted a wife:

> I know he wanted someone to take care of his son, rather than wanting a wife. I think that way. He gave me that impression...for him, he just wanted a family, and someone to take care of his son. (M03(2),24)

The husbands of the stepmothers were not actively involve in family activities
As pointed out at the beginning of this Chapter (p.147), the spouses of these stepmothers were in their mid 30s to mid 40s. The spouses were middle-aged men and, because their work was demanding, they needed rest and participated little in family activities, either at home or on outings. For example, Mrs. Lau reported:

> He likes sleeping. He pays little attention to things. (M03(3),14)

Her husband had to travel between Hong Kong and Mainland China for his work. He only had Sundays off and spent them resting at home.

Another stepmother, Mrs. Lee, also described a similar pattern. She said:

> When he has time, he prefers to go into our bedroom to watch T.V. ...he expects me to watch T.V. with him. (M06(2),28)

Another stepmother Mrs. Lam noted that her husband did not like to go out on Sundays which were his only days off. She said:

> He doesn't like eating out...when he is home, he likes to heat up the dish and rice from the night before. I take the kids out, and he repairs the electronic appliances. (M05(3),8)

Stepmothers were older than average when they married   Many of the stepmothers in this study married later than did other women who married for the first time. They had clear life goals and perceived themselves as having a good job and high pay. They found more satisfaction at work than in doing household chores and taking up child care responsibilities. They were ambivalent about taking on child care roles but felt pressure from their families to find a mate before it was too late. Mrs. Lam, who married at 40, told me:

> He hoped that I would marry him...so I thought, I am older and am not like females in their 20s who would be cheated by men...maybe that was a stage of life. If I got married, my mother would not have to worry about me. (M05(1),6)

She explained further:

> ...everyone reaches a certain stage in life. I had reached this step. Maybe it is because I have older generation at home, and I don't want them to worry about me and say, 'Why has she still not married? Everyone is getting married, why not her?' I don't want them to worry about me. (M05(2),4)

Another stepmother, Mrs. Ho, reported that she lived a carefree life and did not want to marry too soon:

> I had never married before. I liked travelling and I was independent...before I met my husband, another man also wanted to date me. I never wanted to settle down then...I met him when I was over 30. I did not think of marriage at that time, I liked to be free.... (M01(1),22)

184

Career women do not easily give up their career for marriage. Another stepmother, Mrs. Chan, told me about her struggle:

> I had my career, and a carefree life. I went on a trip every year, and there was no need to ask for anyone else's permission. Why should I be bound by a family? If I wanted to go on holiday, I took one and then went back to work. I have done this many years and I enjoyed this. (M08(3),2)

She married her husband when she was 41 years old and she recalled that people were pleased that she had found a mate at that age:

> They were happy for me that I could marry at this age and find someone nice. We are similar in age, and there is no big age gap...they think it is good to have a nice husband, who has a good income, a maid, and there is no need to do housework. (M08(3),30)

Stepmothers would like to see their role performances recognized
Stepmothers have various roles to play; the main ones are the roles of wife and mother. They are often over-loaded by these roles (refer to Chapter 2, pp.22-25). The stepmothers I interviewed were aged in their mid 30s to mid 40s, which is a time when career women are working hard for advancement, and housewives are busy managing their school-age children and responding to their needs as they grow. Those women who held full time jobs and were also responsible for child care and housework after office hours were thus doubly loaded. I shall give some examples below to illustrate the fact that these overloaded stepmothers wanted recognition for their hard work, but they were rarely rewarded. Mrs. Chan reported:

> At first I thought I only had to treat him well. I thought it was very simple, but it ended up being...very difficult. Sometimes it is not a matter of one just treating others well and behaving according to one's conscience, which makes one feel good. Sometimes this is not the case. One could feel bad too. In this process, however, if one walks alone, one finds it difficult to take; it requires your husband to walk with you to make it better. (M04(2),13)

185

She further expressed:

> I was very unhappy. I worked hard and was not appreciated. I should not have done it in the first place. (M04(2),18)

Another stepmother, Mrs. Chan, also felt that her hard work was not recognized and she was frustrated. She said:

> Nowadays kids are difficult to teach and manage, and my role makes these tasks more difficult. I feel that. Is my existence necessary or not? I have mixed feelings. I think...I ask myself, am I married to my partner, or to the whole family? ....when I mentioned the incident [the misbehaviour of her stepchild] to him, he made no response, no facial expression...whether he was happy or not, he would not show any response. (M08(2),19)

Another stepmother, Mrs. Lau, also voiced her feelings about the failure to recognize her needs:

> My husband does not recognize how well I treat his son. He thinks I should treat his stepson well...this is very difficult to tolerate. I can accept his son, but his son does not accept me, but my husband does not consider it from my angle...if I have done something wrong, he doesn't give me encouragement, he should at least love me, so that I can love his son more. I need to be given more encouragement...He never says, 'You are feeling miserable, I know how difficult it is for you to take all this.' He doesn't encourage me or say nice things. He never does. (M03(1),28)

Common needs of stepchildren: they wished to be loved but had difficulties building up close relationships with their stepmothers The social workers and teachers perceived that younger stepchildren accepted a substitute parental figure more easily because their basic needs could be satisfied more readily than their other needs by relating to a replacement parent. Older children had difficulties relating to stepparents, but they had social outlets to meet the needs which were not met at home (refer to Chapter 5, p.132). An examination of stepmothers' reports show that the common need of stepchildren was identified to be loved, but they had difficulties building

186

close relationships with their stepmothers. The following are some illustrations. When asked about whether her stepson wanted to be close to her, Mrs. Lau said: 'He would. In fact he likes to be close to me, as does his younger brother'. She noted his ambivalence to physical proximity: 'When he was little, he would avoid me by pulling his body away. When he took initiative to be physically close to me, he was afraid that I wouldn't accept him, and he was uneasy. He is older now. He won't draw close to me physically. We mutually reject each other' (M03(2),4).

Another stepmother, Mrs. Lee, observed that her stepson wanted to be close to her but felt that he would not be accepted. She said:

He always wants to hold my hand, I thought, 'You hold me because you want me to buy things for you'. (M06(1),25)

According to this stepmother, her stepson felt he was an outsider:

If he goes out with me, he likes to hold my hand. But when his father is present, he automatically walks behind us, just to follow me and his father. (M06(2),5)

Mrs. Lau's stepson felt intense loss after his biological mother suddenly disappeared from his life without saying goodbye to him probably. This happened when the stepson was seven or eight years old. When he reached 16, he still had not recovered from the emotional wound. According to Mrs. Lau, he had become withdrawn from family relationships and was unable to accept a new mother in his life. Neither the stepson's need to be mothered nor the stepmother's needs to mother were satisfied. Mrs. Lau noted:

I treat him much better than his own mother did, but my reward is that nobody thinks that I am treating him well, including the child himself, he feels that his mother is better than me. (M09(2),3)

The Impact of Need-fulfilment on Parents and Children and Parenting Behaviours in Stepfamilies

Different family members have different needs. If the needs of parents and children in stepfamilies are denied, parent-child relationship problems may develop and parenting performance is affected.

Firstly, working women are ambivalent about taking the role of a career woman or that of a child-carer/housekeeper. Many of these stepmothers had gone through a period of ambivalence in making the decision about which role to take. In fact, many of them had to take up dual roles. These women married late and had worked for many years, and they had, therefore, developed individual-oriented values, such as personal satisfaction and financial independence from their spouses. These values had affected how they perceived their roles and their role performance. For example, they may put their careers higher on their list of priorities and if they are frustrated in child care and housekeeping, they may seek satisfaction from their work outside their families rather than by making more effort to improve their parenting performance.

Secondly, conflicts in the needs of husbands and wives were noted. Both of them were mature adults or in middle age. Men wished to have a harmonious family managed by their wives, with child care responsibilities left in the hands of loving and caring mothers. Women who married late hoped to have a loving partner with whom they could walk together on the life path. They wished to be loved because it had taken them a long time to find their spouses. Therefore, conflicts arose because men wanted 'care' while women wanted 'love'. As these needs may be due to a difference in expectations to start off with, they are unlikely to be satisfied in practice. The frustration caused by the failure to fulfil these needs will affect their parenting behaviours. Figure 6.2 below illustrates their expectations.

Figure 6.2
The Expectations Couples Have of
Marriage and Family Life in Stepfamilies

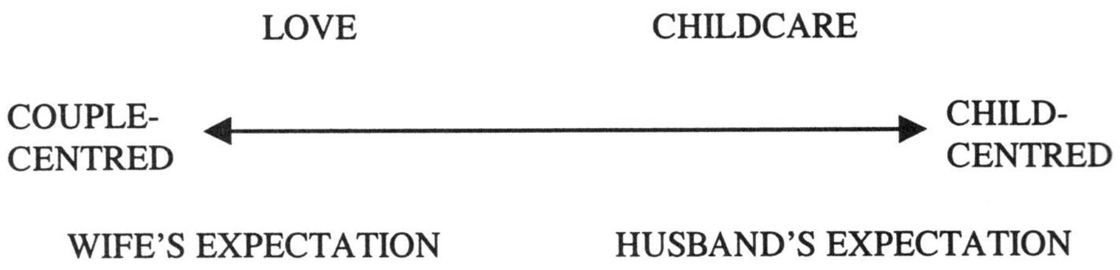

LOVE   CHILDCARE

COUPLE-   ◄————————————►   CHILD-
CENTRED   CENTRED

WIFE'S EXPECTATION   HUSBAND'S EXPECTATION

Thirdly, the stepmothers had problems of role strain because they felt that they were overloaded with responsibilities. There were troubles arising from family dynamics which added further difficulties to their lives and they had to cope with many challenges, therefore, they might not have the energy to develop parenting skills and to enhance parent-child relationships.

Fourthly, the children in these stepfamilies had the common basic needs to be loved and taken care of, which is the same for all children. Their turbulent experience in life which were brought about by loss of a parent or parental divorce, meant that they had difficulties in building trusting relationships with their stepmothers.

Fifthly, a distinction should be drawn between the difficulties arising from the formation of a new family with the mixture of old and new 'cultures' and those resulting from normative development in a stage of life. For example, the problems of teenagers in relating to their stepmothers can be explained as the difficulty every family member experiences when a family is undergoing reorganization and reconstitution, or as a result of the difficulties every child has to tackle during adolescence, or as a combination of the two.

Equity and Authority in Stepfamilies

The concepts of equity and authority have been discussed in Chapter 2 (pp. 38-44). There are two major areas relating to equity in stepfamilies which warrant closer examination. They are: the dividing of parental tasks between couples, and parental treatment of their biological children and stepchildren.

Equity in Stepfamilies

Dividing parenting and housekeeping tasks: stepmothers do not see 'fair play' Stepmothers were often overloaded with work in child care and housekeeping. A typical example is the heavily loaded stepmother (a real case) described in vignette #4 (Appendix 5A) in the interview guide for teachers and social workers. Mrs. Lau had to live with the relatives of her husband and cook for a large number of them every night; one of the paternal relatives even expected her to include her maid in their 'daily family supper (M09(1),9).

189

The stepmother I have described above was a full time housewife and she felt overloaded, therefore, Mrs. Chung, who took up dual roles, felt more pressurize both at work and at home. As she worked as an insurance agent, she worked long and irregular hours and some days she did not return home until almost mid-night. She did ask her husband to involve himself more in child management. She said to him: 'I am very busy at work. Not only should I should play a part in the kids' lives, you must also.' She thought that she had contributed to the passive involvement of her husband by '...taking up too many duties in the past. I think I have made him less responsible in the family. I think I should let him take over some of the duties' (M07(2),20).

Mrs. Lee was another career woman who worked long hours and had to support her stepfamily financially. Her husband did not earn enough money to pay the family's monthly expenses. She said that she had complied with her mother's suggestion to marry a divorcee who had a child so that the couple's background would be the same and 'equal'; she sighed:

So I did what she [her mother] asked. But it won't work if we depend on one parent only. He doesn't pay much attention to his son, he relies on me to do everything and he doesn't support me, so problems arise...his parents, and friends don't understand. Problems arise. (M06(1),28)

Parenting a biological child and a stepchild: stepmothers want to be fair but blood is thicker than water   Some stepmothers believe in instant love and that if they work harder on building stepparent-stepchild relationships, eventually there will be desirable outcomes (refer to Visher & Visher 'myths of stepfamilies' in Chapter 2, p.21). These stepmothers had had good intentions to parent during the formative stage when stepfamilies were built. They had, however, under-estimated the difficulties they would encounter in building stepparent-stepchild relationships and they were frustrated and felt that there was difference between rearing someone else's child and rearing one's own: 'blood is thicker than water'. The following are some examples to illustrate this. Mrs. Lee told me that she felt sorry for her stepson but admitted that she could not be close to him. She said:

It's sad if one doesn't have a mother. I pity him [her stepson]...but I can't hug or kiss him in a genuine way. Although he does things well, I can't show affection such as 'You are good, you are smart'. For my own children, however, I can do so naturally. When they are ill, I hug them, but I can't hug him [her stepson], although I wish I could... (M06(1),24).

She admitted:

I think it is difficult to feel like a biological mother, it can't be that way. Stepmother is just a name, and one's attitudes towards one's own son and towards him [her stepson] are different. Even if one doesn't have children but has some later, and the children are from the same father, one still would favour one child against the other. Favouritism makes a big difference. Children will be treated differently. I can honestly say that, I treat my own son better than I treat his son. (M06(1),17)

Mrs. Lau also reported that she treated her stepson differently to her own children. She admitted:

I can behave intimately when playing with my kids...I can hug and kiss them, the way I want to. But I don't behave like that with my stepson. When he was little, I held his hand on outings...other than that, I did not relate to him intimately. With my children, I can hug, and tickle them...there are two different ways. (M09(3),19)

Another stepmother, Mrs. Lau, was also aware that she treated her own son and her stepson differently. She told me:

Oh yes, they are somewhat different. I don't care about being criticized for favouritism...After I spanked my own son, I would say nicely to him, 'Do you think you were right?' Then I would kiss him. I wouldn't do this to my older son [her stepson]. When he was little, I didn't do that either. I don't know why, I rejected him, and he rejected me. (M03(1),15)

There are other examples which show that stepmothers favoured their own children. For instance, Mrs. Ho was very caring and loving to her pre-school age son but was very harsh and demanding to her stepdaughter (M01); Mrs. Lam was lenient to her infant son and was very strict and overly demanding to her stepdaughter (M05).

191

There was one exception. Mrs. Lau (M09) was frustrated at not being given the chance to care for her stepson, who had rejected her since his biological mother had disappeared without saying goodbye. Mrs. Lau changed her focus to become extremely harsh and demanding to her own daughter, to the point that she needed help from a child protection agency. She later came to realize that she wanted to prove to the paternal kin that she was able to parent and that her daughter achieved more than her stepson:

> I feel that it is unfair. I treat him [her stepson] so well. I think: 'I do everything for you [her husband], but in the end I don't come first in your heart. I am not regarded the second either. I am not satisfied, I want to be the first.' Maybe I like to win, or otherwise I would not have forced my daughter to win, or forced her to act like that. I 'want to win all the time' (好勝). I think: 'you don't teach your son very well, I shall teach my daughter so she will be better than your son.' I want to compete. (M09(3),40)

Authority in Stepfamilies

It has been suggested that remarried men give in to their wives more when there are disputes (refer to Chapter 2, pp.42-44), but that does not mean that wives have authority in stepfamilies. From the data I collected, five out of the ten stepmothers' fathers-in-law had died, and one father-in-law was living in Beijing. Three fathers-in-law were in Hong Kong, but they were not living with the stepfamilies, and were not involved in the child care of their grandchildren. Only one father-in-law was living with the stepfamily (M04), and he helped in child care and cooking, as reported by the stepmother, it was his wife who interfered in child management and was manipulative, causing conflicts in the family. It is obvious that, mothers-in-law have authority; and after a divorce, non-custodial biological parents often lose their authority over parenting decisions. The following examples illustrate these points.

The mothers-in-law of the stepmothers claim, 'I am powerful' Mrs. Chan lived with her parents-in-law. She married Mr. Chan two years after the death of his wife and became the stepmother of a pre-school age stepson. According to her, her mother-in-law bossed her around in the house; for example, she would make a suggestion and expect Mrs. Chan to carry it out

192

without considering whether the timing was right or whether she was fit to do so. Mrs. Chan recalled that one day she felt ill with morning sickness not long after she had discovered she was pregnant with her younger son, but her mother-in-law gave her an order:

> My mother-in-law said that her grandson wanted to go to the Ocean Park, and my brother-in-law had suggested that we went...she said to me, 'Today you will go to Ocean Park with John.' She did not ask for my opinion. She decided. (M04(2),6)

Another incident occurred during a meal time. She recalled:

> My mother-in-law said, 'Ah So [the named used by Chinese parents-in-law to address a daughter-in-law], get him [the stepson of the informant] some fish.' I picked some for him, but he looked at it as if it were poison. He wanted to cry. My mother-in-law then said, 'Oh, there is no need to eat it. Don't eat it.' How did I feel? One wants to catch a thief, and then one wants to let the thief go. I was very unhappy. (M04(2), p.18)

Another stepmother, Mrs. Ho, reported that her mother-in-law always caused trouble in the family. She recalled what her mother-in-law said: I like to quarrel, and I like to do what I like. I'm one of the owners of this flat, your name is not included (M01(1),8). Once she wanted to move back to live with Mrs. Ho's family. She said to her son, 'When I move back, ask Ah Ling [the informant's first name] not to work and to take full care of me' (M01(1),10).

Mrs. Lau's husband was grateful to his mother for taking care of his son during his divorce. He felt that he owed her a lot. His mother was given power. Mrs. Lau told me:

> He [her husband] treats his mother very well. She took care of his son and he would not want to do anything against her will. He also feels that if he doesn't treat him [his son] well, his mother would blame him. (M09(1),16)

She further explained to me how powerless she was in parenting her stepson:

I am only his mother in name. I am not given the chance to discipline him. Not only can I not punish him, but I am not expected to confront him when he does something wrong. (M09(3),6)

Biological parents who were unfaithful should be out of sight forever When biological parents lose the right to custody of the child, they may also lose the power to negotiate for involvement in decision-making for the child. Wives who are divorced from their husbands due to their infidelity find that their power is further taken away because the older generation usually consider their behaviour to be immoral and unacceptable. They are unlikely to be allowed to maintain contact with their child(ren). Six out of the seven divorces which were experienced by the husbands of the stepmothers in this study were due to their wife's adultery. The reactions of the family members were intensively negative and the non-custodial mothers were not welcome to visit or telephone their children. The attitudes of the paternal kin were so negative that most of these mothers were discouraged from visiting their children even though they had visiting rights. They stopped visiting a short while after the divorce (M03, M05, M06, M09, M010). The following is an example to illustrate this.

Mrs. Lam met her husband's former wife on a ferry and the latter requested an arrangement to be made so that she could see her two sons. Mrs. Lam felt sorry for the woman and thought it was a pity that the biological mother and her son could not meet. Her husband knew about the plan and forbode her from arranging any contact between his ex-wife and his sons. She told me:

> She [her husband's ex-wife] discussed it with me over the phone. I consented to her request of taking her sons on outings, but my husband would not allow it. He said she was tricky. He said if something happened to his sons, he would not forgive me for the rest of his life (M010(1),12).

Mr. Lam was afraid that his ex-wife would take his sons away and make them live with a stepfather.

There are several points which are important to note. First, inequity in the division of labour can lead to role strain and the development of negative feelings. In the stepfamilies under study, the husbands of the stepmothers were not actively involved in child management and housekeeping. The stepmothers usually had dual roles. Irrespective of whether the stepmothers had the resources or not, they had to do more housework than their husbands. This is different from the theory of the 'Relative Resources Model' (refer to Chapter 2, p.39) which suggested that the one who has greater resources or power in a family is given a lesser load. Although some of the women in these stepfamilies did bring in a good family income (M05, M06, M07), they did not have the power to decide to take fewer tasks. Therefore, it seems that the Ideology Model (refer to Chapter 2, pp.39-40) can explain the observations better. It is the beliefs of people that determine how labour is divided in these stepfamilies. According to Chinese cultural values, women are supposed to take heavier child care and housekeeping responsibilities, and this rules out the possibility of some women having to work outside the family, and they also have less time for fulfilling those tasks. Moreover, although it is noted that these stepmothers were frustrated because their hard work was not recognized, it seems to fit with the traditional thought on the gender-role division of labour, as women are expected to do these tasks, people around them assumed that they would do them, without considering their feelings towards this overwork.

Secondly, in Chinese families, it is a fundamental family belief that it is important to carry on the family name of the paternal line. In the stepfamilies, members have to face changes and challenges when the family is undergoing reorganization and they undergo a process of sorting out the membership into the 'insiders' or 'outsiders' in order to maintain the status quo. In Chinese stepfamilies, 'insiders' are the blood-tie members and males are more important than females. They exclude the outsiders for fearing of contaminating the 'blood'. Stepparents and stepchildren are the 'outsiders' and they are psychologically and physically-rejected.

Thirdly, the mothers-in-law are the people with power in stepfamilies. Most of them were widows. As noted by Chao (1983), 'the emotional relationship of mother and son is threatened when he marries. It often occurs that the mother becomes jealous of the young wife because the latter takes away the attachment of the son; it is jealousy that gives rise to difficulties between mother and daughter-in-law. There is a common saying: "A son is lost when he is married"'. (Chao, 1983, p.54). When a woman has lost her husband, she also 'loses' her son when he is married. When the son remarries, the mother 'loses' her son a second time, which intensifies her feelings of loss and this may lead to the rejection of her second daughter-in-law. In addition, the power of mothers-in-law is further strengthened if they had offered to assist with child care during their son's divorce. In order to return the favour, the sons would allow their mothers to retain a powerful position, even after the new families are formed.

Lastly, according to the seven grounds for divorce in traditional Chinese culture, adultery is the most offensive kind of behaviour and brings great disgrace to a family. In contemporary divorce law, no-fault divorce is advocated, but the stigma brought by the adultery of an unfaithful wife is still strong. They are not welcome to continue their visits to their biological children. It seems that exclusive parenting is the pattern chosen by most of the stepfamilies if the former marriages were dissolved due to adultery. In so-doing, they may hope to lessen the psychological and emotional pain according to the myth, 'out of sight, out of mind'.

From the above discussion we can see that stepmothers are loaded with parental and household duties; the beliefs and practices leading to the different treatment of biological children and stepchildren; the dominance of mothers-in-law; and the exclusion of non-custodial biological mothers from parenting are all factors affecting parenting in stepfamilies. Role strain leads to frustration; favouritism leads to different approaches to child management'; power struggles create conflicts; and feelings of separation cause psychological barriers to accepting new relationships. These will affect parenting functions and performance in stepfamilies.

Communication and Conflict Management in Stepfamilies

The following will examine how members of stepfamilies communicate and how conflicts are resolved in the stepfamilies studied. The last part will focus on the impact of communication and conflict management on parenting behaviours in stepfamilies.

It is through communication that people get to understand each other and interaction is facilitated. Communication is affected by a person's perception because, following the receipt of a message, he/she is likely to interpret messages guided by his/her perceptions which, in turn, affect the actions he/she will take.

Communication between the couples: expectations and conflicts   From the information reported by the stepmothers, we know that they tended to romanticize their marital relationships (refer to earlier section of this chapter on p.171). It is common to observe from the data that wives wished that even if their husbands could not show them much affection or love, they could, at least, talk to them and be an understanding listener. Their husbands seemed to be too tired after work and they just hoped that their wives would maintain a harmonious family atmosphere and join them in quiet past-times. These couples had something in common: they both wanted understanding from each other, but they expected this to be achieved in different ways. The following are some examples.

In the case of Mrs.Lau, her husband worked in Mainland China most time of the week, and she felt burdened and unsupported during his absence. When he was at home, she wished that he would talk to her about the problems brought about by stepparenting. However, Mrs. Lau reported:

> He let me have the sole responsibility in parenting. When I used the wrong approach, he didn't comment.... (M03(1),14)

She expressed her feelings:

> He doesn't speak out...he would not say, 'You are miserable, I know how difficult it is for you to do all this'. (M03(1),28)

She wished to be understood and comforted.

Another stepmother, Mrs. Lee, reported the difference in the expectations of her and her husband because they did not communicate well and frequently enough. She said:

We don't have time to relate to each other. I expect him to get involved with everybody in the family, and then I would feel more at ease. The only time when all the family members are there is meal times. I love to talk about our lives but he doesn't. He likes watching T.V. I object to that and I scold him. Everybody becomes quiet. He walks away. He can't make a good family atmosphere. It is so quiet at meal times. I don't like it. (M06(2),29)

She further added:

He expects me to watch T.V. with him...after the kids have gone to bed, he is asleep and I can't talk to him about anything. (M06(2),28)

Mrs. Lam told me that her husband needed to travel daily to a city on the border of Mainland China and Hong Kong and he was exhausted by the time he returned home. She said:

He is busy, or I am busy. When he returns home on Sunday, he needs rest, he doesn't want go anywhere...so at the weekend he rests, I may go out with children...we don't have a 'world for two' since we were married. Very rarely. Only when they [the kids] are asleep, we may chat for a while. (M05(2),17)

Another stepmother, Mrs. Chung, said that her husband was 'pragmatic', he did not feel comfortable 'sharing' and saw 'sharing' as a waste of time (M07(3),20). She added: He won't share his inner world with others. He doesn't want others to understand what he thinks....'. She said her husband was aware of his communication pattern which covered his feelings. He said to his wife at bedtime: 'In fact, I don't have a loving heart'. His wife responded, 'You are not without it, you just hide it deep inside.' (M07(3),21)

Parent-child communication: stepmothers felt rejected and the biological fathers were not skillful Many stepmothers discussed their attempts to build relationships with their stepchildren but the responses they received were rather apathetic, if not rejecting. For example, Mrs. Chung found that her stepdaughter was quite an introverted person, she seldom initiated talk and responded only when spoken to. She reported:

The most difficult problem I faced in my role as a stepmother is the feeling that I can't help her [her stepdaughter] to open up...she has a psychological barrier. If she opens up a little, it will be better for both of us. (M07(2),16)

Other examples reveal the same concern. Mrs Lam's stepsons did not greet her until six months after the stepfamily was formed (M010); Mrs. Ho noted that her stepdaughter only liked the attention of her father (M01). The stepmothers were frustrated by such responses. The following is an example given by Mrs. Lau:

If I talk to him [her stepson] about things concerning him, he does not respond and I lose interest. I am not a patient person by nature...if he drags on talking, I will lose interest in carrying on a conversation with him. (M03(1),6)

The stepmothers noted that the fathers who were busy at work and had limited time, lacked the skills to communicate with their children. The patterns of communication affected the quality of parent-child interaction and parenting behaviours. For example, Mrs. Lau said distancing of parent-child relationship had affected father-son communication. she reported:

He [her stepson] can't communicate with his father. It is not because they are not on the same key [she meant they are not in conflict with each other], but they don't talk on the same level. When his father sees him, he does not talk to him, he acts the same when he sees his father. They are always like that. (M03(1),6)

Mrs. Lau also noted that the father and son in her family communicated badly. She reported:

He [her stepson] doesn't speak to him [father]. He walks out as if he is a stranger...in fact, at heart his father is very good to him [his son], but he would not greet him [his son] without him doing so first. And he [father] is very disappointed in him [his son] now. (M09(3),12)

Mrs. Lee, a remarried stepmother, did not stop her son from contacting his biological father, but her son did not want to communicate with him:

> My son always wants my attention. It is not like that between my son and his father...I asked my son why he didn't telephone his dad, he said, 'He would scold me'. In his mind, his daddy would always scold him. In fact, he would. His father was fierce to him. (M07(2),20)

Another stepmother, Mrs. Lee, said her husband did not easily show his feelings and was uneasy about showing affection openly. She reported:

> In fact, I know my husband loves his own son better. It is just that he can't communicate his feeling so other people would think that he loves his elder son better. I think he does not want to let his own son know that he loves and cares about him. (M06(3),9)

Conflict Management in Stepfamilies

Conflicts in the stepfamilies I studied arose mainly during child management. Firstly I will examine parent-child conflicts, and then conflicts between siblings and between stepmothers and their in-laws, and finally the husbands' role in conflict management will be explored.

Stepmother-stepchild conflicts and resolutions   The main sources of conflicts were the monitoring of stepchildren's school performance, their behaviour and rivalry between siblings. Stepmothers expected their children and stepchildren to do well at school and they saw this as their major parenting task (M01, M03, M04, M05, M06, M07). There were three stepmothers who had high expectations of the performance of their stepdaughters (M01, M05) and of their own daughter (M09). It was usually over a disagreement on child management in relation to academic performance that marital conflicts arose:
In the case of Mrs. Ho, she demanded that her stepdaughter finish her homework before she was allowed to go to bed. In this situation, her husband would do some of the homework for his daughter. Mrs. Ho described the conflict:

The situation was not easy for me to control. My husband always protects her, if not for that, I would not have questioned her as if we were in a court room. I wanted a reason from her. I would not easily lay a hand on her at the beginning, but if the two adults did not agree and one was prohibiting the other from hitting her [the stepdaughter], it would make the other adult very angry, and disciplining action had to be taken. (M01(3),10)

Mrs. Ho would demand her stepdaughter's compliance and she expected her husband to deal with the conflict with her as a team. She said:

If I asked her [the stepdaughter] something and she answered at once, I would not be angry. I think parents have to teach their children, and one parent should act as the nice one while the other acts as the disciplinarian. I think this is the way. (M01(3),10-11)

Mrs. Ho thought the best way was for her husband to complement her role. Mrs. Lam was very strict with her stepdaughter, who had to concentrate on finishing her homework and was very rarely allowed to watch television even after she had completed all her assignments. She was then told to practise the piano. Once her father let her go to a library after her school work was complete but Mrs. Lam found out about it and was angry. She thought her stepdaughter should stay at home to revise what had been taught in class. Her husband felt sorry for his daughter and tried to reason with his wife but Mrs. Lam felt:

My husband thought I was too strict with her for her age. He thought, 'Why don't you care about her and be gentle to her. Why do you teach her in such a strong and strict way?' He thought about me like this. I knew it but I said nothing. I am a person with a strong character, so I don't give up. I don't mind if you think I'm wrong. (M05(1),8)

Mrs. Lam did not want to compromise with her husband. She suggested child management method to her husband and expected him to follow. She asserted:

Men are like that. They don't teach children properly, and they would avoid troubles by letting them have whatever they requested. But they have not thought of the great influence this has on them [children]. So I won't let her have her own way, or stop being strict with her. I won't. I don't care if I don't notice the wrongs in her behaviour, but if I do notice, I can't spoil her by letting them pass. (M05(2),1)

Because of Mrs. Lam's strong determination to manage her stepdaughter in that way, Mr. Lam avoided confrontation and was withdrawn in his parenting role.

Mrs. Lau had a different story. She was upset by her paternal kin not allowing her to manage her stepson and she wanted to prove that she could do better in parenting her daughter. She was overly demanding of her own daughter:

I pressurized her to do her homework, I felt that I could not afford to lose when competing with others. I wanted her to perform better than my stepson. I asked her to study all the time. She might have developed resistance to study. (M09(2),31)

Mrs. Lau was so demanding on her own daughter that Mr. Lau intervened in the hope of protecting his daughter. Mrs. Lau reported:

My husband is a gentle person, and he won't get irritated easily; he is much better tempered than me. In the past I spanked and scolded my daughter, and he was so much on her side that he physically fought with me. He wanted to stop me from losing control, I would,…after all, the kid was innocent. (M09(3),24)

On the other hand, Mrs. Lau's husband would not show his affection to his son from his previous marriage because he was afraid that if he showed his love to his son, it would intensify his wife's jealousy and she would further push their daughter to work hard and excel. Mrs. Lau noted the way her husband dealt with the conflict:

He pretended that he was not good to his son when I was there. When I was not at home, he would treat him well. You know what? On the other hand, when his son was not there, he treated me very nicely, but when the kid [her stepson] was there, he would not treat me as well. He acted that way for the sake of 'avoiding the heavy but opting for the light'

[which means he avoided conflicts] (避重就輕), and he did not want us
to be jealous of each other. (M09(3),5)

The other kind of parent-child conflicts arose from concerns about the
behaviour of the stepchildren. For example, Mrs. Chan was concerned that
her stepchildren were not well-mannered; her husband did not feel that that
should matter. She said:

> I am strict, and I am serious about teaching them [her stepchildren].
> They are not well-mannered. I have the responsibility of pointing this out
> to them. If they are not told, they don't know that it is wrong. My
> husband feels that it does not matter, and that they only do so 'naturally,
> with no intention to upset me'. They have not made big mistakes and
> kids are like that. (M08(2),19)

So the method she chose was tolerance when facing conflicts arising from
parent-child conflicts:

> I must tolerate this for the time being. I want to throw a temper when I
> am frustrated or I am not happy, but then I think, I must take it easy... I
> suppress my feelings and say to myself that I can't go on like that. There
> is conflict. (M08(2),19)

Mrs. Lau's stepson lived with the family of her husband's elder brother
after his parents' divorce. The child was used to their house rules and their
way of life there. Mrs. Lau did not approve of these when she took over the
mothering role. She was concerned about her stepson's inability to respond
to limit-setting. She said:

> Their family is so different from ours: we are two different families.
> We have different rules, and different personalities. They allow him to
> do whatever he likes. He does things as he likes. In this family, he is not
> allowed to and he has to abide by the rules of this family. He has to tidy
> up his things, be clean, study hard...I think my family is normal...it is
> hard for him to relate to me. (M03(1),11)

In order to deal with her stepson's defiance to limit-setting, she resorted to
physical punishment. She said:

I got irritated and spanked him. In my generation, a mother spanked her child. We were scared but were then tamed. I thought I should use the same method to teach him. (M03(1),12)

When asked about the response of her husband to the conflicts resulting from child disciplining, she said:

As I live with him [her husband] for longer, I begin to see that he doesn't know how to teach a kid. He let me take the sole responsibility for parenting. When I used the wrong approach, he didn't comment. If he were to pick on me, I may lose my temper at that moment but, after that, I would think and see my own mistake, I would then change. (M03(1),13)

But he never did.

In addition to parent-child conflicts due to behavioural problems of stepchildren, there were conflicts resulting from sibling rivalry. Mrs. Chui said that her stepson used to bully her own daughter from her last marriage because she had taken some parental love away from him. Mrs. Chui reported:

I knew clearly that he [her stepson] did not treat his stepsister [the informant's own daughter] well. He always acted like a fierce big brother...I find him difficult to teach. He waited until I left home before he beat her. Even if I was at home, he would ask to take her downstairs to buy things, and would beat her inside the lift, but stopped the beating when they stepped out of it. That's something one can't imagine. If I discovered his misdoing, he would beat her harder next time. (M02(3),23)

How should Mrs. Chui deal with this conflict between siblings? Mrs. Chui consoled her daughter and talked patiently to her stepson without blaming him. She recalled what she said to him:

If you do something also like that, your younger sister and brothers will leave you and you will be alone by yourself. What you have done is not what a big brother should do. A real big brother would not beat up his younger sister...because you call them your brother and sister, and you would not let others bully them, you yourself would not bully them yourself. You should try to care about them....

Then Mrs. Chui hit the main point which encouraged him to change his behaviour:

Your younger sister is no better off than you, you think that she has the 'whole mother', and you don't have one...in fact each of you has one parent, you are your father's son. She [his younger sister] does not have a wonderful life either. She has to share her mother with the other siblings in this family. She cannot have all of me. Even if she could have all of me, it depends on whether I decide to let that happen. If I did let her have me to herself, I would not be speaking to you like this today. (M02(3),24)

From an examination of the major management methods used by parents in stepfamilies to deal with parent-child conflicts, several methods were identified. For example, husbands were expected to complement the role of their wives and to deal with the conflict as a team (M01(3),10-11; M02(1),25); or to be a 'bridge' between the stepmother and her stepchild (M07(1),14); or to be the 'last resort' by using their authority to scare the stepchild about behaving undesirably (M06 (3), p.17).

Dealing with conflicts with in-laws: the husbands' role was crucial The second type of conflict in these stepfamilies was caused by disputes between parents-in-law and their daughters-in-law. As pointed out in the section on 'authority in stepfamilies' in this chapter (pp.189-191), it was not the fathers-in-law the contributors to family conflicts but their wives. The husbands of the stepmothers were usually caught in between, and they needed to take on the 'mediator' or 'peace-maker' role. The following are some examples:

Mrs. Lam married into a family in which the mother-in-law had been a widow since she was in her 40s. According to information reported, the mother-in-law was a very capable woman who had raised nine children on her own. Mrs. Lam found it difficult to meet her expectations when she married her son. She said: 'She is very tough. She is so hardworking. I can't work hard, and I can't bear frustrations. I get scolded and am picked upon. I had difficulty adjusting when I first married into this family' (M010(2),19). The mother-in-law called Mrs. Lam names. Mrs. Lam recalled: 'My husband always said to her, "Don't scold her"' (M010(1),6). The scolding stopped only after Mrs. Lam proved to her mother-in-law that she was hardworking.

Another stepmother, Mrs. Lau, had great conflicts with her mother-in-law and the paternal relatives. She noted that her widowed mother-in-law had difficulty accepting her because: 'she had many worries. She was afraid that her son would leave her and I would not treat her and her grandson well. She started to show her negative attitude towards me' (M09(1),12). The mother-in-law did not allow Mrs. Lau to manage her stepson, and at times she created both marital and parent-child conflicts. For example, the stepson asked for a television for his own use but the request was denied by his father, so he telephoned his paternal grandmother and said that he must have one. The grandmother asked her son to buy one for her grandson. It was difficult for Mrs. Lau's husband because he was caught in the middle. He knew that his wife would not agree to this unreasonable request but he found it difficult to say 'no' to his mother. He was a filial son and he was grateful for his mother's help with child care at his divorce. However, the conflicts had not really been resolved because whenever there was a conflict, the husband tended to abide by the wishes of his mother.

There were other mothers-in-law who created conflicts by their interference in child management and who clashed with their daughters-in-law, as in the cases of Mrs. Ho (M01), Mrs. Chui (M02), Mrs. Chan (M04), and Mrs. Lee (M06). Usually the daughters-in-law endured this and the husbands tended to side with their mothers at the time. Some consoled their wives afterwards, but the wives did not feel they were sufficiently supported. Only one daughter-in-law (M04) dared to speak up and was supported by her husband at the time of conflict.

The Impact of Problems of Communication and Conflict Management on Parenting Behaviours in Stepfamilies

The above raises several issues for discussion. Firstly, communication can take many forms. In Chinese families, as pointed out, it may be expressed differently to that in Western culture. However, it should be pointed out that although there are variations, there are similarities too. For example, hugging and kissing a child may not be the common expression of affection from a parent to a child in Chinese culture, but good food is regarded in many cultures as a way for a mother demonstrate her love and care for her children. In Chinese families good cooking is also seen as a way to show love and care to children, and this practice is stronger than in other cultures because not only does the provider of the food regards this an important way to convey a loving message, but the receiver also sees this as a way to return love and practise a filial act. It is evident that many adult married children would say: 'No matter how busy I am, I am going to my parents' home for supper, they will be happy to see me eating all the food they cook for me'. In the stepfamilies I studied, the mothers did not all use good cooking to show their love (except M06 & M010), but I noted that the parents in the stepfamilies followed the Chinese belief that there is 'no need to say it openly, just do it' or 'as long as I am good to someone, no need to show off one's effort by telling that person'. Their feelings for their loved ones were not explicitly shown as they did not see the need to mention it.

As described in the earlier section, stepmothers in this study were heavily loaded with responsibilities and they did not feel that their hard work was recognized. One of the major parenting tasks for many stepmothers was to pressurize their stepchildren to perform well at school. One may say that the competition-orientated education system in Hong Kong has put academic achievement at the top of parents' priority list. However, one should also look at other possible factors leading to this problem: stepmothers may find other parenting tasks, such as building up stepparent-stepchild relationships, or relationships with in-laws, more difficult than focusing upon a more concrete kind of task. Academic achievement can be measured and assessed more easily. This has become the top of the list of tasks to be accomplished by stepparents. It should be noted that if support and assistance were given to help stepparents to deal with the pressure and to build stepparent-stepchild relationships, they may not focus so much of their energy into pushing their children or stepchildren to excel in school work when it is unrealistic for them to expect this.

Conflicts are usually found between mothers-in-law and daughters-in-law and especially between widowed mothers-in-law and the stepmother daughters-in-law. It should be noted that women who have lost their husbands may find it difficult to accept that their sons have been taken away by a second woman. The mothers-in-law in this study had assisted their divorcee sons with child care and they expected the reciprocity of favour and wished to be included in the stepfamily. That seems to be the major reason leading to conflicts. It should also be noted that the influence of mothers-in-law was more intense if they were living in the stepfamilies. Those who had at one time lived with the stepfamilies but who had moved out had weakened their power to influence but they still had great influence upon the parenting practice in stepfamilies. Their methods were varied, e.g. dropping by without notice; sending orders over the telephone; making requests to stay with the family for a period of time, etc. The husbands of the stepmothers were regarded as mediators, but they did not live up to the expectations of their stepmother-wives. They were weak when negotiating with their mothers. Traditional Chinese values may have influenced how these sons handled conflicts between their mothers and wives. As pointed out by Chao (1983), 'to prefer one's wife or children to one's parents is a grave sin' (p.76).

Summary of the Chapter

In this chapter I presented a profile of stepmothers and their families. The parents in stepfamilies were middle aged and their family background ranged from working class to middle class. They had had rather difficult childhoods and turbulent experiences before their present marriage, but their lives continued to be hard after the stepfamilies were formed. They had had to adjust to their new families and to deal with many new and difficult challenges.

Most of the remarried men had not forgotten the pain experienced in their last marriage. Their emotional difficulties meant they did not find it easy to resolve their children's feelings of loss and separation. These two problems had added further tension to the marital relationship and stepparent-stepchild relationships. Parents-in-law and paternal kin were perceived by stepmothers as sources of conflict, especially when they indiscreetly intervened in child management situations. Stepmothers wished to be supported and comforted by their husbands during times of conflict and they hoped that their hard work in child care and housekeeping would be recognized; very few felt that their husband was understanding and caring. The above-mentioned problems are all inter-related.

7   Reflections on the Themes and the Issues

Introduction

In Chapters 2 and 3 the concepts relevant to parenting and stepfamilies from theoretical perspectives and in cultural contexts were discussed. In Chapters 5 and 6 I presented the findings of this study, extracted the significant points and addressed them under several themes. In what follows, I will reflect upon what appears to be the most important themes and issues in this study.

A Framework Developed from the Data Analysis for Reflection

Figure 7.1 (p.210) is based upon an analysis of the data. It summarizes the cultural values and factors which influence the quality of family life, the impact of competing values and the tensions which affect the structure and process of stepfamilies.

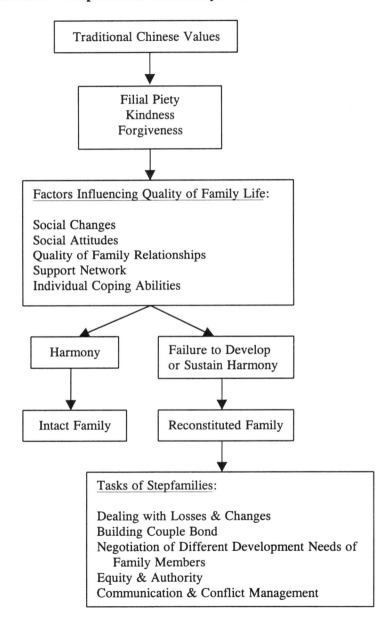

Figure 7.1
Framework Developed from Data Analysis for Reflection

Traditional Chinese Values

Filial Piety
Kindness
Forgiveness

Factors Influencing Quality of Family Life:

Social Changes
Social Attitudes
Quality of Family Relationships
Support Network
Individual Coping Abilities

Harmony

Failure to Develop
or Sustain Harmony

Intact Family

Reconstituted Family

Tasks of Stepfamilies:

Dealing with Losses & Changes
Building Couple Bond
Negotiation of Different Development Needs of
    Family Members
Equity & Authority
Communication & Conflict Management

There are several themes which stand out distinctively.

Theme #1: Some traditional values are still influential in contemporary Hong Kong Chinese families. Stepmothers have taken unconventional roles within a family structure which conflict with the tradition. They are easily scapegoated for their failure to uphold the traditional values.

Chinese families holding traditional values aspire to filial piety, kindness and forgiveness. It is believed that adherence to these values by family members will contribute to the development of family harmony. In contrast to the Western view that 'conflicts in human relationships are inevitable and may be healthy for relationship-building', harmony in Chinese culture is an indicator of the quality of family relationships and family life, as well as an ideal for families. Broken families have failed to maintain this harmony. The stepfamily is viewed as a family system which has experienced the process of breaking into pieces and then is being rebuilt. The scars of conflict and shame still remain and family members have difficulties in adjusting to the newly formed family. Stepmothers, who come into the family with negative labels, are convenient targets for blame.

This study shows that the stepfamilies were perceived as being of less value than the original family; the stepmothers were seen as the 'seconds' and not as good. Traditional Chinese patriarchal-centred familism buttresses the maintenance of rank and order in a family, respect for the older generation through filial piety and sex-role differentiation which perpetuates the subjugation of women. As outsiders coming into a stepfamily, stepmothers are easily scapegoated for destroying the traditions and creating disharmony in the family. They are disadvantaged because they are women and also because their role as stepmothers has a label attached. I shall elaborate on these points.

Searching for Family Harmony and Marital Happiness: the Second Time May Be No Better

As previously discussed, harmony in a family and filial piety are aspired to in Chinese family life. As noted by Roetz, 'the Confucian ideal doubtless is the harmonious family where the young can fulfil their duties without misgivings…however, family harmony based on moral foundations, was an ideal far from reality' (Roetz, 1993, p.56). In stepfamilies where the structure and relationships are complex, it is not easy to have a harmonious family life.

The findings show that remarried men and their parents wish for a harmonious and integrated family. Their unhappy and stressful past experience which was caused by the loss of the adult son's spouse, had made them wish for better when the new family was formed. Nevertheless, conflicts cannot be avoided in a family. It is difficult to practise filial piety and establish couple-bonding simultaneously. The reports of the stepmothers I interviewed indicate that husbands who had widowed mothers were caught in the conflicts between their mother and their wife. When there were conflicts within the family, the sons tended to play the 'mediator' or 'peace-maker' roles, or they simply suppressed negative feelings which arose as a result of the conflicts in the hope of restoring peace to their families. The study showed that husbands felt that they had to reciprocate the favour of their parents who had helped with child care during their divorce, and that they also felt obliged to accept what their parents suggested about child management. Their wives felt that their husbands failed to support them and their power to manage their stepchildren was taken away by their parents-in-law. It is difficult, therefore, to develop and maintain harmony in a stepfamily when husbands must practise filial piety and establish couple bonds simultaneously. One of the triggering factors is child management.

When stepmothers first become members of a stepfamily, they want to be accepted. As noted by Visher & Visher (1988), there are myths such as 'instant love and caring', and 'working hard prevents the development of a wicked stepmother'. The stepmothers in this study believed that by practising 'Jen' (kindness) and 'Shu' (forgiveness), they could build relationships with their in-laws and stepchildren. In situations of conflict, they were inclined to tolerate unreasonable demands from the kin of their husbands, and tried to forgive the defiant behaviour of their stepchildren. By acting in this manner, they aimed to achieve the goal of 'pacifying the matter and bringing peace to everybody' (息事寧人).

Thus, we can see that husbands and their relatives aspire to wider family harmony. The wives set more store by the quality of their marriage. From the husband's point of view, in situations where conflicts had to be dealt with, husbands acted as filial sons. These husbands seemed to abide by the Confucian ethic, i.e. 'the love of parents ought to exceed all others'; 'to

212

prefer one's wife or children to one's parents is a grave sin' (Chao, 1983, p.76); and 'Li' (禮) which advocates 'to receive but not to reciprocate, is not proper manner' (來而不往非禮也). Stepmothers were supported by the Confucian thinking that mothers are thought of as 'Tsu' (慈) which means tender or gentle, and 'loving attention and fondness are the distinguishing qualities of the mother' (Chao, 1983, p.84). Mothers, being tender, gentle and loving, are expected to practise 'Kindness' (仁) and 'Forgiveness' (恕) in parenting. Searching for family harmony and marital happiness is like walking on a road with hidden dangers, since unresolved conflicts are land mines waiting to explode.

The Effects of Moral Judgement and Labelling of the Stepfamily Members

In all three groups of informants, it is clear that infidelity by women is condemned. Not only were the married women who had committed adultery sneered at and regarded as social outcasts following their divorce, but women who married for the first time who chose to marry men who had previously been married were also looked at scornfully. Children born to remarried women in their past relationship bear no physical resemblance to the stepfather and therefore, the child's 'outsider' status is reinforced. These stepmothers and stepchildren were rarely accepted by either insiders or outsiders to the stepfamilies.

Social attitudes are still strongly morally judgemental. Women and children in stepfamilies are prime targets because they are regarded as the weaker members of Chinese society; this is demonstrated by categorizing them as 'ignorant, vulnerable and disadvantaged married women and young children' (無知婦孺). When the pillar of the family -- husband and father -- leaves them, they are easily bullied and belittled. As women who have married into a stepfamily are perceived as 'improper', 'bad' and 'shameful', although they may not have actually done anything to deserve it, they are regarded less favourably no matter how they actually behave. This is the 'cognitive confirmation effect' (Darley and Gross, 1983) which I have mentioned in Chapter 2. Stepmothers are judged morally and regarded negatively, and, therefore, they are not given a place and the power to enact their parenting role in the stepfamily. They feel powerless and pressurized by the unfavourable attitudes of their parents, in-laws, friends, neighbours, and the professionals. Some stepmothers react by adopting a domineering parenting approach to their stepchildren.

My informants said that stepmothers in Hong Kong stepfamilies were not literally described as 'wicked' as in the older Western literature; more often, they were described using colloquial language such as 'fierce' (惡), and 'bad' (唔好). Stepfathers were not only thought of as 'ill-treating' their stepchild, but their abusive behaviour was associated with sexually abusing their stepdaughters. Stepchildren were also described as 'pitiably neglected' and vulnerable to the ill-treatment of their stepmothers. The informants also reported negative attitudes were held towards divorcees and remarried persons by their family members, friends and neighbours. However, the growing number of stepfamilies in society as a result of an increase in divorce was noted. This shows that although they and the people around them acknowledged the existence of stepfamilies as a growing family type, they were strongly influenced by negative social attitudes. The feelings of pain and helplessness which the stepmothers expressed during the interviews were evidence of these strong negative social attitudes.

There is a Chinese saying, 'the gossip of people is something to be feared' (人言可畏). Indeed, this kind of cultural belief profoundly affects marriage and family life in Hong Kong Chinese families and reinforces the labelling of stepparenting and stepfamilies. Not surprisingly, these generally negative attitudes were also held by the professionals interviewed. Regardless of whether they had actual experience in their own family life, or whether they had derived these attitudes from the wider society, they presented a view of stepfamilies as problematic.

What we can see is a vicious circle in which the negative attitudes of a wider society reinforce the difficulties and insecurities of the stepmothers. The process which I have previously described as cognitive confirmation may lead to a kind of self-fulfilling prophecy in that when the person feels unappreciated, they are more likely to develop the very behaviour which is criticized.

Ways of Handling Family Shame

The second point to note is that the 'shame of the family should be kept within the family' (家醜不出外傳). 'If there is any conflict inside the family, it is deliberately handled as a kind of backstage behaviour which should not be brought to the front of the stage where it could be exposed to "outsiders" of the mixed tie' (Bond, 1986, p.245). Marital separation and children who

214

are reminders of the shameful past are buried as the hidden history of the family. This is quite a common way of handling undesirable family secrets in a Chinese family. Family members are discouraged from facing the problems; they are expected not to mention them and 'to forget' about them. Although 'denial' or 'purposeful ignoring' may be used as a defence by people in different cultures when confronted by stressful and shameful events, Chinese people holding traditional values have used these defenses extensively to barr family members from open communication. Suppressed feelings and unresolved issues may have more damaging effects just as a piece of bad meat swept under a carpet would produce a bad smell if it is not dealt with.

Theme #2: The dominating role taken by mothers-in-law in stepfamilies has negatively affected stepmothers' feelings, and marital and parent-child relationships, as reported by the stepmothers.

In contrast to the views of Western researchers about the supportive roles usually taken up by the grandparents when their adult children divorce and remarry (Kalish & Visher, 1982; Kennedy & Kennedy, 1993), most of the parents of the remarried couples in this study created tension rather than giving support. The likely explanation is that older generations in Chinese culture usually possess greater authority and rank higher in a family. In the context of the domestic life of families holding traditional values, it is the grandmothers who have the greatest power in decisions about childrearing and they are the most likely to offer their married children help with child care. If the grandfathers are alive, they influence the major decisions in their children's lives, e.g. choice of education, job, partner, etc. If the older people are of the same gender as the stepmother, role conflicts and power struggles are likely because they are competing for the child-carer role.

In majority of the cases in this study, the paternal grandfathers had passed away, and the influential older generation were their wives. In addition, many of the stepfamilies in this study had female relatives who were 'powerful' and 'influential'. Before they became members of the stepfamily, some of them had mothers who had strongly influenced their thoughts and behaviour. After they entered the stepfamily, they had powerful and dominating mothers-in-law and female relatives on the paternal side. These paternal kin discriminated against both remarried women and women who had married for the first time but who had chosen to marry a remarried man.

Stepmothers were looked down upon. The paternal female relatives felt uneasy because the stepmother had taken over the tasks with which they had been helping their son, brother or brother-in-law. The mothers-in-law had most conflicts with the stepmothers than did other paternal kin, for three reasons. Firstly, most of the mothers-in-law were widows and they expected that their unmet needs would be satisfied by their relationships with their sons and grandchildren. They seemed to be rather demanding of their sons and possessive of their grandchildren. Secondly, the mothers-in-law expected filial piety from their remarried sons and daughters-in-law; they wanted their sons to side with them in conflicts. Thirdly, the mothers-in-law who did not live with stepfamily members would exert control over domestic and child care matters by sudden 'drop-ins' and telephone commands. The stepmothers were affected by these frequent conflicts and thus their marital and parent-child relationships and their parenting behaviours were negatively influenced.

Reflecting on the findings relevant to this theme, the following issue warrants further discussion.

The Penetration of Kin in Stepfamilies: An Additional Strain or a Support?

As pointed out in Chapter 3, traditional Chinese families are not nuclear families, they are familistic groups in which an individual family member is expected to relate to a network of blood-tie relationships. Recent research in Beijing (Yuen, 1997) shows the dependence of working women on grandmothers for child care. In contemporary families in Hong Kong, nuclear families are the predominant family type and comprise slightly more than 60% of families. Nevertheless, the influence of kin cannot be overlooked, and shared mothering is a convenient and acceptable arrangement for families with working parents. Families that have good relationships with their extended families who live apart, maintain close contacts by visiting each other several times a week (or at least have a family gathering to have a meal in a 'tea house' on Sundays), or by buying houses close to each other so they can render mutual support. In families in which members do not have good relationships with their extended families and they do not live together, the older generation may still feel that their children are obliged to pay them attention and satisfy their demands.

It was apparent that even some of the parents of the stepmothers were against the idea of their daughters marrying a divorcee. Three of my informants felt guilty about acting against their parents wishes. However, a number of these stepmothers did receive emotional support and child care assistance from their own kin and from in-laws. Offering 'support', however, may on occasion be viewed as intrusive and be stressful for the stepparents. As Visher & Visher (1982) and Hamon & Thiessen (1990) point out, the older generation may feel a sense of loss of control following the divorce and providing 'support' offers a means of re-establishing that. It was apparent that stepmothers often regarded this support as interference.

Much Western literature supports Cherlin's hypothesis that the stepfamily is an incomplete institution, and also his later observations that the entrance into stepgrandparenthood is inherently ambiguous due to a lack of social norms (Cherlin, 1978; 1981). Nevertheless, grandparents have readily penetrated the lives of the Hong Kong Chinese stepfamilies I interviewed. They do not need a passport to allow them entry into the family system, they cross boundaries and make rules. They are assertive in claiming their rights and in taking over part, if not all, of the parenting duties of the stepparents. It is often because of this failure to let go of their parenting role that conflicts arise between mothers-in-law and their daughters-in-law. If the mothers-in-law are satisfied with playing a grandparent's role instead of the role of a parent, then the parents in stepfamilies may feel more supported than stressed by their involvement. Moreover, it is likely to add strain to stepmother-stepchild relationships when the long-established substitute carer is replaced by a new mother. The stepchild may resent the change of carer, and intense feelings may be provoked when the new mother is replacing his/her lost mother.

Theme #3: The stepmothers feel overloaded. They are discontented with the lack of support from their spouses and paternal kin. These stepmothers reported that such feelings have affected their family relationships and their parenting behaviours.

Stepmothers in this study may not, in fact, have had to work harder than women in other families, but they were living in families where the structure was complicated and relationships were complex. They felt that they lacked support and experienced much tension between the family members, who were competing for attention, affection and power. From my observations, they seemed to be hardworking women who felt isolated and insecure. From the information they shared with me, their parenting behaviours were affected and quite a number of them had adopted a controlling approach to managing household matters and a disciplinary approach to child management. It should be pointed out that although some of these stepmothers thought that the controlling household management style and the disciplining child-rearing approach they adopted were influenced by their feelings of being overloaded and discontented, they may also have had personalities which were controlling and disciplinarian before joining the stepfamiy.

The following discussion further explains how the feelings of the stepmother affect their parenting behaviours.

Marital Relationships are Unsatisfactory: Love Gives Way to Child Care

The development of marital relationships and bonding are seen as primary tasks of the spouses during the initial stage of the marriage. In stepfamilies the honeymoon period is often non-existent and couples have no time for preparation and planning for the arrival of children who are the 'bonus' of the marriage. As pointed out by Goetting (1982), this simultaneous demand of parental and marital roles has usually been found to result in the marital relationship being neglected. It is rather common for child care to be placed high on the agenda of stepfamily tasks in many stepfamilies which was supported by the expectations of the couples as reported by the stepmothers in this study.

Like other institutions and relationships, parenting is socially constructed. Many people held their view that the mother should be the primary carer when the child is in his/her formative years. The expectations of women who play the major parenting role has extended to the years after the child has grown up. Trebilcot argued that the expectations of mothering are designed to perpetuate hierarchical societal arrangements by patriarchies. Those expectations include 'requiring mothers to make children conform to gender roles according to biological sex; to transmit the values of the dominant culture to their children; to reproduce patriarchy in children and also to care for the men who create and maintain it, etc.' (Trebilcot, 1983, p.1). Visher & Visher (1988) also pointed out that there are deep-rooted expectations that 'women are primarily responsible for the ambience of the home and the care of the children, including stepchildren' (p.19). It seems that men want their wives to bear children and take care of them. If we follow this argument, it is not difficult to understand why remarried husbands in stepfamilies designate the child care responsibilities to their wives and why, when their

218

wives abdicate their parental role, they wish to find another wife who could fill the position.

Most of the wives believed that their husbands had remarried primarily because they wanted someone to take on the child care duties. A few of them knew this before they married, but felt sorry for their husbands and took on the child care responsibilities to show their love for their husbands. They believed that by building loving relationships with their husband's children, they would prove their love for their spouses. They were disappointed when they were not rewarded with a loving relationship with their husbands in return for the efforts they had made in child care.

Parents' Reactions to Parenting in Stepfamilies

Stepmothers' Reactions to Parenting

My study does not enable me to write about the characteristics of stepparents as compared with parents in ordinary families, but it is clear that being a stepparent makes parenting tasks more difficult.

Some stepmothers had given up trying to relate to and discipline their stepchildren because they were so tired of their responses to communication or disappointed by their behaviour. For example, one stepmother (M03) had been unable to build a relationship with her school-aged stepson since the stepfamily had formed. She felt that she had tried to relate to him closely but he did not respond as she had expected. Her stepson had repeatedly run away from home, so she had given up confronting or disciplining him. This style of parenting can be described as 'disengaged'.

Other stepmothers were unsure of their role; they wanted to be close to their stepchildren but also wanted to protect themselves from being rejected. For example, one stepmother (M08) did not know how to play her role and was struggling to establish her position as the 'stepmother', but at times felt that she would rather continue in her former role as an 'aunt of her niece and nephew', which she had before the stepfamily was formed. Another stepmother (M06) was stressed by the marital and financial problems. She felt more at ease and happier when her husband was not at home and she said she could then relate more closely to her stepchildren. The above illustrates another style of parenting which can be termed 'ambivalent'.

Several of the stepmothers could play their parenting roles adequately. For example, one stepmother (M04) recognized the difficulties of mothering her pre-school aged stepson and had tried hard to build a relationship with him. She had been successful and had overcome the interference of her resident parents-in-law in child management. She reported that her success was due to support from her husband. Another stepmother (M07) was a busy career woman but she had spent as much time as she could in trying to relate to her teenage stepdaughter. She was sensible and sensitive to feelings. She told me that she had won the trust of her introverted stepdaughter. These two are examples of a 'committed' style of parenting.

Contrary to the parenting style described above, half of the stepmothers were either so eager to perform well in parenting that they overplayed their part or they presented an authoritarian image in order to make their stepchildren comply with their expectations. As an example of the first case, there was one (M010) who wished to establish relationships with her two stepsons before they were ready. She spoilt them. In the second case, there was one stepmother (M05) who excessively controlled the daily routine of her school-aged stepdaughter, demanding her total effort so that she would excel academically. This was a way for her to cover up her inadequacy in relating intimately to her stepdaughter. These two types of parenting can be described as 'overly involved/controlling'. They tended to do too much and the end results were not as expected.

Fathers' Reactions to Parenting

I have reported and discussed the feelings of the stepmothers and the ways in which they perceive the situation. There are many difficulties confronting them which are no different from those facing 'ordinary' mothers and their families. For example, the whole issue of 'shared parenting' between husband and wife is of general significance. The absence of the fathers placed a particularly heavy responsibility on stepmothers whom, as have already seen, were in insecure and ambivalent positions.

Most of these stepmothers reported that their husbands/spouses worked long hours to support their families, and most of them left the child care to their wives and had little involvement. For example, one husband (M03) worked in the border city of Shenzheng and was usually only at home on Sundays. He did not play with his children, let alone discipline them. Another husband (M05) also worked outside Hong Kong. When he was at home at the weekends, he would rather stay alone indoors fixing electrical household appliances and asked his wife to take their children to the park or to the teahouse for lunch. These are illustrations of the 'disengaged' parenting style that most fathers had adopted, as was reported by their wives. Only one father (M04) was reported to have great love for his family and to be actively involved in child care.

It may be that this finding -- that fathers had little involvement in parenting -- was linked to their career stage. People have different needs at different life stages. Fathers in stepfamilies seem to be work-oriented, although this may also be a means of escaping from child care responsibilities and problems in the family. They are at the life stage of career advancement and work is important to them. Two of the husbands in the stepfamilies I studied had financial problems -- one did not have enough work (M01) and the other did not earn enough (M06). It is important to note that stepfamilies are usually larger in family size and there are many mouths to feed. The resolution of tangible problems, such as improving their financial stability and the quality of daily life, may save them energy and time so that they would have greater motivation to deal with relationship and emotion-related problems in their families. It may, however, be more deeply rooted in assumptions about gender-roles in child care.

Reflections on the Parents' Reactions to Parenting in the Stepfamilies

From the above observations, most stepmothers employed 'overly involved' or 'controlling' parenting styles, while their husbands adopted a 'disengaged' style. These two styles seem to be at the two extreme ends of the spectrum and this raises concerns as to the impact of parenting on parent-child relationships and the development of the children in stepfamilies. The above observations indicate that one parent was doing too much while the other was insufficiently involved in relating to their children. There were problems arising from role strain of the stepmothers, who took on heavier responsibilities in child management. The fathers were rather withdrawn when relating to their children and could be regarded as the weaker parent by their children, who had no choice but to ask the stronger parent, i.e. the stepmother, for her approval of any requests they might have. The children might, however, be so reluctant to ask for their stepmother's permission that they just simply did not raise the request at all. In the former situation, the children might feel angry with their father for not taking up the primary decision-maker role and it was likely that they would be driven into conflicts with their stepmother if their requests were not first answered by their father. In the latter case, stepchildren did not like communicating with their stepmothers and relationships would be difficult to build.

There was only a small number of stepmothers who appeared to be contented in parenting. What made them feel that they had been successful in relationship-building? As described in the earlier paragraphs about 'committed parenting', two stepmothers (M04, M07) appeared to be reasonable and sensitive. They reported that they listened patiently to their stepchildren, felt supported by their husbands who shared parenting with them as far as they were able and were able to overcome the emotional difficulties and conflicts arising from the complicated relationships. These were the attributes and conditions which had facilitated the building of stepparent-stepchild relationships.

Other Issues Concerning Parenting in Stepfamilies

Involvement of the Biological Parents

Due to the influence of Chinese patriarchal familism, the biological son has the mission to carry on family name of his father. If a divorced father is granted custody of his son, the biological mother has difficulties in being involved in parenting even though she may have the right to do so by court order. In this study, few of the divorced biological mothers visited her children, let alone became involved in parenting or decision-making for their children. Moreover, the biological mothers who were divorced from their husbands because the former had committed adultery were not allowed to see their children again. The feelings of the children who experienced this abrupt separation were not dealt with.

It is rare for Chinese divorced couples to be friendly towards each other after the end of their marriage, as compared with cases I observed in Western societies. Many husbands in this study did not want their ex-wives to visit their child, let alone share parenting, because they wished to forget the shame and pain brought by their unhappy marriages and their ex-wives' adultery. In this study, most local stepfamilies did not want to practise inclusive parenting.

Remarriage is a major life event. At such times, the adults involved are making important decisions in their lives, and the children in these families may or may not be asked to take part in the process. Western culture regards children as important family members; parents who aspire to liberal child management believe that the involvement of children in the discussion of family matters and decision-making is not only healthy for the development of their children, but also for the family as a whole. In fact, however, not all of the children, even in the families where parents are concerned about the well-being and rights of their children, are invited to give their opinions on their parents' remarriage. Some of them are simply taken to the newly formed family without prior notice. This raises questions. Firstly, supposing that children will benefit from participation in family decision-making, what should be taken into consideration when they are asked to take part? Should there be any consideration of their age or their abilities to comprehend and decide upon the matter? Could there be situations where children should be prevented from giving opinions? Secondly, does the involvement of children simply mean 'talking the matter over with them'? Considering the idiosyncrasy of a family's interaction and communication pattern, and that of its individual family members, could there be other forms or methods of communication to deal with the family matter? In my opinion, people who have been exposed to Western culture may find the involvement of children in family decision-making appealing; however, the idea should not be blindly followed because each family has its own established interaction and communication patterns. A practice which is good in theory may be unworkable in certain families and it would not contribute to the well-being of the members. Moreover, the age of the children and their ability to cope should be carefully assessed before involving them in the discussion of sensitive family matters.

The idea of allowing children to be involved in family affairs and giving them chances to voice their opinions is foreign to Chinese parents. In Chinese culture where parents holding traditional values have ultimate authority over children's rights, 'the best interests of the child' are not usually considered. In Chinese stepfamilies the adults may have been so involved in attending to their problems and needs that the children have been neglected. Parents may not recognize that children's feelings have to be dealt with delicately and in time before they can adjust well into the stepfamily.

Although parents in some other cultures may also share few of their children's feelings, this may be more so in Chinese families because children are expected to take orders from their parents. The parents do not need to discuss feelings before they decide upon matters which affect their children. As pointed out by Redding (1993), the Chinese learn to 'read people' when relating to them. The young generation are, therefore, expected to read the messages which are given by the older generation in their non-verbal expressions, rather than have the messages discussed openly in dialogues.

The Gender of Children in Stepfamilies and Its Possible Impact on Stepmother-Stepchild Relationships

In the Western literature it appears that boys have more difficulties than girls in accepting parental divorce, while girls have more difficulties than boys in accepting their mothers' remarriage. As mentioned earlier, most stepmothers commented very little on this point, but the age at which the children acquired a stepmother seemed relevant to their adjustment. As evidenced in the report of one stepmother (M04), children who had had stepmothers since their pre-school years seemed to accept them well and trusting stepmother-stepchild relationships were possible. In other cases (M01, M010), between latency and teenage years proved to be a more difficult time for the adjustment.

The Contribution of Parental Expectation of Academic Performance to Parent-Child Relationship Problems

Quite a number of stepmothers pressed their stepchildren to excel academically. As pointed out earlier, they may feel that it is an objective to exercise parental supervision over homework assignments. The education system in Hong Kong also contributes to the pressure on students to do well at school; parents push their children to perform well in order to obtain places at elite schools in the hope of getting good jobs later. Stepparents and stepchildren feel a triple amount of pressure, i.e. from the education system and social aspirations; from parental and family expectations (intact families experience these too); and from stepparents who want their stepchildren to excel academically to prove that they are able and dutiful parents. In view of the above, it is important to note the tensions generated by the over-emphasis on the academic achievement of stepchildren, which will negatively affect the stepparent-stepchild relationship and the development of the stepchild.

Summary of the Chapter

In this chapter I have described the major themes emerging from the findings, i.e. the impact of traditional Chinese patriarchy on the sex-role problems in stepparenting; scapegoating of stepmothers for destroying harmony in families; the dominating role of mothers-in-law in stepfamilies which has negatively affected the feelings of stepmothers, and marital and parent-child relationships; and the lack of sufficient support for stepmothers from their husbands and their paternal kin. I reflected on these themes and discussed the issues arising from each theme. It was found that traditional Chinese values and beliefs were still held by many of the stepfamilies I interviewed. Those values had contributed to the formation of negative self-images, and difficulties in marital, parent-child and in-law relationships.

8 Implications for Social Work Practice

Introduction

From the reports of the stepmothers, social workers and teachers, there are four salient points which have implications for social work practice. First, women are positioned as weaker family members in Hong Kong Chinese families holding traditional values. The stepmothers are doubly jeopardized because of their gender, and because of cultural stereotyping and negative social attitudes. Second, the paternal kin, especially the mothers-in-law in stepfamilies, are powerful. The latter intervene in child management and create family relationship problems. Third, the fathers in stepfamilies are disengaged in parenting. They do not support their wives in child care. Their wives felt maritally dissatisfied. Finally, the children in stepfamilies have not been given any help to cope with their emotional difficulties arising from the loss, separation, divorce and remarriage of their parents. There are potential risks that the children will develop emotional and family relationship problems.

Before making suggestions as to what and how these problems should be tackled, it is important to make contextual reflections and to review the current debates concerning these issues.

Ideology Issues

Contextual Reflections

Views about stepfamilies are built upon perceptions and attitudes towards family and family life. These are socially constructed and they change according to different place and time. Social changes have challenged the notions of a 'normative family' and a 'normative family life'.

As have been discussed earlier, there is evidence of a much greater increase in marital breakdown and remarriages in the United Kingdom than in Hong Kong. In the United Kingdom, according to Social Trends 1997, the number of divorces in 1994 was more than double the figures for 1971 (Government Central Statistical Office, 1997, p.46). Moreover, Britain 1997 recorded that in 1993, some 25.1% of marriages were remarriages where one or both parties had been divorced. There is also evidence of a growing number of cohabitations. This is particularly high among divorced women (28%) but recently the largest increase has been for single women (Central Office of Information, 1996, pp.30-31). In Hong Kong the number of decrees absolute granted in 1975 was 668, but by 1997 it had risen to 10,492. There are no official figures on the number of remarried families or cohabitations, but the impressions from social workers suggested that these are also on the increase, as are single parent families. It should be recognized that in both the West and Hong Kong, ethical and religious codes have emphasized stable and lasting relationships. In the United Kingdom, where the influence of religion on both individual and family lives is powerful, many churches are still reluctant to remarry couples; and some people choose cohabitation, otherwise the number of remarriages would be even greater. These changes have been visible in the United Kingdom for several decades and especially since the Divorce Reform Act came into force in 1971. People are uneasy about the growth of atypical family structures and unstable relationships, but they are gradually developing greater acceptance of them.

The prevailing views of Hong Kong people towards stepfamilies are different, mainly because people who come from families which hold traditional values are still influenced by the Confucian beliefs about family life. Confucianism is a moral teaching and people who believe in it aspire to an intact family, harmonious family relationships and life-long marriage. People have value conflicts which develop because liberal thoughts about marriage and divorce are currently growing while the traditional Chinese values remain in the background.

While Confucianism continues to influence family life, there are three forces in the current scene which interact with the traditional thought. These dynamics perpetuate the labelling of families as being different from the mainstream ones and promote traditional Chinese values. Firstly, there has been a growth in the number of divorces and diversified family types; secondly, there have been changes to law in an attempt to regulate marriage and family life; and thirdly, the policy address of the Chief Executive of the new Government of Hong Kong indicates support for the on-going influence of Confucian values.

As regards the first force, and as pointed out earlier, the growing number of divorces in Hong Kong has led to more single parent families and to increases in cohabitation and remarriage. The number of stepfamilies in Hong Kong has not increased as rapidly as in the West, and there have been two consequences of this. On the one hand, there has not been the alarm and fear about the instability of nuclear families which has been seen in the West. On the other hand, because stepfamilies are still relatively uncommon, the stigma and negative labelling is still powerful.

As regards the second force, polygamy was permitted for many years in China and Hong Kong, whereby one man could take a number of wives, but this simply reinforced gender inequality and male power. Even though this was abolished in Mainland China (1950) and Hong Kong (1971), attitudes towards women in sexual matters remain much harsher than towards men. Furthermore, earlier patterns of polygamy did not make it any easier to accept stepfamilies or even remarriage as 'normal'.

As regards the third force, stepfamilies are embedded in a society which is undergoing transformation and the new Chief Executive has voiced his support for the traditional Chinese values of harmony and intact families (Chapter 3, p.71-72). The promotion of these values will have an impact upon the ideologies of family and family life, and it may reinforce the negative labelling of stepfamilies.

Current debates on the ideology issues   At the beginning of this chapter I pointed out the major points discovered in this study; all of these are problems relating to the value stance people hold which, in turn, affects their behaviour. The reluctance to accept families which are different from the 'ideal' or the 'mainstream' raises the following issues.

Underlying any consideration of stepfamilies, there are complex questions about social expectations of the patterns and structures of family life and about how families are socially constructed: the answers vary greatly between cultures, generations and families. They also vary with time, and especially when, as in the case in contemporary Britain, family life is in a state of flux and a number of different patterns can be observed, with varying degrees of acceptability. This is also true of Hong Kong, but it seems that there is, as yet, a stronger acceptance of the traditional patterns were discussed earlier. Those who view stepfamilies as somehow 'deviant' may compare their behaviour and family life unfavourably with those observed in mainstream families. The 'Child Protection: Messages from Research' pointed out, however, that behaviour which are thought of as 'normal' because they are exhibited by the majority of parents, are not necessarily 'optimal'.

Being a researcher who is a Chinese social work educator in Hong Kong, I too am affected by the prevailing norms and values but I am also strongly influenced by the Western views on family life. Therefore, I have had to be aware of these dual influences which could affect the way in which I perceived and interpreted the evidence from my data.

The most difficult aspect of this has been to disentangle what might be specific to the dynamics and problems of stepfamilies, from those which are part and parcel of family life generally and not attributable to the fact of being a stepfamily. Behind this, of course, may lie an unexplored assumption that family life in stepfamilies is not 'normal' as in intact, mainstream families.

When discussing the findings, I always reminded myself not to use a 'deficit-comparison paradigm' and tried not to fall into the trap of viewing stepfamilies as inherently less good or abnormal. I also bore in mind the fact that I did not have a control group with which to compare the difficulties and problems experienced by the stepfamilies. At the same time I was cautious not to overlook the possibility that stepfamilies may have specific problems attributable to their being stepfamilies. The best way to handle this is to take aspects of family life which are manifestly different in stepfamilies and see what stepfamilies say about them, for example, the adjustment that they have to make in daily living when a new family is formed; the handling of 'loss' in this context by all concerned; the impact of traditional values (such as filial piety and harmony in relationships) on a 'new' family; etc.

Ideology issues affecting social work practice Stevenson (1997) suggests that good professional judgements involve the interaction of values, knowledge or theory and skills. 'Our values influence what knowledge/theory we want to learn, ...knowledge/theory gives us evidence or offers hypotheses to inform our understanding of our basic concern...and knowledge/theory may form a basis for the development of skills' (Stevenson, 1997, p.2). In relation to stepfamilies, Chinese social workers will need to attend to all three dimensions. Their values are affected by Confucianism. Culturally they were taught to aspire to an intact family, harmonious family relationships and life-long marriage. However, these values conflict with the growing liberal thoughts about marriage and divorce and the traditional Chinese values remain in the background. Their own personal experiences as stepfamily members would have a further impact on their conflicting values, and in turn their professional values would be challenged. For example, these values may make them reluctant to admit that family breakdown in particular cases is inevitable and they are, therefore, unable to support adults in their decision to separate. Secondly, the knowledge base concerning stepfamilies is quite inadequate. For example, research findings (Lam, 1998) show that difficulties in stepparenting are related to power conflicts between daughters-in-law and mothers-in-law and information such as this will sensitize social workers to handle underlying relationship problems which are caused by the wider family. Thirdly, knowledge is essential to the develop of practice skills, knowledge about the stages and areas of difficulty experienced by stepfamilies will motivate concerned social workers to find ways to intervene. For example, when it is noted that the women and children in stepfamilies are in weaker positions, social workers will adopt appropriate strategies in order to achieve a better balance of power.

Moreover, social workers should not just take professional principles, such as 'non-judgemental', 'acceptance', 'controlled emotional involvement', for granted. They need to gather information about stepfamilies, understand them, and acknowledge and deal with the feelings of negativism they may have had built up about their clients prior to their intervention. For example, paternal mothers-in-law and relatives were found to be contributors to stepfamily conflicts which were triggered by child management disputes. Social workers should have a balanced view and note their positive contributions. Their practical help with child care at the time of their adult child's divorce should be recognized and they should be helped to deal with their difficulties in accepting the stepmother, who they regard as a competitor taking over their child care role. Moreover, from the information provided by the social workers, it seems that parents-in-law were not usually included in counselling because they were reluctant to be involved and they refused to own the problem; social workers also felt that the older generation were difficult to work with because they had fixed ideas. Social workers must come to terms with their anxieties and refine their skills in working with older people.

Last but not least, it is important to help the children in stepfamilies to deal with their feelings of loss so that they can build relationships in the new family. Social workers may find it difficult to understand and handle the children's complex feelings and at times they may over-identify with the children as victims and therefore develop biased views towards their parents and stepparents. They must understand the dynamics of the stepfamilies they work with, enhance their sensitivity in order to empathize with the children who have experienced emotional turmoil, and develop skills to work at their level.

Policy and Service Issues

Contextual reflections The governments of the United Kingdom and Hong Kong have recently shared the common view that the state should intervene as little as possible in family life. Fox-Harding (1996) pointed out that the state both controls and supports families. The models of the family-state relationship she suggested reflect the possible policy choices of the government based upon the different degrees of control and intervention in family life. With the excepting of the two models at the extremes of the seven suggested, the remaining five models, namely, the enforcement of responsibilities in·specific areas; the manipulation of incentives; working within constraining assumptions; substituting for and supporting families; and responding to needs and demands, are not mutually exclusive. These models can be grouped into three broad categories: control of family life by law (e.g. custody arrangements after divorce); by financial means (e.g. enforcing the contribution to children's upkeep from divorced parents); and by the supervision of children's welfare (e.g. by the enforcement of the law which regulates behaviour towards children by normative standards). The last of these is the sphere of activity in which social workers are most engaged but the first two contribute significantly to shaping family life. Furthermore, social work action is greatly affected by, some might say governed by, the legal framework within which it must work.

The official policy of the United Kingdom Government in power from 1980-1997 was one of 'minimal intervention' in family life. Adults were encouraged to take care of themselves and help would not be offered unless it was asked for. It is only 'where family responsibilities are not "properly" met, a number of state responses may come into play' (Fox-Harding, 1996, p.108). Paradoxically, although the previous government of the United Kingdom stressed minimal intervention, it put in place a new focus which widens the scope for intervention. Since the introduction of the Children Act 1989, child protection has been at the top of the policy agenda. After several years in operation, the findings of the child protection research pointed out the need to shift the focus from the protection of child abuse victims to the wider concern of helping more 'children in need'. The policy-makers and social workers had narrowly defined child protection as protecting children who were suffering from child abuse, which unnecessarily drew many children into the child protection system, whereas children in need were not given timely support and services (Gibbons, 1997). It remains to be seen whether this can be translated into effective action with sufficient resources. Until now, stepfamilies have not been the focus of any special initiatives, although arrangements for the custody of children and access for natural parents have been the focus of more attention as their numbers have increased.

Intact nuclear families and extended families are still the major family types in Hong Kong. There are not as many stepfamilies but they need the support of policy and the provision of services in the same way. Moreover, when governmental policies are reviewed by looking at the White Papers on social welfare since 1965, it is not surprising to note that since the first White Paper entitled 'Aims and Policy for Social Welfare in Hong Kong', the Government has strongly encouraged families to stay intact and to strengthen support of the natural family unit so that a family can be self-contained without relying on outside resources. For example, social welfare should aim to 'help families to remain intact as strong natural units and to care for their children and handicapped or aged members...the constant endeavour should be to rely to the maximum extent on the natural family unit...' (Hong Kong Government, 1965, p.10). In the most recent White Paper, the policy-makers pointed out that 'the traditional roles of the different constituents which make up the family unit and in particular the role of women are changing', but the overall objectives of family welfare services were still to 'preserve and strengthen the family as a unit' (Hong Kong Government, 1991, p.19). The needs of families which are different from the mainstream are not recognized by resource provision. Thirty years after the announcement of the first social welfare policy, the 1995 five-year welfare plan reflected the same message, that is, 'the overall objectives of family welfare services are to preserve and strengthen the family as a unit' (Hong Kong Government, 1995, p.16) with no recognition of the diversified family types and their need for services.

Social workers were among the first professionals to note the needs and problems of stepfamilies. In mid-1996, the Hong Kong Council of Social Services organized a conference on 'Families in Disadvantaged Situations', which included stepfamilies as one of the areas of concern as well as other 'out-of-mainstream families', such as split families, families which have experienced extra-marital affairs, single parent families, and families with unemployed family members. It was the first open forum to draw public attention to the needs and difficulties of stepfamilies. The failure to recognize the needs of stepfamilies perpetuates the provision of services at a remedial level rather than developing services based on preventive and developmental considerations.

Thus, we can say that stepfamilies have received no explicit attention in Hong Kong. As in the United Kingdom, they have been ignored. Whilst there is a case for arguing that they should not be picked out as necessarily having more needs and problems than 'first time' families, it seems that this reflects the denial of a significant social change and its implications for the State.

It was pointed out at the beginning of this chapter that women, especially stepmothers, feel oppressed in Hong Kong Chinese families with traditional values. Stepmothers said that most of their husbands expected their wives to take on the child-carer role but gave them no support so that their wives felt maritally dissatisfied. The paternal kin, and especially the mothers-in-law, were powerful and influential in child management in stepfamilies which held traditional values. The children in stepfamilies were often not given the chance to express their feelings caused by family transitions. Such an analysis requires reflection by social workers. Ideology issues arising from these observations are greatly relevant to policy and services, and they should be examined before suggestions are made.

Some of the work which needs to be done with stepfamilies involves shifting to some extent the balance of power between family members. From the findings the balance of power in stepfamilies seemed to tilt strongly in favour of husbands and mothers-in-law. The wives and children in stepfamilies are positioned as weaker family members. This is, of course, part of a wider agenda concerning empowerment and especially within that context particular constellations between people involved: husband and wife; mother-in-law and wife; adults and children. When we think about these interwoven, complex relationships, important questions have to be asked and answered before considering empowering the clients. The first question is, how far can, and should, social workers seek to alter a balance of power which is, at least in part, culturally normative? As analysed in earlier chapters, traditional values in Chinese culture are male dominant and the older generation is powerful. Whilst social workers may believe that it is desirable to shift the balance of power, they must first appreciate that this may be perceived by the family as undermining traditional values, and, secondly, that such changes may cause disequilibrium within the family system. There is also a question about the attitudes of the policy-makers in social work agencies. We should note that the notion of empowerment has ever wider implications for the workers and agencies and thus for the method for working directly with families. Social workers may be sensitive to the needs of their clients for empowerment and their assessment may be accurate, but they need a supportive supervisor to endorse an innovative intervention plan.

'If empowerment is our aim, we will find ourselves questioning both our public policy and our role relationship to dependent people' (Rappaport, 1985, p.18). As professional helpers, social workers need to confront this issue and reflect on policy and practice, because empowerment is a challenge to the existing approach which requires changes to the role of the service provider and his/her relationship with the service user. Consideration should be given in order to focus upon strengthening the service user. Stevenson (1994) explained 'the translation of ideals such as empowerment into practice requires sophisticated rigour as one seeks to move at the pace and in the way which the user needs and to balance protection and autonomy' (p.187). 'It is not easy to think how needs might be met differently or, indeed, sometimes to articulate needs which are more deeply felt and not immediately definable in terms of service' (Stevenson & Parsloe, 1993, p.34). Earlier, we noted that children in Chinese families holding traditional values are in a weak position and they are not given the opportunity to participate in family discussions. However, parental attitudes towards children have been changing due to the influence of Western culture and the reduction in family size. The former influences parents to adopt a more liberal child-rearing method, whereas the latter encourages parents to focus their attention on the single child and thus many children are spoilt. In sum, the parenting approach adopted by many educated, middle class, mainstream families is quite close to that adopted by their Western counterparts. The more obvious cultural difference seems to be the way parents share their feelings about painful and shameful experiences. Chinese parents are not used to opening up about their feelings and their children are also discouraged from openly expressing their feelings. This should have an impact on stepfamilies where there are many emotional issues 'swept under the rug'. Children's feelings of loss of their biological parents and their ambivalence towards their stepparents have not been adequately handled. Thus there are issues concerning the balance of power which require both cultural sensitivity and sensitivity to the needs and capacities of individuals.

Current debates on the policy and service issues   The core of this study is to understand parenting practice in some of the stepfamilies in Hong Kong. We should take a closer look at the relationship between parenting and the well-being of children, and the beliefs underpinning policy.   Optimal child development depends on the optimal quality of parenting. As the United Nations Convention on the Rights of the Child (1989) states: 'The family is the fundamental group of society and the natural environment of growth and well being of all its members and particularly children'. However, the approach to working with families has changed in line with the notions of empowerment discussed above. According to Hearn (1997), 'Working with rather than on families in the interests of children is essential for a healthy society' (Parton, 1997, p.225). A recent policy document of the Kent Social Services pointed out that the development of child welfare depends on working jointly with the families. They advocated supporting children in their families and community because that is where their roots are, and it is the base from which they can most satisfactorily grow into adult life. From the above there were indications of a re-affirmation of the importance of family in child welfare, which prompted actions to examine the existing policy agendas on which unbalanced policies and practices of child protection and child welfare have been developed. The current debates in the United Kingdom on child protection versus child welfare in the context of family welfare stimulated me to consider how stepfamilies can best be helped.

Social workers in the United Kingdom have been concerned about the protection of children in a narrow sense, and there has been a failure to achieve a balance between protection and the welfare of children. Furthermore, as the 'Child Protection: Messages from Research' pointed out, 'A bias in the service towards assessment rather than prevention and treatment was noted by several researchers and their findings underline the need to tackle the wider welfare requirements of children and families' (Dartington Social Research Unit, 1995, p.48). The messages were loud and clear that children in need should be considered in the context of children's general quality of life, which can only be enhanced when the quality of their family life is improved (Dartington Social Research Unit, 1995; Parton, 1997). It is important 'to work alongside families rather than disempower them, to raise their self-esteem rather than reproach families, to promote family relationships where children have their needs met, rather than leave untreated families with an unsatisfactory parenting style' (Dartington Social Research Unit, 1995, p.55).

Following this argument, then, a shift from child-focused assessment and problem-focused orientation to that of a family-focused, strength-focused orientation will require a re-thinking of the 'what' and 'how' in intervention. According to Hearn (1995), 'Family support is about the creation and enhancement, with and for families in need, of locally based (or accessible) activities, facilities and networks, the use of which will have outcomes such as alleviated stress, increased self-esteem, promoted parental/carer/family competence and behaviour and increased parental/carer capacity to nurture and protect the children' (Parton, 1997, p.238). To take this suggestion a step further, 'the focus should be on identifying and assessing need, then producing flexible and non-stigmatizing services...more emphasis should be placed on prevention and less on reactive interventions...' (Parton, 1997, p.4). It is with examining the concept of prevention in order to ascertain its use in helping stepfamilies. It is a proactive, positive family support agenda for the promotion, development and delivery of services (Frost, 1997). According to the pre-Children Act literature, there are three levels of prevention -- primary, secondary, and tertiary (Parker, 1980; Holman, 1988; and Hardiker, Exton & Baker, 1991). Primary prevention comprises those services which provide general support to families and reduce the problems to which they might otherwise be exposed. Secondary prevention is restricted to those who are assumed to be at 'special risk' or whose circumstances warrant special priority. Tertiary aims to avoid the worst consequences of a child having to be placed in substitute care (Parker, 1980).

Hardiker et al develop this model further. They suggest that prevention services can be classified into four levels. The first level is the help needed to prevent a person from acquiring 'client' status; the second level involves helping clients in the early stages of their problems to restore their 'non-client status'; the third level is to help families with severe/well established problems to prevent family breakdown; and the fourth level is help to restore/reconstitute families or permanency planning (Hardiker, Exton & Barker, 1995, p.27).

In Hong Kong the role of a social worker within the education system has developed differently from that in the United Kingdom. School social workers are employed by the family service centres of non-governmental organizations, and many of them service secondary schools as well as being family caseworkers in a family service centre belonging to a multi-service agency. The school social workers who are not re-deployed to family casework duties work very closely with the family caseworkers and family life education workers in the same agency or with those from the other agencies. School social workers are not employed by the Education Department and their main duties are not to find school placements for pupils. They conduct counselling sessions to deal with the pupils' problems relating to learning and their work may sometimes involve teachers and the pupils' families. They also run groups or mass programmes at preventive, developmental or remedial levels for pupils.

As there are various levels of intervention for helping stepfamilies, consideration should be given as to how inter-agency cooperation and the co-ordination of services can be facilitated. At present, only a small group of professionals who are mostly social workers and teachers who have experience in working with stepfamilies are concerned about them. Their need for services is not established in the minds of policy-makers. However, stepfamilies can benefit from a wider range of services provided by different agencies, which are the same as those that can be acquired by other families in the community. Social workers and teachers could advocate that support be provided by their employers and join other professionals and organizations to develop innovative programmes for families, which include stepfamilies in the agenda. For example, school students would be more likely to accept stepfamily members if a social-work-minded school principal is willing to allocate manpower and time for teachers to promote family life education with a family service social worker in his/her school. Furthermore, coordination is needed between services to deal with complex family systems. Some stepfamilies may require multi-level services and therefore, social policy initiatives are needed in different services, such as social services, education, health, psychological services, taxation advice. Efforts made by coordinating services at different levels and various departments can widen the networking of help available and presents a caring image. For example, social work agencies can design educational programmes which promote an understanding of family life and life transitions for use in schools and health care settings. Professionals from different disciplines can work together to offer preventive services at different levels to meet the various needs of stepfamilies. The 'holistic help' concept is thus incorporated into the preventive services.

Policy and service issues affecting social work practice   As regards of what value is the idea of prevention in helping stepfamilies, the assumptions need to be made explicit. It should be agreed that prevention is better than remedial work, and it is better for the problems and difficulties of stepfamilies to be addressed by prevention programmes. If this is agreed, then from the policy point of view, people should be offered services if they encounter difficulties in family life before the difficulties snowball to the point of needing remedial attention. Therefore, the services offered to families to deal with the problems of family life should also be extended to stepfamilies. However, stepfamilies should not be picked out and made to carry a 'special need', 'stigmatized' label. They are simply families which have particular needs at particular times.

Primary prevention offers general support to families in order to enrich their family life and enhance their family relationships. Since the late 1970s, Hong Kong has had family life education, which is community education in the form of mass programmes or small groups. Family life education programmes are funded by the government and are usually planned and organized by social workers in the family service centres of the non-governmental organizations. Understanding of family lives, including those experienced by the stepfamilies, can be launched by a multi-service social work agency such as the Caritas-Hong Kong. This has the advantage of promoting an understanding of family life without treating a stepfamily as if it were a family with special needs and problems. It serves the purpose of educating the public with a view to increasing their acceptance of stepfamilies, but at the same time, stepfamily members who have joined the programmes may be attracted to other services, e.g. marital counselling, social groups for children, sessions with a psychologist, etc., if the need arises.

The second level of prevention is for the clients 'at risk.' Whilst the families in my study were not in crisis, they might have benefited from some kind of help during difficult times. For example, quite a number of the stepmothers who asked for help from social workers were having difficulties with stepparent-stepchild relationships or the behavioural problems of their stepchildren. It should be noted that it is not uncommon for mothers in Hong Kong to reach out to social work services. Fathers are reluctant to share the problems and it is also common for 'parent-child relationships' and 'child behaviour problems' to be put forward by the clients to cover up their underlying problems. Owing to the sensitive nature of the difficulties confronting stepfamilies, it is understandable that stepparents would not initially reveal their 'real' problem at intake and they feel more comfortable using the presenting problem to connect with professional help. In the United Kingdom, there is anxiety about families involving themselves with social workers from the statutory sector. However, non-governmental organizations in Hong Kong such as the Caritas play a much more significant role in family services than do the non-governmental organizations in the United Kingdom. In Hong Kong there are opportunities to develop family services in ways which will include stepfamilies. Consequently, secondary prevention seems to be the most feasible means to answer the needs of stepfamilies which have experienced difficulties in their family life but which have not yet come to the point of crisis. Multi-service agencies in Hong Kong have a role to play in providing services for stepfamilies which do not stigmatize them. From the practice point of view, social workers who provide second level prevention services have to remind themselves that the difficulties experienced by stepfamilies are also problems encountered by other families, and, therefore, these clients should not be treated as having special problems or labelled because of the negativism generated by cultural stereotyping. Their use of child-related problems as entry points for the social work service should be sensitively accepted with a view to helping them to deal with their more extensive or deep-rooted problems. Children in need should be given due attention so that their feelings of loss or split loyalty conflict can be dealt with before the problems worsen during their developing years. Efforts should also be made to reach out to their wider family. The significant in-laws, especially the paternal mothers-in-law, should be included in the counselling or given group work services in order to improve family relationships.

The third level is tertiary prevention. When families are breaking down or have broken up, social workers have a delicate and difficult task in helping the family to decide whether it is best to reunite as a family again or to break up. Services at this level require intensive remedial intervention by the social workers. The limited number of informants participating in this study provided insufficient evidence to conclude that stepfamilies in Hong Kong do not need services at this level. I imagine that stepfamilies are the same as other families in that there must be some who need more intensive professional help than others, although the findings of the present study do not indicate such a need.

To conclude, prevention services for stepfamilies in Hong Kong should be planned and organized at the primary and secondary levels. At present the government is not responding to the needs and problems of stepfamilies. There are very few non-governmental social work organizations which are concerned with stepfamilies; although some are becoming aware of the growing number of stepfamilies and their problems, their hands are tied because they lack the funding support needed to launch services. Caritas-Hong Kong has played the most active part in responding to stepfamilies. Shortly after I asked if they could introduce me to possible informants, they established data banks in family service centres in different districts to gather profile information about the various kinds of families with which they work. Stepfamilies are one of their targets. As previously discussed, obtaining knowledge can help to identify the needs and difficulties of clients and such information can assist in the development of better services. The example of Caritas-Hong Kong demonstrates how stepfamilies can be helped in a positive way. As stepfamilies are negatively labelled by people holding traditional values, the provision of special services for stepfamilies can only further reinforce negative social attitudes. Professional helpers should, therefore, have special sensitivity to the problems faced by stepfamilies, but they should not necessarily provide special services for them. A multi-service agency can take the lead to launch services for families in need and can include stepfamilies in their agenda. Parents in stepfamilies will find it easier to use services which are established in a non-stigmatizing setting and which are staffed by understanding and accepting professionals; a multi-service agency will also provide them with the opportunities to make use of a range of preventive, developmental and remedial services at their own pace and readiness. Agencies where there are parent groups will provide a venue for the parents of stepfamilies in which they can express their feelings. Services for children such as interest groups and after school care programmes will ease the childminding responsibilities of parents in stepfamilies. These can be used to satisfy the social and emotional needs of the child as well as providing a break for the parent, which will eventually help to improve the parent-child relationship. A family weekend fun camp organized by family life education workers which is targeted at families may also attract stepfamilies and their kin. It is an opportunity to promote better understanding among family members without the fear that their problems may be exposed before they are ready. Satisfied users of these prevention programmes will be more likely to reach out for counselling or other more intensive and personal programmes should the need arise.

Suggestions for Social Work Practice

Suggestions for Policy-makers

- It is important that policy-makers should recognize the diversity of family types, including the needs and problems of stepfamilies; they should respond accordingly, with particular reference to the impact on children.

- Consideration should be given to the policy for prevention and provision of family support to those families who have not reached the point of needing remedial services.

- The importance of interagency and interprofessional work in this area should be emphasised.

- The underlying principle of empowerment and an emphasis on working in partnership with families need to be accepted by those who frame policy.

- A social worker's own value stance with women and stepmothers should be gender-sensitive and culture-sensitive.

- Social workers should facilitate better relationships between in-laws and stepparents and most particularly the relationships between the mothers-in-law and the stepmothers.

- Social workers can keep children within the stepfamilies by helping them to express and deal with the changes and with conflicts of loyalty and the sense of loss.

- The role of social workers in the context of primary prevention should be to promote 'good fathering', which assumes gender sensitivity, should be encouraged.

- Social workers should support and relate to the key agencies which impinge on stepfamilies, particularly schools, in order to encourage a more sympathetic approach to stepfamilies.

Epilogue: Peeling an Onion: The Exploration of Stepfamilies Needs to Continue

This study began as a result of the researcher's concern about the soaring number of divorces and broken families in Hong Kong and her curiosity to uncover the untold stories of an emerging family structure -- the stepfamilies. The literature review, presentation and thematic analysis of the findings of this exploratory study have been documented in the earlier chapters of this book. They are followed by critical reflections based upon the findings and the process of this study and, in the final chapter, the conclusions of this study and recommendations for social work policy and practice are presented.

This book is a record of an intellectual exercise, supported by empirical investigations, into the perceptions and life experiences of the informants about social attitudes towards stepfamilies, their perceptions of parenting in stepfamilies and the parenting behaviours of stepfamilies. The findings reveal that the informants believed that social attitudes towards stepfamilies and stepparenting were rather negative in Hong Kong. The parental perceptions and parenting behaviours in the stepfamilies under study are in turn affected. Marital relationships, parent-child relationships, and sex-role differentiation in child care and domestic duties in these stepfamilies are in need of improvement. Spousal support and understanding from the in-laws of the stepmothers would strengthen marital bonding and facilitate the building of stepmother-stepchild relationships.

All of the five objectives set for this study were achieved. There was another promotional and educational objective which was not one of the initial objectives but can be said to be a 'secondary gain' of this study. In the process of recruiting respondents, I contacted a number of the people in charge of the social work agencies and some 60 teachers. These professionals were made aware of the growing number of stepfamilies and ideas were exchanged with regard to the service needs of these families. I also made use of the opportunities to promote the idea of detecting the difficulties of children from stepfamilies in the classroom.

The information collected in this study has increased the knowledge and understanding of stepfamilies, which are currently ignored in Hong Kong. The current interventions by the formal organizations focus upon helping single parent families and dealing with marital problems resulting from extra-marital affairs. Knowledge-building on stepfamilies through research activities should be promoted in order to accumulate evidence to support the arguments for the development of policy and services. This study provides information which is new and was previously unknown, but it is limited because social attitudes have so negatively affected stepfamily members that some key members are not yet ready to be interviewed; it is partly due to the Chinese cultural belief in 'not washing dirty linen in public'. Therefore, the information collected is based upon the first-hand reports of stepmothers only, and not from all the family members. I have been involved at every step of the process of this study and I am, therefore, fully aware of its limitations. Now that the first layer of the onion has been peeled off, it is hoped that more studies will be conducted to find the core of the problem. Further studies to interview more stepmothers, their family members and extended kin are needed. The professionals who provide help will benefit from acquiring the knowledge to understand the difficulties of local stepfamilies, and the need will be established for services supported by state policy. Knowledge-building can also be accumulated by consultation with peers and by reflecting upon work experiences. Social workers and professionals who have worked with stepfamilies may contribute to the sharing of knowledge through staff development and training programmes. It is only when knowledge has been built and shared that stepfamilies can be better understood and helped.

Appendix 1
Major Problems Faced by Stepfamilies Which Receive Family Services in Hong Kong

Problem	Year	Percentage
MARITAL RELATIONSHIP	1991	19.5%
	1992	22.0%
	1993	26.7%
	1994	25.9%
	1995	26.2%
	1996	30.1%
CHILD CARE	1991	14.1%
	1992	16.3%
	1993	14.5%
	1994	12.8%
	1995	13.9%
	1996	13.2%
PARENT-CHILD RELTIONSHIP	1991	11.9%
	1992	13.1%
	1993	13.2%
	1994	12.5%
	1995	11.8%
	1996	10.7%

Source: Hong Kong Council of Social Service Clientele Information System's statistics on family counselling/casework service of the years from 1991 to 1996.

Appendix 2
Hong Kong Child Protection Registry Statistics on Active Child Abuse Cases Involving Stepparent-abusers Handled by the Social Welfare Department and the NGOs

Year	Active Cases*	Total Cases
1996	54 (8.6%)	629 (100%)
1997	66 (8.6%)	770 (100%)

* Active cases with stepparent-abusers handled by social workers of the social service units of the governmental Social Welfare Department and the non-governmental organizations.

Source: 1996 and 1997 Child Protection Registry Statistical Report published by the Hong Kong Social Welfare Department in 1997 and 1998.

Appendix 3
Against Child Abuse's Annual Statistics (June 1979 – March 1997): Number of Stepparent-abusers Receiving Casework Service

Year	Stepfather (a)	Stepmother (b)	No. of (a) + (b)	Total No. of Abusers (c)	% : (a) + (b) ÷ (c) x 100
Jun. 1979 - Mar. 1980	3	3	6	143	4.2
Apr. 1980 - Mar. 1981	1	1	2	87	2.3
Apr. 1981 - Mar. 1982	Stats. not available	Stats. not available	--	130 (cases)	--
Apr. 1982 - Mar. 1983	Stats. not available	Stats. not available	--	96	--
Apr. 1983 - Mar. 1984	Stats. not available	Stats. not available	3	298	1.0
Apr. 1984 - Mar. 1985	0	7	7	292	2.4
Apr. 1985 - Mar. 1986	0	2	2	209	1.0

(Cont'd)

Year	Stepfather (a)	Stepmother (b)	No. of (a) + (b)	Total No. of Abusers (c)	% : (a) + (b) ÷ (c) x 100
Apr. 1986 - Mar. 1987	1	2	3	138	2.2
Apr. 1987 - Mar. 1988	0	3	3	148	2.0
Apr. 1988 - Mar. 1989	0	3	3	103	3.0
Apr. 1989 - Mar. 1990	0	2	2	127	1.6
Apr. 1990 - Mar. 1991	2	3	5	128	4.0
Apr. 1991 - Mar. 1992	1	4	5	153	3.3
Apr. 1992 - Mar. 1993	2	7	9	171	5.3
Apr. 1993 - Mar. 1994	0	6	6	164	3.7
Apr. 1994 - Mar. 1995	0	3	3	143	2.1
Apr. 1995 - Mar. 1996	0	0	0	0	0.0
Apr. 1996 - Mar. 1997	0	0	0	34*	0.0

* Number of abusers only. Number of potential abusers is not combined with the number of abusers as from this year.

Source: Annual Reports, Against Child Abuse, Hong Kong (1979/80 - 1996/97).

Appendix 4
Tasks and Difficulties of Stepfamilies

Tasks	Major Areas of Difficulty	Especially Important Intervention Strategies
1. Deal with losses and changes	Coping with loss and change Unrealistic belief systems	Relate past family experiences to present Make educational comments Use genograms Use accurate language
2. Negotiate different developmental needs	Life cycle discrepancies Power issues	Restructure / reframe Teach negotiation
3. Establish new traditions	Unreaslistic belief systems Insiders / outsiders Closeness / distance	Teach negotiation Make educational comments
4. Develop solid couple bond	Insiders / outsiders Loyalty conflicts Boundary problems Power issues	Use genograms Relate past family experiences to present Teach negotiation Make educational comments Reduce a sense of helplessness

Tasks	Major Areas of Difficulty	Especially Important Intervention Strategies
5. Form new relationships	Unrealistic belief systems Insiders / outsiders Loyalty conflicts Closeness / distance	Fill in past histories Encourage dyadic relationships Separate feelings and behavior Make educational comments
6. Create parenting coalition	Loyalty issues Unrealistic belief systems Power issues Dealing with losses and change	Relate past family experiences to present Make educational comments Restructure / reframe
7. Accept continual shifts	Boundary problems Closeness / distance Unrealistic belief systems	Use genograms Reduce sense of helplessness Make educational comments Make specific suggestions
8. Risk involvement despite little societal support	Closeness / distance Dealing with losses and changes	Encourage dyadic relationships Make educational comments

Source: VISHER, E.B. & VISHER, J.S. (1988), *Old Loyalties, New Ties - Therapeutic Strategies with Stepfamilies*, N.Y.: Brunner / Mazel.

Appendix 5(A)
Interview Guide for Interviewing Stepmothers

Session 1

Objectives:

(1)   to build up initial working relationship with the stepmother;
(2)   to gather the background information of the stepmother and her family; and
(3)   to explore the stepmother's perception on stepparenting and difficulties of parenting in her family.

Duration: About 1 hour to 1.5 hours.

Schedule and Interview Guide:

Although the following will be presented as structured sequence, the researcher will bear in mind that the sequence will not necessarily follow its order. She will attend to the responses and readiness of the stepmother to facilitate natural flow of information.

1. **Briefing** on the purposes of the study and the expectations of her involvement.

2. **Face Sheet**: The researcher will collect the background information of the stepmother and her family (including family of origin) through asking all the items on the face sheet. Questions may not follow the sequence of the items on the face sheet, and if the respondent is not ready, she will be asked when she is more ready in the next interview.

Session 2

Objectives:

(1) to explore the stepmother's perception on stepparenting and difficulties, needs of parenting in her family;
(2) to explore the sex-role differentiation pattern of parenting in the stepmother's family; and
(3) to explore how feelings underlying parental perception have affected parenting behaviours and feelings of the children aroused by the parenting behaviours as reported by stepmother.

Duration: About 1.5 hours to 2 hours.

Schedule and Interview Guide:

1. **Free Association**: The stepmothers will be asked about what would the words strike her when she hears of 'step', 'stepfamily', 'stepmother', 'stepfather', 'stepchild'. The purpose is to tune her in the core subject matter and start where she is -- let her impressions lead her expression of feelings and information-giving. (Chinese characters written on cards will be shown.)

2.   **Statements by Western Stepmothers** for triggering the stepmother's opinions and feelings in relation to four aspects, namely, social attitudes (SA), parental perception (PP), stepparent's roles (SR), and stepparent's tasks (ST). (Informants will be shown cards on which statements in Chinese are written.)

SA(1): 'My mother was thrilled for me when I told her I was going to marry, but her manner changed completely when I told her he had a child. She was wary for me, she wanted me to think about it. It was not the dream she had for my marriage.' (Smith, 1990, p.30)

SA(2): 'Some people are embarrassed when I mention that I am a stepparent. It has connotations of failure [divorce], being second best [second wife], and it is a challenge to the myth of the "happy family". People either tend not to want to know, or to want to know all the intimate details.' (Smith, 1990, p.10)

SA(3): 'Society's attitude to stepmothers is unrealistic, on the one hand there is only one adjective which springs to mind and that is "wicked". On the other hand, stepmothers are expected to behave as if they were biological mothers.' (Smith, 1990, p.51)

SA(4): 'You can see people trying to put you into the mother position, sizing you up and evaluating your age, and whether the children look like you.' (Smith, 1990, p.23)

PP(1): 'You feel very alone in it... In the first year you have to give and give and take kicks from the kids and not let your own needs show, even when you feel like an abandoned child yourself.' (Smith, 1990, P.30)

PP(2): 'I must admit I don't like to think of myself as stepmother, but they are my life. I don't want to compete with their mother... and I don't want people to make mistaken assumptions. They [the children] would resent that more... [to another stepmother] I would say. Give of yourself but don't expect too much back, because you never get back what you really want. Be a little distant because there is a lot of hurt, a lot you don't know. Let them be themselves.' (Smith, 1990, p.67)

SR(1): 'It's in hard word, stepmother. Recently one of my stepchildren introduced me to a whole group of her friends in a pub as her stepmother. I felt I wanted the floor to swallow me. I never wanted to be their mother; I first happened to be married to their father. I wanted to know them, be a friend....' (Smith, 1990, p.23)

SR(2): 'There was a moment, very early on, when I had to caution one of the children to be careful, not to do something, and he shouted back to me, "You are not my mother - you can't tell me what to do!"' (Smith, 1990, p.72)

SR(3): 'I heard my stepson on the phone to his mother say to her, 'I love you', and it hurt so much!... There is no automatic right of caring or receiving care back from your stepmother. She is hire only for this time and purpose. Your mother's your mother forever.' (Smith, 1990, p.62)

SR(4): 'He [the husband] did not expect me to take over like a mother. He expected me to be friendly, have a good relationship with his son, and that is all....' (Smith, 1990, p.75)

SR(5): 'I made it very clear I was their stepmother. I respected their mother's right to be remembered.' (Smith, 1990, p.61)

SR(6): 'I think I have always wanted to impose more rules and structures than my partner thought necessary. When they [the children] were young I regarded the children as unruly and difficult to correct, whereas my partner regarded them as free and spontaneous! I have always had some difficulties in finding an appropriate role. I have always felt rather redundant to them - they have never been lacking in love and attention from either parent and at the beginning there seemed to be no role for me to slip into.' (Smith, 1990, p.75)

ST(1): 'I must admit I'd never really thought of myself as a stepmother. It's in hard word... My role is to look after them. I say to other people that they are not my children and that I look after them. But I am a typical mum in what I do. I ask about homework, bend their ear about bedrooms....' (Smith, 1990, p.67)

ST(2): 'I am there in their home and they are there in my life. I help with homework and go shopping for them, and with them. I prepare good for them. I think about them and I'm concerned about them, but I cannot control their behavior... Their father disciplines and sets standards. When he is out I sometimes withdraw if they misbehave and leave them to it.' (Smith, 1990, p.88).

ST(3): '... he (the stepchild) was very difficult. He was clingy, then tantrums, then clingy again. His mother had left very abruptly, but he didn't appear to be shattered; instead he because very withdrawn... I felt I was succeeding with him after about a year... the only problem is disciplining. That is better now as I have learnt not to interfere [when father is disciplining]....' (Smith, 1990, p.85)

ST(4): 'I disapproved of some of the things (the stepdaughter) did and wanted to indicate that. I discovered that... too many adults were telling her what to do....' (Smith, 1990, p.76)

ST(5): 'There's a lot of guilt. You cannot do what you would normally do with your own child, so you feel guilty, but if you do have a normal reaction and get angry, you feel guilty about that, too. You are always so afraid you will be unfair....' (Smith, 1990, p.42)

ST(6): 'Her father and I did not agree ... He never disciplined her, never structured her. I tried to, but the more he did nothing, the more I nagged... I worked all day and made dinner... but (the father) would get up and clear the table stead of asking her to do it, because he was afraid I would have an agreement with her... She always knew when her father was coming, and her behaviour would immediately change.' (Smith, 1990, p.76)

Reference: Smith, Donna Stepmothering, NY: Harvester/Wheatsheaf, 1990 (for all statements quoted above).

3. **Sharing of opinion and feelings triggered by vignettes:** After showing the stepmothers cards for 'free association', 'statements by western stepmothers', the subject will be shown cards on which eight local cases are described in Chinese. They will be used to trigger the subject's sharing of own opinion and feelings when told cases of other stepfamilies.

Vignette #1: The mother of a F.1 school girl complains that her daughter does not accept the stepfather. She is so disrespectful to him that she does not even greet him 'good morning'. This is the sixth month after the stepfamily is formed but despite much of her effort to build closer relationship between daughter and her new husband, she fails. The daughter is only looking forward to seeing her natural father who takes her out once a month. (This vignette tries to illustrate Visher and Visher's concept on task#1 'dealing with losses and change'. This means that family members carry with them experiences and feelings from the past, they need time to cope with losses and changes, and deal with feelings when relating to the old ties and new relationships.)

Vignette #2: A middle-aged man remarried a woman who likes to play the housewife role, unlike his former wife who was a career woman and disliked housekeeping and caring of children. The man feels very contented after work when greeted by his wife who cooks great dinner for him and manages his home well. His two children, aged 13 and 10, complains that their new mother is always on their back and they hate her. (This vignette tries to illustrate Visher and Visher's concept on task#2 'negotiation of different developmental needs', which means that the couple may have needs in their own developmental life state, they have to negotiate and restructure the priorities for their needs, and to deal with power issues when they arise).

Vignette #3: A 35 years old woman remarries an older man hoping to 'make her marriage work this time'. She loves this man because she thinks that he is mature and is a good-planner for his life and career. He can make her feel secure. Her 11 year old daughter finds her stepfather too strict on setting rules and she complains of him always limiting her on the number of telephone calls each day, setting rules for lights out at bedtime and demanding church-going on Sunday. (This vignette tries to illustrate Visher and Visher's concept on task#3 'establishing new traditions'. This means the stepparents may wish to speed up the building up of the new family by introduction of new ways of family life, they may overlook the fact that evolvement of stepfamily will take time and it will require understanding of the old traditions and needs of individual family members).

Vignette #4:   John has a daughter from his former marriage and remarries Susan who has a son from her last marital relationship. Four of them live together. Both John and Susan have busy jobs and they come home late. The household work is left to a live-in domestic helper. Susan has to spend time with her son who seemingly has deteriorated in school performances since the stepfamily was formed three months ago. John complains that Susan does not attend to the needs of his daughter nor does she spend time with him. He said, 'I talked with you more when I was dating you before our marriage, now you only spare the time for your own son.' (This vignette tries to illustrate Visher and Visher's concept on task#4 on 'developing solid couple bond'. This means biological parents may be enmeshed with their own child and they have to work on a balanced but permeable boundary between the marital dyad system and the parent-child system.)

Vignette #5: The stepmother complains to her husband about his pre-school age daughter Mary: 'I love you and I love your daughter too. See my son Peter, he respects you a lot and is close to you. But Mary is different, she doesn't accept me, whenever I buy Peter something, I always buy things for her. She is so ungrateful for what I do for her.' (This vignette tries to illustrate Visher and Visher's concept on task#5 'forming new relationship'. This means that stepparents may have frustrations over their stepchildren for not being able to build up relationships with them as far as they wish, they may overlook the loyalty conflicts issues which they have to deal with.)

Vignette #6: The father said to his daughter who is living with him and the stepmother: 'Your stepmother is treating you so nicely, when you buy the Mother's Day gift for you own mother, don't forget to buy one for your stepmother too.' The daughter said, 'Why should I? You buy stepmother everything she wants but my mother gets nothing. If I buy her a gift, my mother will be angry.' (This vignette tries to illustrate Visher and Visher's concept on task#6 on 'creating a parenting coalition'. This means that parents have to be understanding of the child's feelings towards the non-custodial parents and they have to make effort to deal with split loyalty issues.)

Vignette #7: A middle-aged man divorced his wife, remarries his business partner who is a young, pretty woman in her mid-20s. They are living in the same house with three teenage children of the man's former marriage. His children are Lily, age 17, Helen, age 15, and John, age 13. The father and the stepmother are often on business trips and they leave the housekeeping to Lily. The father allows his ex-wife to keep an eye on the children when he and his wife are away from Hong Kong. The stepmother does not cook or take up housework, nor does she speak to the children when she is at home. (This vignette tries to illustrate Visher and Visher's concept on task #7 'accepting continual shifts'. That means that there are boundary problems in a rather open family system where family members come and go, it is difficult for the family members to build up a sense of belonging and develop identity to the stepfamily.)

Vignette #8: The stepfather said to his wife at bedtime: 'You know what your daughter said to me today? You are not my father, you will never be. I live here because I feel pity for my mother who has lost her last husband. And don't you ever hug me again. I will tell the social worker at my school that you've sexually molested me.' The wife said, 'I shall talk to her about this tomorrow. She must have read the "stepfather raped the stepdaughter case" in the newspaper a few days ago and have developed some wrong ideas. How can she say something like that to you?' (This vignette tries to illustrate Visher and Visher's concept on task#8 'risk involvement despite little societal support', this means that stepparents may have to deal with their stepchildren's strong feelings of loss and build up parent-child relationship with the support and understanding of their spouse.)

Note: After the stepmother is shown the above eight cards one by one, she will be allowed time to free flow her opinions and feelings after reading them. If she has difficulties to give opinion or express feelings, she will be asked these questions: (1) How do you feel when you read this case? (2) What are the problems of this family? (3) Are there any problems in parenting? (4) Who should be the key person responsible for causing the problems of parenting and why?

258

The researcher does not need to change the gender of the parents in the case illustration to match the informant. The purpose of discussion by using vignettes is to facilitate the informant to talk about the difficulties she sees in taking up the role of stepparent, so the views expressed will not be limited to stepmothering.

Session 3

Objectives:

(1)   to further explore the parental tasks undertaken by the stepmother and her spouse in her family;
(2)   to explore the difficulties of the parental tasks taken by the stepmother and the causes of these difficulties;
(3)   to explore the sex-role differentiation pattern of parenting in the stepmother's family; and
(4)   to explore the kinds of help needed by the stepmothers and her family.

Duration: About 1.5 hours to 2 hours.

Schedule and Interview Guide:

The following are research questions to be asked in this session, they do not necessarily follow a sequential order.   The stepmothers should be interviewed at their pace and readiness.

•   What were your expectations of the role of a parent in a stepfamily before it was formed? What are your expectations now?
•   How were those expectations formed?   Was there anybody who influenced you in developing those expectations?   Who was/were he/she/they?
•   Do you know the expectations of the role of parent in a stepfamily held by your husband / partner before this stepfamily was formed? What are his expectations now?

- How were his expectations formed? Was there anybody who influenced him on developing those expectations? Who was/were he/she/they?
- Do you think those expectations have affected the ways in which you and your husband / partner parent? Could you give me an example?
- What are the parenting tasks undertaken by you in this family? Could you explain to me in your role as a parent, what are your responsibilities in a typical day?
- Do you have any difficulties when carrying out your roles and tasks? If so, what are they?
- In your view, what may have caused the difficulties?
- What are the parenting tasks undertaken by your husband / partner in a typical day? Do you think he has difficulties to carry those out?
- If you have children of your own and stepchildren living with you, do you see your parenting responsibilities different? Could you give me an example of a daily life encounter which can illustrate the difference?
- How would your husband / partner handle the same situation? Do you agree with him on how he handles the situation?
- If you have children of different sex, would you undertake different parenting tasks? How would it be different as compared with the current situation? Could you give me an example so that I can understand this better?
- How would your husband/partner handle the same situation? Do you agree with him on how he handles the situation?
- What are the parental tasks which would arouse feelings when carrying them out? Do you think your children/stepchildren's feelings will be affected too? How?
- What are the parental tasks which would arouse your husband/partner's feelings when carrying them out? Do you think your children/stepchildren's feelings will be affected too? How?
- Would you say you are a 'strict' or 'lenient' parent? Could you give an example as to how you would handle a difficult disciplining situation?
- Would you say your husband/partner a 'strict' or 'lenient' parent? Could you give an example as to how he would handle a difficult disciplining situation?
- If your usual disciplining method fails, how would you handle the situation then?

- If the usual disciplining method used by your husband/partner fails, how would he handle the situation then?
- What other parenting difficulties and feelings you may have in addition to what you have described earlier?
- What other parenting difficulties and feelings your husband / partner may have in addition to what you have described just now?
- What kinds of help do you think you would need to solve the above-mentioned problems? Are you getting any help now? If not, would you like some?
- What kind of help do you think your husband/partner may need?
- Whether you are reaching out for some help or have decided not to reach out, what have made you decide whether or not to seek help? Has this decision anything to do with the way you perceive yourself, your family, or your encounters with others who know you are from a stepfamily?
- What do you think are the views of people on stepfamily and stepparenting? Would their views affect the ways how they relate to you and your family, or prevent you and your family from getting the kind of help that you may need?
- What kinds of service you and your family would like to obtain?
- Is there anything you would like the Government do to help your family or stepfamilies in general?
- Do you think your husband/partner would suggest the same? What are some of the other things which you think your husband/partner would suggest to obtain help for your family and the stepfamilies in general?

Appendix 5(B)
Interview Guide for Interviewing Social Workers and Teachers

Objectives:

(1)   to gather brief background information of the informant;
(2)   to explore the informant's perceptions on stepfamilies and stepparenting; and
(3)   to explore the roles the informant has played or would like to play in helping the stepfamilies.

Target:

Eight social workers from NGO Family Services Centres (four males, four females who have handled stepfamily cases).
Eight teachers from primary, secondary, and special schools (four males, four females who have contacts with members of stepfamilies at work).

Duration of the Interview: About 1.5 hours.

Interview Guide:

1. **Briefing** on the purposes and schedule of the interview.

2. **Face Sheet**: the researcher will collect the background information of the informant.

3. **Free Association**: As a warm-up exercise, the informant will be asked about what the following words strike him/her when he/she sees them. The purpose is to tune him/her in the core subject matter but start where he/she is, let his/her impressions lead him/her to express feelings and views on the subject matter.

    The words will be presented in Chinese, written on cards :

    *   step;
    *   stepfamily;
    *   stepmother;
    *   stepfather; and
    *   stepchild.

4. **Sharing of opinion and feelings triggered by vignettes**: The informant will be shown cards on which five local cases are described. They will be used to trigger the informant's responses by sharing of his/her opinion and feelings when seen case illustrations of stepfamilies.

    Vignette #1: The mother of a F.1 school girl complains that her daughter does not accept the stepfather. She is so disrespectful to him that she does not even greet him 'good morning'. This is the sixth month after the stepfamily is formed but despite much of her effort to build closer relationship between daughter and her new husband, she fails. The daughter is only looking forward to seeing her natural father who takes her out once a month. (This vignette tries to illustrate Visher and Visher's concept on 'dealing with losses and change'. This means that family members carry with them experiences and feelings from the past, they need time to cope with losses and changes, and deal with feelings when relating to the old ties and new relationships.)

Vignette #2: John has a daughter from his former marriage and remarries Susan who has a son from her last marital relationship. Four of them live together. Both John and Susan have a busy job and they come home late. The household work is left to a live-in domestic helper. Susan has to spend time with her son who seemingly has deteriorated in school performance since the stepfamily has been formed three months ago. John complains that Susan does not attend to the needs of his daughter nor does she spend time with him. He said, 'I talked with you more when I was dating you before our marriage, now you only spare time for your own son.' (This vignette tries to illustrate Visher and Visher's concept on 'developing solid couple bond'. This means biological parents may be enmeshed with their own child and they have to work on a balanced but permeable boundary between the marital dyad system and the parent-child system.)

Vignette #3: A middle-aged man remarried a woman who likes to play the housewife role, unlike his former wife who was a career woman and disliked housekeeping and caring of the children. The man feels very contented after work when greeted by his wife who cooks great dinner for him and manages his home well. His two children, aged 13 and 10, complain that their new mother is always on their back and they hate her. (This vignette tries to illustrate Visher and Visher's concept on 'negotiation of different developmental needs', which means that the couple may have needs in their own developmental life stage, they have to negotiate and restructure the priorities of their needs, and to deal with power issues when they arise.)

Vignette #4: A woman, in her late 20s, married a divorcee who has a seven year old son. The husband is the eldest son of his widowed mother. The divorced younger sister of the man is also living in the flat with her son. So although the flat is owned by the women's husband, she shares it with her mother-in-law, stepson, husband, his divorced younger sister and her son. At night the younger brother of her husband, his wife, and two of the man's younger sisters would come to the flat for supper, and there is a child of the man's younger sister, childminded by the mother-in-law, all have supper at this woman's flat. One night the woman's sister-in-law came for supper and said to the woman's mother-in-law: 'My Filipino maid will arrive Hong Kong tomorrow, from tomorrow night and on, I shall take her here to have supper too. It's too troublesome to cook at home.' (This vignette tries to illustrate the concept of 'power and equity'. Firstly, the concept of gender-biased division of household tasks. As pointed out by Demo and Acock (1993), mothers in remarried families did not differ from mothers in first marriages in the amount of household they did, and both groups of women did far more than their husbands. Secondly, the concept of 'latent function hypothesis' by Clingempeel el al (1992) speculates that the stress of divorce and new remarriage might activate grandparents to become involved in the lives of their divorcing child and grandchildren.)

Vignette #5: A middle age woman married a man whose wife died and he has a seven year old daughter. The paternal mother-in-law has lived with them since the beginning of their marriage but she does not accept the new daughter-in-law. She calls her 'stepmom' in front of her stepdaughter. Once the stepmother punished her stepdaughter out of anger, the mother-in-law took out a stick and shouted provokingly, 'Hit her, hit her to death.' She opened the door, punched her own chest so neighbours could react and show sympathy to her. That night the couple had a wedding banquette to go to. The mother-in-law made things difficult by demanding the couple to take the girl to the banquette too or else they were not allowed to go. The stepmother said to her, 'You think you could threaten me with this? I may buy additional gift for the newly-wed so I could take the girl there too.' She ordered the stepdaughter to get dressed and blamed her for initiating the incident. The husband said, 'Leave her alone. she had gone to a picnic yesterday and today she has experienced this, she would be too tired to go.' (This vignette tries to illustrate the concept on 'communication and conflict management'. It is commonly believed that remarried couples fight with each other more than couples in first marriages. Hobart (1991); Messinger (1976) point out that the primary topics that remarried couples argue about are issues related to children from prior relationships, e.g. rules for children's behaviour, discipline techniques. According to Ganong and Coleman, there are a number of moderating and mediating variables potentially influence the dynamics of remarriages. Among them there is one which is named 'contact and support from extended kin'. This vignette reflects that conflict with extended kin may contribute to marital and parenting difficulties.)

265

5. Perceptions on stepfamilies and stepparenting

The subject will be asked the following questions.

- Should people remarry after the death of their spouse?
- Should people remarry after divorce?
- Should people remarry if they have children from their previous marital relationship?
- How would you address a stepparent, a stepchild?
- Should father be the primary disciplinarian? Mother be the carer in a family?
- What are your expectations of the roles of a parent and a stepparent in a stepfamily?
- What are your expectations of stepmothers in their parenting role?
- How were these expectations formed?
- If you have to deal with the problem of a child / student who is a stepchild, which parent would you talk to on his / her problem, and why?
- In your views, what are the needs and difficulties of the members in a stepfamily, i.e. the stepparent, parent, stepchild, child?
- Would there be any difference in their needs and problems depanding upon whether the stepparent is male or female? What are these differences and why?
- How can you tell whether a child / student is a stepchild or not? What are the characteristics they may have?
- If you know that the child / student is a stepchild, would you change your attitude in relation to him / her? Why?
- Would there be any difference in the needs and problems depending upon whether the stepchild is a boy or girl? What are the differences and why?
- Would there be any difference in their needs and problems if the stepchild is a younger or older child? What are the differences and why?
- In your role as a teacher / social worker, what kind of help do you think you can offer to the stepparent, parent, stepchild or child in a stepfamily?
- Is there anything you think your school / agency can do to help them?

- Is there anything the Government can do to help them?
- Any other opinion or suggestion you may have in helping stepfamilies, stepparents or stepchildren?

Appendix 6
Reflections of a Hong Kong Stepmother*

Being a stepfather or a stepmother is not easy nowadays. They have to face great pressure. In the eyes of many people, they are viewed as fierce, they have no loving hearts, and, they are selfish. Many stepfathers and stepmothers at first do hope to relate genuinely and lovingly to their stepchildren with love and they wish to live harmoniously with them together. But their relatives [of the stepchildren] think that the love shown by the stepparents is not genuine, so the stepchildren would not accept their stepparents easily. In the eyes of the kin, children are always 'the weak', they will be bullied, they need to be protected, they are miserable, etc.

People usually wish that their marriages are happy and perfect. During the period when they are newly wedded, they hope to have sweet times for two people only, keeping them for beautiful memories. But if these two people are stepparents, their marital life starts from the beginning is a 'three people's world', or a 'multi-people's world', and in this three people's or multi-people's world there are many problems. For example, stepparents try to do all the good things to please their stepchildren so as to make them accept them, but most of the children would not accept another person to be their father or mother, and the result is that at the end the stepparents have made great effort but they fail to build the relationship.

Being stepparents, they do not only have to face the above problems, they have to face pressure from the relatives of their spouse, for example, from the parents, siblings, friends of his/her spouse, and the children's biological parents, etc. These people, most of them, are siding with the children, they

268

are watchful of whether the stepparents are treating the children fairly, but no one would pay attention to whether the children are respectful to the stepparents and whether they accept their stepparents. Biological parents of the stepchildren should be aware of their responsibilities to develop their children healthily, they should not just place the responsibilities on the stepparents' shoulders. If they love their children, they should think of their children first before deciding on matter of their welfare. They have to think whether they could tolerate and forgive the other party for the sake of their children, they should not let themselves do wrong thing, leading to broken marriage and divorce, then place the responsibilities onto the stepparents' shoulders. They hope that other people would take care of their children. They demand a lot from the stepparents, they would not sacrifice for their children, but shifting the responsibilities to the stepparents. For example, they hope other people would take their children as if they were borne by them, they expect that their children to be taught to become an achiever, when their children have psychological, behavioural, physical or academic problems, the children's biological parents, relatives and general public would think that those are due to the stepparents' failure to fulfil their responsibilities. On the other hand, they would not teach their children to respect their stepparents, same as what they will do when relating to their own parents. If the stepparents have psychological problems caused by pressure, they do not only have no sympathy, they think that the stepparents have brought those problems on themselves. I feel this is most unfair.

I believe that one who is prepared to take on the stepparent's role must love their spouse very much, so they are willing to bear the name of 'stepfather' or 'stepmother', bear the pressure imposed by general public, relatives and friends when starting their marital life. They must place their spouse at the most important position in their mind: say, for everything you do, you hope to see happiness in your husband or wife, and to trade for his/her concern to you. But may be at the end one will find that the concern of his/her spouse is whether his/her children would live with the stepparent happily, but not him/her living happily with the stepparent as happy married couple. In their hearts, children are most important, not the spouse. If so, this may lead to his/her second failure of marriage. If children's parents have to remarry, please think carefully about one's own needs: do you wish to find a caring parent for your children? Or do you wish to have a new start? If you wish your children to be cared for by both parents, one must think very carefully before proceeding for divorce, because it is very difficult to find replacements for biological parents. Before remarriage, one has to ask his/her future spouse to think over it very carefully, can he/she be the parent

269

of one's children, ask himself/herself whether he/she can tolerate, forgive and accept children who are not his/her own. If one wants a new start for oneself, but one's future husband/wife cannot accept one's children, please do not force him/her to, one should sit down and talk calmly on the arrangement and plan, so that the person, his/her future husband/wife and his/her children can live happily.

(* The stepmother was an informant of my study. She had written a full two-page message reflecting on her feelings regarding the role of being a stepparent. This English version is translated from the original version which was in Chinese language.)

Appendix 7(A)
Personal Particulars of the Social Workers Interviewed

Code	Name	Sex/ Age	Years of Work	Marital Status	No. of Childrens	Type of Family of Origin	Religion
S01	Ko	F/27	4	Single	N/A	Intact	Catholic
S02	Liu	F/27	2½	Single	N/A	Intact	Catholic
S03	Lo	F/34	10	Married	N/A	Broken (Parents Divorced)	Protestant
S04	Yu	M/28	3	Married	N/A	Broken (Parents Divorced)	Protestant
S05	Ng	F/28	6	Married	N/A	Intact	Protestant
S06	Wong	M/29	7	Single	N/A	Intact	N/A
S07	Tang	M/38	9	Married	One	Broken (Parents Deceased)	Protestant
S08	Kong	M/29	5	Single	N/A	Intact	N/A

Appendix 7(B)
Personal Particulars of the
Teachers Interviewed

Code	Name	Sex/ Age	Years of Work	Marital Status	Number of Children	Type of Family of Origin	Religion
T01	Mok	F/29	4	Married	N/A	Intact	N/A
T02	Lai	F/35	13	Married	One	Intact	Catholic
T03	Ng	M/32	8	Married	N/A	Intact	N/A
T04	Sin	M/42	12	Married	Three	Intact	Catholic
T05	Wong	F/34	10	Single	N/A	Remarried (one parent deceased)	Catholic
T06	Hui	M/29	7	Single	N/A	Intact	Protestant
T07	Tsui	F/30	6	Single	N/A	Intact	N/A
T08	Lau	M/30	6	Single	N/A	Remarried (one parent deceased)	Protestant

Bibliography

Against Child Abuse (1996), *Against Child Abuse Annual Report 1995-96*, HK: Against Child Abuse.

Against Child Abuse (1997), *Against Child Abuse Annual Report 1996-97*, HK: Against Child Abuse.

Ahrons, C.R. & Wallisch, L. (1987), 'Parenting in the binuclear family: Relationships between biological and stepparents', in K. Pasley & M. Ihinger-Tallman (eds), *Remarriage and Stepparenting: Current Research and Theory*, NY: Guilford.

Ahrons, C. & Rodgers, R.H. (1988), *Divorced Families: A Multidisciplinary Development View*, NY: Norton.

Alexander, J.F. (1973), 'Defensive and supportive communication in normal and deviant families', *Journal of Consulting Clinical Psychology*, 40, pp. 223-31.

Allport, G. (1954), *The Nature of Prejudice*, Cambridge, MA: Addison-Wesley.

Amato, P.R. (1987), 'Family processes in one-parent, stepparent, and intact families: The child's point-of-view', *Journal of Marriage and the Family*, 49, pp. 327-37.

Amato, P.R. & Keith, B. (1991), 'Parental divorce and the well-being of children', *Psychological Bulletin*, 110, pp. 26-46.

Aquilino, W.S. (1991), 'Family structure and home leaving: A further specification of the relationship', *Journal of Marriage and the Family*, 53, 999-1010.

Astone, N.M. & McLanahan, S.S. (1991), 'Family structure, parental practices and high school completion', *American Sociological Review*, 56, pp. 309-20.

Aulette, J.R. (1994), *Changing Families*, CA: Wadsworth.

Baker, H.R.D. (1979), *Chinese Family and Kinship*, London: Macmillan.

Barber, B.K. & Rollins, B.C. (eds) (1990), *Parent-adolescent Relationships)*, Lanham, MD: University Press of America.

Baumrind, D. (1966), 'Effects of authoritative parental control on child behaviour', *Child Development*, 37, pp. 887-907.

Baumrind,D. (1971), *Current Patterns of Parental Authority*, Development Psychology Monographs, 4 (1, pt. 2)

Baumrind, D. (1991), 'Parenting styles and adolescent development', in J. Brooks-Gunn, R. Lerner, and A.C. Petersen (eds), *The Encyclopedia of Adolescence*, NY: Garland.

Bernard, J. (1956), *Remarriage*, NY: Dryden Press.

Birenbaum, H. (1988), *Myth and Mind*, Lanham, MD: University Press.

Bohannon, P. (1970), 'Divorce chains, households of remarriage, and multiple divorces', in P. Bohannon (ed), *Divorce and After: An Analysis of the Emotional and Social Problems of Divorce*, NY: Doubleday.

Bond, M. (1986), *The Psychology of the Chinese People*, HK: Oxford University Press.

Bond, M.H. & Hwang, K.K. (1986), 'The social psychology of Chinese people', in M.H. Bond (ed) *The Psychology of the Chinese People*, HK: Oxford University Press.

Bowlby, J. (1953), *The Roots of Parenthood*, London: National Children's Home.

Bowlby, J. (1980), 'Loss: sadness and depression', in Vol. III of *Attachment and Loss*, London: International Psychoanalytic Library, Hogarth & the Institute of Psychoanalysis.

Boys' and Girls' Clubs Association of Hong Kong (1990), *Participation of Fathers in Household Activities in Hong Kong*, HK: BGCA.

Boys' and Girls' Clubs Association of Hong Kong (1994), *The Relationship between Parenting Styles and Adolescents' Behaviour*, HK: BGCA.

274

Bray, J. (1988) 'Children's development during early remarriage', in E.M. Hetherington & J.D. Arasteh (eds), *Impact of Divorce, Single Parenting, and Stepparenting on Children*, Hillsdale, NJ: Erlbaum.

Bray, J., Berger, S.H., Silverblatt, A.H. & Hollier, A. (1987), 'Family process and organization during early remarriage: A preliminary analysis', in J. P. Vincent (ed) *Advances in Family Intervention, Assessment, and Theory*, Greenwich, CT: JAI.

Brody, E. (1974), 'Aging and family personality: A developmental view', *Family Process*, 13, pp. 23-37.

Browning, S. (1994), 'Treating stepfamilies: Alternatives to traditional family therapy', in K. Pasley & M. Ihinger-Tallman (eds), *Stepparenting: Issues in Theory, Research & Practice*, Westport: Greenwood Press.

Bruner, J.S. (1960), 'Myths and identity', in H.A. Murray (ed), *Myth and Mythinking*, Boston: Beacon Press.

Bryan, L., Coleman, M., Ganong, L. & Bryan, S. (1986), 'Person perception: Family structure as a cue for stereotyping', *Journal of Marriage and the Family*, 48, pp. 169-74.

Burgoyne, J. & Clark, D. (1981), 'Parenting in stepfamilies', in Chester, R., Diggory, P. & Sutherland, M.B. (eds), *Changing Patterns of Child-bearing and Child-rearing*, NY: Academic Press.

Burgoyne, J. & Clark, D. (1984), *Making-a-Go-of-it*, London: Routledge & Kegan Paul.

Capaldi, F. & McRae, B. (1979), *Stepfamilies: A Cooperative Responsibility*, NY: New Viewpoints/Visions Books.

Caritas and the University of Hong Kong (1995), *Study on Marriages affected by Extramarital Affairs*, HK: Caritas Family Service.

Carter, E.A. & McGoldrick, M. (eds) (1980), *The Family Life Cycle: A Framework for Family Therapy*, NY: Gardner Press.

Central Office of Information (1996), *Britain 1997*, London: Stationery Office.

Chan, W.T. (1963), *A Source Book in Chinese Philosophy*, Princeton, NJ: Princeton University Press.

Chang, J. (1991), *Wild Swans*, London: Flamingo.

Chao, P. (1983), *Chinese Kinship*, London: Kegan Paul International.

Cherlin, A. (1978), 'Remarriage as an Incomplete Institution', *American Journal of Sociology*, 84, pp. 634-50.

Cherlin, A. (1981), *Marriage, Divorce, Remarriage*, Cambridge, MA: Harvard U. Press.

Cherlin, A. & Furstenberg, F. (1986), *American Grandparenthood*, NY: Basic Books.

Cheung, F.M., Chau, B.T.W. & Lam, M.C. (1990), 'Caregiving techniques and pre-school children's development in Hong Kong families', A monograph published by the Centre for Hong Kong Studies, HK: The Chinese University of Hong Kong, Institute of Social Studies.

Choi, Y.W. (1987), 'Exploring the current values of adolescents', in *The Problems of Adolescents living in Hong Kong and Mainland China* (in Chinese), HK: The Hong Kong Federation of Youth Groups, pp.1-7.

Cissna, K.N., Cox, D.E. & Bochner, A.P. (1990), 'The dialectic of marital and parental relationships within the stepfamily', *Communication Monographs*, 57(1), pp. 44-61.

Clingempeel, W.G., Brand, E. & Ievoli, R. (1984), 'Stepparent-stepchild relationships in stepmother and stepfather families: A multimethod study', *Family Relations*. 33, pp. 465-73.

Clingempeel, W.G., Brand, E. & Segal, S. (1987), 'A multilevel-multivariable-developmental perspective for future research on stepfamilies', in K. Pasley & M. Ihinger-Tallman (eds), *Remarriage and Stepparenting Today: Current Research and Theory*, NY: Guilford.

Clingempeel, W.G., Colyar, J., Brand, E. & Hetherington, E.M. (1992), 'Children's relationships with maternal grandparents: A longitudinal study of family structure and pubertal status effects', *Child Development*, 63, pp. 1404-22.

Coleman, M. & Ganong, L. (1985a), *Childbearing and Stepfamilies: Effects on Half-siblings*, Unpublished Raw Data.

Coleman, M. & Ganong, L.H. (1987a), 'The cultural stereotyping of stepfamilies' in Pasley, K. & Ihinger-Tallman, M. (eds), *Remarriage and Stepparenting Today: Current Research and Theory*, NY: Guilford.

Coleman, M. & Ganong, L. (1989), 'Financial management in stepfamilies' *Life Styles: Family and Economic Issues*, 10, pp. 217-32.

Colmey, J. (May, 1997), 'Everything you wanted to know about the Handover (but were afraid to ask)', *Time Magazine Hong Kong 1997 Special Souvenir Issue*, HK: Time Magazine.

Combrinck-Graham, L. (ed) (1989), *Children in Family Contexts: Perspectives on Treatment*, NY: Guilford.

Conroy, R. (1987), 'Patterns of divorce in China' in *Australian Journal of Chinese Affairs*, (Jan.), 17, pp. 53-75.

Coverman, S. (1989), 'Women's work is never done, the division of domestic labor', in J. Freeman (ed). *Women: A Feminist Perspective*, CA: Mayfield, pp. 356-70.

Crosbie-Burnett, M. (1994) 'The interface between stepparent families and schools: Research, theory, policy, and practice', in K. Pasley & M. Ihinger-Tallman (eds), *Steppparenting: Issues in Theory, Research and Practice*, Westport: Greenwood Press.

Crosbie-Burnett, M. & Giles-Sims, J. (1991), 'Marital power in stepfather families: A test of normative-resource theory', *Journal of Family Psychology*, 4, pp. 484-96.

Crosbie-Burnett, M. & Giles-Sims, J. (1994), 'Adolescent adjustment and stepparenting styles', *Family Relations*, 43, pp. 394-99.

Dainton, M. (1993), 'The myths and misconceptions of the stepmother identity', *Family Relations*, 42, pp. 93-98.

Dartington Social Research Unit (1995), *Child Protection: Messages from Research*, London: HMSO.

Dallos, R. (1992), *Family Belief Systems, Therapy and Change*, Milton Keynes: Open U. Press.

Darley, J. & Gross, P. (1983), 'A hypothesis-confirming bias in labelling effects', *Journal of Personality and Social Psychology*, 44, 20-33.

Demo, D.H. & Acock, A.C. (1993), 'Family diversity and the division of domestic labor: How much have things really changed?', *Family Relations*, 42, pp. 323-331.

Demo, D.H., Small, S.A. & Savin-Williams, R.C. (1987), 'Family relations and the esteem of adolescents and their parents', *Journal of Marriage and the Family*, 49, pp. 705-715.

Denzin, N. (1970), *The Research Act in Sociology*, London: Butterworth.

Denzin, N.K. (1978b), *The Research Act: A Theoretical Introduction to Sociological Methods*, NY: McGraw-Hill.

Denzin, N.K. & Lincoln, Y.S. (eds), (1994), *Handbook of Qualitative Research*, Thousand Oaks, CA: Sage.

Duberman, L. (1975), *The Reconstituted Family: A Study of Remarried Couples and Their Children*, Chicago: Nelson Hall.

Duvall, E.M. & Miller, B.C. (eds) (1985), *Marriage and Family Development* (6th ed.), NY: Harper & Row.

Ehrlich, H.J. (1973), *The Social Psychology of Prejudice*, NY: Wiley.

Erikson, E.H. (1950), *Childhood and Society*, NY: Norton.

277

Espinoza, R. & Newman, Y. (1979), *Stepparenting*, Washington, DC: US Government Printing Office.

Express News (December 11, 1996), HK: Express News.

Fagot, B.I., Leinbach, M.D. & O'Boyle, C. (1992), 'Gender labeling, gender stereotyping, and parenting behaviors', *Developmental Psychology*, 28, 2, pp. 225-30.

Fan, Y.K. & Skeldon, R. (1995), 'Introduction', in R. Skeldon (ed) *Emigration from Hong Kong*, HK: The Chinese U. Press.

Fine, M.A. (1986) 'Perception of stepparents: Variation in stereotypes as a function of current family structure,' *Journal of Marriage and the Family*, 48, pp. 537-43.

Fine, M.A. & Kurdek, L.A. (1992), 'The adjustment of adolescents in stepfather and stepmother families', *Journal of Marriage and the Family*, (Nov.), 54, pp. 725-36.

Fine, M.A. & Kurdek, L.A. (1995), 'Relation between marital quality and (step) parent-child relationship quality for parents and stepparents in stepfamilies', *Journal of Family Psychology*, 9(2), pp. 216-23.

Fine, M.A. and Schwebel, A.I. (1991), 'Stepparent stress: A cognitive perspective', *Journal of Divorce and Remarriage*, 17(1/2), pp. 1-15.

Fine, M.A., Voydanoff, P. & Donnelly, B. (1993), 'Relations between parental control and warmth and child well-being in stepfamilies', *Journal of Family Psychology*, 7, pp. 222-32.

Fiske, S.T. & Taylor, S. (1984), *Social Cognition*, Reading, MA: Addison-Wesley.

Fluitt, M.S. & Paradise, L.V. (1991), 'The relationship of current family structures to young adults' perceptions of stepparents', *Journal of Divorce and Remarriage*, 15, pp. 159-73.

Fox Harding, L. (1996), *Family, State and Social Policy*, Houndmills: Macmillan.

Frost, N. (1997), 'Delivering family support: Issues & themes in service development', in N. Parton (ed), *Child Protection & Family Support*, London: Routledge.

Furstenberg, F.F. Jr., & Nord, C.W. (1985), 'Parenting apart: Patterns of childrearing after marital dissolution', *Journal of Marriage and the Family*, 47, pp. 893-904.

Ganong, L. & Coleman, M. (1993), 'An exploratory study of stepsibling subsystems', *Journal of Divorce and Remarriage*, 19(3/4), pp. 125-41.

Ganong, L. & Coleman, M. (1983), 'Stepparent: A pejorative term?', *Psychologist Reports*, 52, pp. 919-22.

Ganong, L., Coleman, M., & Kennedy, G. (1990), 'The effects of using alternate labels in denoting stepparent or stepfamily status', *Journal of Social Behaviour and Personality*, 5, pp. 453-63.

Ganong, L., Coleman, M. & Mapes, D. (1990), 'A meta-analytic review of family structure stereotypes', *Journal of Marriage and the Family*, 52, pp. 287-98.

Ganong, L.H. & Coleman, M. (1994), *Remarried Family Relationships*, Thousand Oaks, CA: Sage.

Gibbons, J. (1997), 'Relating outcomes to objectives in child protection policy', in N. Parton (ed) *Child Protection and Family Support*, London: Routledge.

Giles-Sims, J. (1984), 'The stepparent role', *Journal of Family Issues*, 5, 1, pp. 116-30.

Goetting, A. (1982), 'The six stations of remarriage: Development tasks of remarriage after divorce', *Family Relations*, 31, pp. 213-22.

Golan, N. (1974) 'Crisis Theory', in F.J. Turner (ed) *Social Work Treatment: Interlocking Theoretical Approaches*, NY: The Free Press, pp. 420-56.

Goode, W.J. (1993), *World Changes in Divorce Patterns*, New Haven, CT: Yale U. Press.

Government Central statistical Offic (1995), *Social Trend 1995*, London: HMSO.

Government Central Statistical Office (1996), *Social Trends 1996*, London: HMSO.

Government Central Statistical Office (1997), *Social Trends 1997*, London: HMSO.

Guisinger, S., Cowan, P.A. & Schuldberg, D. (1989), 'Changing parents and spouse relations in the first years of remarriage of divorced fathers', *Journal of Marriage and Family*, 51, pp. 445-56.

Haley, J. (1981), *Reflections on Therapy and Other Essays*, Chevy Chase, MD: Family Therapy Institute.

Hamon, R.R. & Thiessen, J.D. (Nov.1990), 'Coping with the dissolution of an adult child's marriage', paper presented at the National Council on Family Relations Annual Meeting, Seattle, WA.

Hanson, T.L., McLanahan, S.S. & Thomson, E. (1996), 'Double jeopardy - - parental conflict and stepfamily outcomes for children', *Journal of Marriage and the Family*, 58(1), pp. 141-54.

Hardiker, P., Exton, K. & Barker, M. (1995), 'The prevention of child abuse: A framework for analyzing services', London: The National Commission of Inquiry into the Prevention of Child Abuse.

Hardiker, P., Exton, K. & Barker, M. (1991), *Policies and Practices in Preventive Child Care*, Aldershot: Gower.

Hearn, B. (1995), '*Child and Family Support and Protection: A Practical Approach*, London: National Children's Bureau.

Hearn, B. (1997), 'Putting child and family support and protection into practice', in N. Parton (ed), *Child Protection and Family Support*, London: Routledge.

Henry, C.S., Ceglian, C.P. & Ostrander, D.L. (1993), 'The transition to stepgrandparenthood' *Journal of Divorce and Remarriage*, 19(3/4), pp. 25-44.

Hetherington, E.M. (1987), 'Family relations six years after divorce', in K. Pasley & M. Ihinger-Tallman (eds), *Remarriage and Stepparenting: Current Research & Theory*, NY: Guilford.

Hetherington, E.M., Cox, M. & Cox, R. (1978), 'The aftermath of divorce', in J.H. Stevens, Jr. & M. Matthews (eds), *Mother-child, Father-child Relations*, Washington, DC: National Association for the Education of Young Children.

Hetherington, E.M., Cox, M. & Cox, R. (1982), 'Effects of divorce on parents and children', in M.E. Lamb (ed), *Non-traditional Families*, Hillside, NJ: Erlbaum.

Hetherington, E.M., Cox, M. & Cox, R. (1985), 'Long-term effects of divorce and remarriage on the adjustment of children', *Journal of the American Academy of Child Psychiatry*, 24, pp. 518-30.

HMSO (1995), *Marriage and Divorce Statistics of England & Wales - 1993*, London: HMSO.

Ho, D.Y.F. (1974), 'Face, Social Expectations, & Conflict Avoidance', in J.L.M. Dawson & W.J. Lonner (eds), *Readings in Cross-cultural Psychology*, HK: University of Hong Kong Press.

Ho, Y.F. (1986), 'Chinese Patterns of Socialization: A Critical Review', in M.H. Bond (ed), *The Psychology of the Chinese People*, HK: Oxford University Press.

Holman, R. (1988), *Putting Families First*, London: MacMillan.

Hong Kong Council of Social Service Committee on International Year of the Family (1993), *Reference Paper on Major Family Concerns*, HK: Hong Kong Council of Social Service.

Hong Kong Council of Social Service Committee on International Year of the Family Working Group on Research (1994), *Role of The Family in Community Care*, HK: Hong Kong Council of Social Service.

Hong Kong Council of Social Service (1995), *Clientele Information Service for Family Counselling/Casework Service 1992-1993*, HK: Hong Kong Council of Social Service.

Hong Kong Census & Statistics Department (1996), *Hong Kong 1996 Population By-Census Summary Report*, HK: Hong Kong Government Printer.

Hong Kong Census & Statistics Department (Dec.1996), *Hong Kong Monthly Digest of Statistics*, HK: Hong Kong Government Printer.

Hong Kong Census & Statistics Department (1998), *Hong Kong Annual Digest of Statistics 1997*, HK: Hong Kong Government Printer.

Hong Kong Census & Statistics Department (April, 1998), *Demographic Statistics*, HK: Hong Kong Census & Statistics Department.

Hong Kong Census & Statististics Department (July, 1998), *Hong Kong Monthly Digest of Statistics*, HK: Hong Kong Government Printer.

Hong Kong Government (1965), *Aims and Policy for Social Welfare in Hong Kong*, HK: Hong Kong Government Printer.

Hong Kong Government (1991), *White Paper on Social Welfare into the 1990s and Beyond*, HK: Hong Kong Government Printer.

Hong Kong Government (1995), *Governor Policy Address*, HK: Hong Kong Government Printer.

Hong Kong Social Welfare Department (1997), *Child Protection Registry Statistical Report 1996,* HK: Hong Kong Government Printing Department.

Hong Kong Social Welfare Department (1998), *Child Protection Registry Statistical Report 1997*, HK: Hong Kong Government Printing Department.

Hsu, F.L.K. (1971), 'Psychological homeostasis and Jen: Conceptual tools for advancing psychological anthropology', *American Anthropology*, 73, pp. 23-43.

Hsu, J. & Tseng, W.S. (1974), 'Family relations in classic Chinese opera', *International Journal of Social Psychiatry*, 20, pp. 159-72.

Hutchison, J. & Hutchison, K. (1979), 'Issues and conflicts in stepfamilies', *Family Perspective*, 19, pp. 111-21.

Ihinger-Tallman, M. & Pasley, K. (1987), 'Divorce and remarriage in the American Family', in K. Pasley & M. Ihinger-Tallman (eds), *Remarriage and Stepparenting: Current Research and Theory*, NY: Guilford.

Ihinger-Tallman, M. & Ishii-Kuntz, M. (1988), 'Explaining divorce among married and remarried couples', Paper presented at the meetings of the American Sociological Association, Atlanta, GA.

Ishii-Kuntz, M. & Coltrane, S. (1992), 'Remarriage, stepparenting and household labor', *Journal of Family Issues*, (June), 13(2), pp. 215-33.

Jacobson, D. (1980), 'Crisis intervention with stepfamilies', *New Directions for Mental Health Services*, 6, pp. 35-42.

Johnson, C.L. (1988), 'Postdivorce reorganization of relationships between divorcing children and their parents', *Journal of Marriage and the Family*, 50, pp. 221-31.

Johnson, H.C. (1980), 'Working with stepfamilies: Principles of practice', *Social Work*, 25, 304-8.

Jones, S.M. (1978), 'Divorce and remarriages, a new beginning, a new set of problem', *Journal of Divorce*, 2(3), pp. 217-27.

Kalish, R.A. & Visher, E. (1982), 'Grandparents of divorce and remarriage', *Journal of Divorce*, 5, pp. 127-40.

Kamo, Y. (1988), 'Determinants of household labor', *Journal of Family Issues*, 9, 177-200.

Kaufman, S.R. (1994), 'In-depth interviewing', in J.F. Gubrium & A. Sankar (eds), *Qualitative Methods in Aging Research*, London: Sage.

Kennedy, G.E. & Kennedy, C.E. (1993), 'Grandparents: A special resource for children in stepfamilies', *Journal of Divorce and Remarriage*, 19, 3/4, pp. 45-68.

Ketcham, D. (1987), *Individualism and Public Life*, Oxford: Blackwell.

King, A.Y.C. (1985), 'The individual and group in Confucianism: A relational perspective', in D. Munro (ed), *Individualism and Holism: Studies in Confucian and Taoist Values*, Michigan: The U. of Michigan Ann Arbor Centre for Chinese Studies.

King, A.Y.C. & Myers, J.T. (1977), *Shame as an Incomplete Conception of Chinese Culture*, HK: The Chinese University of Hong Kong, Social Research Centre.

Koller, J.M. & Koller, P. (1991), *A Sourcebook in Asian Philosophy*, NY: Macmillan.

Kompara, D. (1980), Difficulties in the socialization process of stepparenting', *Family Relations*, 29, pp. 69-73.

282

Kubler-Ross, E. (1970), *On Death and Dying*, London: Tavistock.

Kupisch, S. (1987), 'Children and stepfamilies', in A. Thomas & J. Grimes (eds) *Children's Needs: Psychological Perspectives*, Washington, DC: National Association of Psychologists.

Kurdek, L.A. & Fine, M.A. (1993), 'Parent and nonparent residential family members as providers of warmth and supervision to young adolescents', *Journal of Family Psychology*, 7, pp. 245-49.

Lam, G.L.T. (1998), 'Stepmother-abusers: Wicked or not?', *Mental Health in Hong Kong 1996/97*, HK: Mental Health Association of Hong Kong.

Lam, L.Y. (1991), *The Life River of the Chinese*, Taipei: Zhang Lao Zhi Publishing Co.

Lam, M.C. (1982), *Changing Pattern of Childrearing: A Study of the Low-Income Families in Hong Kong*, HK: The Chinese University of Hong Kong.

Larson, J.H. & Allgood, S.M. (1987), 'A comparison of intimacy in first-married and remarried couples', *Journal of Family Issues*, 8, pp. 319-31.

Law, C.K. et.al. (1995), *Contemporary Hong Kong Families in Transition*, HK: The University of Hong Kong.

Law Reform Commission of Hong Kong (1992), *Report on Grounds for Divorce and the Time Restriction on Petitions for Divorce within Three Years of Marriage*, HK: Hong Kong Government.

Lee, M.K. (1991), 'Family and Social Life', in S.K. Lau et.al. (eds), *Indicators of Social Development: Hong Kong 1988*, HK: The Chinese University of Hong Kong, Institute of Asia Pacific Studies.

Leslie, G. (1982), *The Family in Social Context* (5th ed.), NY: Oxford University Press.

Lit, T.K.Y. et.al. (1991), *Fatherhood in the 1990s: implications for service needs*, HK: Department of Applied Social Studies, City Polytechnic of Hong Kong.

Louie, K. (1980), *Critique of Confucius in Contemporary China*, NY: St. Martins.

Luborsky, M.R. (1994), 'The identification and analysis of themes and patterns', in J.F. Gubrium & A. Sankar (eds), *Qualitative Methods in Aging Research*, London: Sage.

Maccoby, E.E. & Martin, J.A. (1983), 'Socialization in the context of the family: parent-child interaction', in E.M. Hetherington (ed), *Handbook of Child Psychology* (4th ed.), vol. 4, NY: Wiley.

MacDonald, W.L. & DeMaris, A. (1995), 'Remarriage, stepchildren, and marital conflict: Challenges to the incomplete institutionalization hypothesis', *Journal of Marriage and the Family*, (May), 57, pp. 387-98.

Maddox, B. (1976), *The Half Parent: Living with Other People's Children*, London: Andre Deutsch.

Maddox, B. (1975), *The Half-parent*, NY: New American Library.

Margolin, G. (1981), 'The reciprocal relationship between marital and child problems', in J.P. Vincent (ed), *Advances in Intervention, Assessment and Theory*, Greenwich, CT: JAI.

Margolin, G. & Patterson, G.R. (1975), 'Differential consequences provided by mothers and fathers for their sons and daughters', *Developmental Psychology*, 11(4), pp. 537-38.

Marris, P. (1974), *Loss and Change*, London: Routledge & Kegan Paul.

Mead, M. (1970), 'Anomalies in American postdivorce relationships', in P. Bohannan (ed) *Divorce and After*, NY: Doubleday.

Messinger, L. (1976), 'Remarriage between divorced people with children from previous marriages', *Journal of Marriage and Family Counseling*, 2, pp. 193-200.

Miller, G. (1997), 'Building bridges: The possibility of analytic dialogue between ethnography, conversation analysis and Foucault', in D. Silverman (ed) *Qualitative Research: Theory, Method and Practice*, London: Sage.

Mills, D. (1984), 'A model for stepfamily development', *Family Relations*, 33, pp. 365-72.

Minichiello, V., Aroni, R., Timewell, E. & Alexander, L. (1990), *In-depth Interviewing: Researching People*, Melbourne: Longman Cheshire.

Minuchin, S. (1985), 'Family and individual development: Provocations from the field to family therapy', *Child Development*, 56, pp. 289-302.

Munro, D.J. (1985), 'The family network, the stream of water, and the plant: Picturing persons in Sung Confucianism', in D. Munro (ed) *Individualism and Holism: Studies in Confucian and Taoist Values*, Michigan: The U. of Michigan Ann Arbor Centre for Chinese Studies.

Murray Parkes, C. (1986), *Bereavement, Studies of Grief in Adult Life*, (2nd ed.), Harmondsworth: Pelican.

Nyaw, M.K. & Li, S.M. (eds) (1996), *The Other Hong Kong Report 1996*, HK: The Hong Kong University Press.

O'Brian, C. & Lau, L.S.W. (1995), 'Defining child abuse in Hong Kong' in *Child Abuse Review*, 4, pp. 38-46.

Oakley, A. (1974), *The Sociology of Housework*, NY: Pantheon.

Out of Home, Preventive, and Alternative Care (OHPAC) (1995), *OHPAC Planning and Co-Co-ordinating Committee Literature Review*, England: OHPAC.

Papernow, P.L. (1993), *Becoming a Stepfamily: Patterns of Development in Remarried Families*, San Francisco: Jossey-Bass.

Parker, R. (1980), *Caring for Separated Children*, London: MacMillan.

Parton, N. (ed) (1997), *Child Protection and Family Support*, London: Routledge.

Pasley, K. (1987), 'Family boundary ambiguity: Perceptions of adult members', in K. Pasley & M. Ihinger-Tallman (eds), *Remarriage and Stepparenting: Current Research and Theory*, NY: Guilford.

Pasley, K. & Ihinger-Tallman, M. (1982), 'Remarried family life: supports and constraints', in G. Rowe (ed) *Building Family Strengths*, Lincoln: University of Nebraska Press.

Pasley, K., Ihinger-Tallman, M. & Lofquist, A. (1994), 'Remarriage and stepfamilies: Making progress in understanding', in K. Pasley & M. Ihinger-Tallman (eds), *Steppparenting: Issues in Theory, Research and Practice*, Westport: Greenwood Press.

Patton, M.Q. (1990), *Qualitative Evaluation and Research Methods* (2nd ed.), Newbury Park, CA: Sage.

Pearson, V. (1990), 'Women in Hong Kong', in B.K.P. Leung (ed), *Social Issues in Hong Kong*, HK: Oxford University Press.

Pearson, V. & Leung, B.K.P. (eds) (1995), *Women in Hong Kong*, HK: Oxford University Press.

Petersen, V. & Steinman, S.B. (1994), 'Helping children succeed after divorce', *Family and Conciliation Courts Review*, Jan. 32(1), 27-39.

Peterson, G.W. & Rollins, B.C. (1987), 'Parental-child socialization', in M. Sussman & S. Steinmetz (eds), *Handbook of Marriage and the Family*, NY: Plenum.

Pleck, J.H. (1983), 'Husband's paid work and family role', in H. Lopata & J. Pleck (eds), *Research in the Interweave of Social Roles*, Greenwich, CT: JAI.

Potter, S.H. & Potter, J.M. (1993), *China's Peasants: The Anthropology of a Revolution*, Cambridge: Cambridge U. Press.

Pringle, M.K. (1980), *The Needs of Children* (2nd ed.), London: Hutchison.

Prosen, S.S. & Farmer, J.H. (1982), 'Understanding stepfamilies: Issues and implications for counselors', *The Personnel and Guildance Journal*, 60, pp. 393-97.

Rallings, E.M. (1976), 'The special role of the stepmother' *The Family Coordinator*, 25(4), pp. 445-50.

Rappaport, J. (1985), 'The power of empowerment language', *Social Policy*, Fall, pp. 15-21.

Redding, S.G. (1993), *The Spirit of Chinese Capitalism*, NY: Walter de Gruyter.

Robinson, M. (1980), 'Stepfamilies: A reconstituted family system', *Journal of Family Therapy*, 2:49-53.

Robinson, M. (1993), *Family Transformation through Divorce and Remarriage: A Systemic Approach*, London: Routledge.

Robinson, M. & Smith, D. (1993), *Step by Step: Focus on Stepfamilies*, NY: Harvester/Wheatsheaf.

Roetz, H. (1993), *Confucian Ethics of the Axial Age: A Reconstruction under the Aspect of the Breakthrough towards Postconventional Thinking*, NY: State University of New York Press.

Rutter, M. (1982), *Maternal Deprivation Reassessed* (2nd ed.), Middlesex: Penguin.

Sager, C.J., Brown, H.S., Crohn, H., Engel, T., Rodstein, E. and Walker, L. (1983) *Treating the Remarried Family*, NY: Brunner/Mazel.

Santrock, J.W. & Sitterle, K.A. (1987), 'Parent-child relationships in stepmother families', in K. Pasley & M. Ihinger-Tallman (eds), *Remarriage and Stepparenting: Current Research and Theory*, NY: Guilford.

Santrock, J.W., Sitterle, K.A. & Warshak, R.A. (1988), 'Parent-child relationships in stepfather families', in P. Bronstein & C.P. Cowan (eds), *Fatherhood Today: Men's Changing Role in the Family*, NY: Wiley.

Santrock, J.W. & Warshak, R.A. (1979) 'Father custody and social development in boys and girls', *The Journal of Social Issues*, 35, pp. 112-25.

Santrock, J.W., Warshak, R., Linbergh, C. & Meadows, L. (1982), 'Children's and parents' observed social behaviour in stepfather families', *Child Development*, 53, pp. 472-80.

Sauer, L.E. & Fine, M.A. (1988), 'Parent-child relationships in stepparent families', *Journal of Family Psychology*, 1, pp. 434-51.

Schneider, D., Hastorf, A. & Ellsworth, P. (1979), *Person Perception*, Reading, MA: Addison-Wesley.

Schulz, R. & Rau, M.T. (1985), 'Social support through the life course', in S.Cohen & S.L. Syme (eds), *Social Support and Health*, Orlando, FL: Academic Press.

Schwebel, A.I., Fine, M.A., & Renner, M.A. (1991), 'A study of perceptions of the stepparent role', *Journal of Family Issues*, 12, pp. 43-57.

Sha, K.C. (ed) (1995), *Status of Women in Contemporary China* (in Chinese), Beijing: Beijing University Press.

Shon, S.P. & Davis, J.A. (1982), 'Asian families', in M. McGoldrick, J.K. Pearce & J. Girodano (eds), *Ethnicity and Family Therapy*, NY: Guilford.

Shulman, G. (1972), 'Myths that intrude on the adaptation of the stepfamily', *Social Casework*, 49, pp. 131-39.

Shulman, G. (1981), 'Divorce, single parenthood and stepfamilies: Structural implications of these transactions', *International Journal of Family Therapy,* (summer), pp. 87-112.

Shum, S.L. & Yeung, S.W. (eds) (1995), *Studies of Families in Contemporary Cities of China* (in Chinese), Beijing: China Social Science Publishing Company.

Sigel, I.E., McGillicuddy-DeLisi, A.V., & Goodnow, J.J. (eds) (1992), *Parental Belief Systems: The Psychological Consequences for Children*, (2nd ed.), NJ: Lawrence Erlbaum Associates.

Simons, R.L., Whitbeck, L.B., Conger, R.D. & Melby, J.N. (1990), 'Husband and wife differences in determinants of parenting: A social learning and exchange model of parental behaviour', *Journal of Marriage and the Family*, (May), 52, pp. 375-92.

Skeen, P., Covi, R.B. & Robinson, B.E. (1985), 'Stepfamilies: A review of the literature with suggestions for practitioners', *Journal of Counselling and Development*, (Oct.), 64, pp. 121-25.

Smith, W.O. (1953), *The Stepchild*. Chicago: University of Chicago Press.

Steinhauer, P.D., Santa-Barbara, J. & Skinner, H. (1984), 'The process model for of family functioning', *Canadian Journal of Psychiatry*, 29, pp. 77-88.

Stevenson, O. (1994), 'Social work in the 1990s: empowerment - fact or fiction?', *Social Policy Review*, 6, UK: Social Policy Association.

Stevenson, O. (1997), 'Child welfare in the UK: The exercise on professional judgements by social workers', paper presented to BASPCAN Congress at Edinburgh, England in July, 1997.

Stevenson, O. & Parsloe, P. (1993), *Community Care and Empowerment*, York: Joseph Rowntree Foundations.

Strauss, A. & Corbin, J. (1990), *Basics of Qualitative Research*, Newbury Park, CA: Sage.

Strong, B. & DeVault, C. (1993), *Essentials of the Marriage and Family Experience*, Mineapolis, MN: West.

Thomson, E., McLanahan, S.S. & Curtin, R.B. (1992), 'Family structure, gender and parental socialization', *Journal of Marriage and the Family*, (May), 54, pp. 368-78.

Thurston, A.F. (1984), 'Victims of China's Cultural Revolution: The invisible wounds Part I', *Pacific Affairs*, (Winter), 57(4).

Thurston, A.F. (1985), 'Victims of China's Cultural Revolution: The invisible wounds Part II', *Pacific Affairs*, (Spring), 58(1).

Tein, J.Y., Roosa, M.W. & Michaels, M. (1994), 'Agreement between parent and child reports on parental behaviours', *Journal of Marriage and the Family*, 56, pp. 341-55.

Trebilot, J. (1983), *Mothering: Essays in Feminist Theory*, NJ: Rowman & Allanheld.

United Nations (1989), *Convention on the Rights of the Child*, NY: United Nations.

United Nations (1995), *United Nations Demographic Yearbook - 1993*, NY: United Nations.

Visher, E.B. & Visher, J.S. (1988), *Old Loyalties, New Ties -- Therapeutic Strategies with Stepfamilies*, NY: Brunner/Mazel.

Visher, E. & Visher, J. (1979), *Stepfamilies: A Guide to Working with Stepparents and Stepchildren*, NY: Brunner/Mazel.

Visher, J.S. (1994), 'Stepfamilies: A work in progress', *The American Journal of Family Therapy*, (winter), 22(4), pp. 337-44.

Vogel, E.F. (1965), 'From friendship to comradeship: The change in personal relations in Communist China', *China Quarterly*, Jan.-Mar., #21.

Vuchinich, S., Hetherington, E.M., Vuchinich, R.A. & Clingempeel, W.G. (1991), 'Parent and child interaction and gender differences in early adolescents' adaptation to stepfamilies', *Developmental Psychology*, 27, pp. 618-26.

Wald, E. (1981), *The Remarried Family: Challenge and Promise*, NY: Family Service Association of America.

Walker, R. (ed) (1985), *Applied Qualitative Research*, Aldershot: Gower.

Wallerstein, J. & Kelly, J. (1980), *Surviving the Breakup: How Children and Parents Cope with Divorce*, NY: Basic Books.

Walsh, W.M. (1992), 'Twenty major issues in remarriage families', *Journal of Counselling and Development*, July/Aug., 70, pp. 709-15.

White, L. & Booth, A. (1985), 'The quality and stability of remarriages', *American Sociological Review*, 50, pp. 689-98.

White, L., Brinkerhoff, D. & Booth, A. (1985), 'The effects of marital disruption on child's attachment to parents', *Journal of Family Issues*, 6, pp. 5-22.

Wilks, C. & Melville, C. (1990), 'Grandparents in custody and access disputes', *Journal of Divorce*, 13, pp. 1-14.

Winnicott, D.W. (1964), *The Child, the Family and the Outside World*, London: Penguin.

Wong, S.L. (1986), 'Modernization and Chinese Culture in Hong Kong', *The China Quarterly*, (June), 106, pp. 306-25.

Wu, Y.H. (1981), 'Child abuse in Taiwan', in J.E. Korbin (ed), *Child Abuse and Neglect: Cross-cultural Perspectives*, Berkeley: U. of California Press.

Yeung, C. and Kwong, W.M. (1995), *Attitudes toward Marriage in a Time of Change: A Survey Study of the Attitudes of Secondary School Students toward Marriage in Hong Kong*, HK: City University of Hong Kong and the Hong Kong Catholic Marriage Advisory Council.

Young, John D. (1988), 'Modernization in Hong Kong: The cultural factor', *Hong Kong Chu Hai Journal*, (Oct.), 16, pp. 734-40, 42.

Young, K. (1993), *Marriages Under Stress*, HK: Department of Social Work, University of Hong Kong.

Young, K. (1994), 'Long distance marriages: The Hong Kong China Interface', in N. Rhind (ed), *Empowering Families*, HK: Hong Kong Family Welfare Society.

Young, K.P.H. et.al. (1995), *Study on Marriages affected by Extramarital Affairs*, HK: Caritas Family Service and the University of Hong Kong.

Yuen-Tsang W.K.A. (1997), *Towards a Chinese Conception of Social Support,* Aldershot: Ashgate.